Youth Offending and Restorative Justice
Implementing reform in youth justice

Adam Crawford and Tim Newburn

WILLAN
PUBLISHING

Published by

Willan Publishing
Culmcott House
Mill Street, Uffculme
Cullompton, Devon
EX15 3AT, UK
Tel: +44(0)1884 840337
Fax: +44(0)1884 840251
e-mail: info@willanpublishing.co.uk
website: www.willanpublishing.co.uk

Published simultaneously in the USA and Canada by

Willan Publishing
c/o ISBS, 5824 N.E. Hassalo St,
Portland, Oregon 97213-3644, USA
Tel: +001(0)503 287 3093
Fax: +001(0)503 280 8832
e-mail: info@isbs.com
website: www.isbs.com

First published 2003

ISBN 1-84392-012-3 (cased)
ISBN 1-84392-011-5 (paper)

British Library Cataloguing-in-Publication Data
A catalogue record for this book is available from the British Library

Project management by Deer Park Productions
Typeset by GCS, Leighton Buzzard, Beds
Printed and bound by T.J. International, Padstow, Cornwall

Contents

List of figures and tables

Figures

Tables

Acknowledgements

The research reported in this book is drawn from a Home Office evaluation of the implementation of the referral order and youth offender panel pilots. The evaluation was undertaken by a consortium from Goldsmiths College and the Universities of Leeds and Kent. We would like to thank and acknowledge the important contribution of the rest of the evaluation team to the research, namely Rod Earle, Shelagh Goldie, Chris Hale, Guy Masters, Ann Netten, Robin Saunders, Karen Sharpe and Steve Uglow. The quality of the research is in large part due to the collective efforts of the team. The invaluable group discussions during the research contributed enormously to our thinking. We would also like to thank Arabella Campbell and Angela Hallam for their contribution to the data collection and Julie Latreille for her assistance with sorting a large amount of data throughout the research.

We also wish to acknowledge the vital co-operation and support received from all the staff involved in the implementation of the referral order pilots, most particularly the Youth Offending Team members and the community panel members. We are grateful to all the magistrates and clerks to the Youth Court in the pilot areas who took the time to complete the questionnaires sent to them. Particular thanks are due to the young people, parents and victims who gave up their time to speak with us and discuss their experience of referral orders and youth offender panels.

Thanks are also due to the Youth Justice Board and Referral Order Steering Group and to the Home Office for their support for the evaluation. We are grateful to Simon King, Dorothy Gonsalves and Olivia Mcleod of the Juvenile Offenders Unit and most particularly to Siobhan Campbell in the Home Office Research, Development and Statistics Directorate for helping us see the evaluation through to its conclusion.

We would also like to thank Declan Roche for his valuable comments on the draft manuscript.

As ever, Brian Willan has been an encouraging, supportive and responsive publisher and the world of criminology publishing is a better place as a result of his tireless efforts. To our respective families we owe immense thanks for their support and for helping keep us sane during the realisation of this project. In particular, Adam wishes to thank Susan, Alex and Kirsty, and Tim would like to thank Mary, Gavin, Robin, Lewis and Owen.

Introduction

This book offers an empirically informed, theoretically grounded account of the recent radical changes to the youth justice system in England and Wales. As such, it serves to fill a gap in the British criminological literature which tends either to focus upon policy pronouncements, often from a critical perspective, with little regard to their operation in practice or to describe the evaluation of practical developments with little regard to theory. In this book, we examine recent attempts to introduce elements of restorative justice into the heart of the youth justice system in England and Wales through the implementation of referral orders and youth offender panels as provided by the Youth Justice and Criminal Evidence Act 1999. Though there were restorative elements in the Crime and Disorder Act 1998, the 1999 Act goes much further down the restorative justice path. Together, they constitute what has been described by both critics and proponents alike as the most radical overhaul of the youth justice system in the last half century, so significant as to constitute a 'new youth justice' (Goldson 2000). Indeed, the government presented its reform package as fundamentally changing the underlying values of the system 'away from an exclusionary punitive justice and towards an inclusionary restorative justice capable of recognising the social contexts in which crime occurs and should be dealt with' (Muncie 2000: 14).

The book explores the implications of these changes by using the lens of a detailed study of the implementation of referral orders and youth offender panels to explore wider issues about youth justice policy and the integration of restorative justice principles therein. In so doing, the book draws upon the findings of an in-depth 18 months' study of the pilots established prior to the national roll-out of referral orders in April 2002.

Chapter 1 provides an introduction to the origins and development of youth justice in England and Wales, and contrasts this with some Scottish experiences. It places the recent reforms in their historical context and outlines the contemporary politics and practice of youth justice as well as the competing ideological and penological forces that have shaped them. It charts the development of the modern juvenile justice system in England and Wales, focusing particularly upon changes to youth justice over the past three decades. The genesis, aims and rationale of the 'New Youth Justice' reforms introduced by the Labour Government are explored, focusing particularly on the Crime and Disorder Act 1998.

Chapter 2 provides an introduction to restorative justice ideals and the international growth of restorative practices, specifically victim–offender mediation, family group conferencing, 'healing' and sentencing circles, community peace committees and restorative boards. It provides an overview of key developments around the world as an insight into similarities and differences between models of restorative justice. In the light of this survey of restorative justice practices and the ideals that inform them, Chapter 3 explores a number of critical issues concerning restorative values and their implementation. It considers debates concerning key salient aspects of restorative justice ideals with regard to both processes and outcomes. It questions the relationship between restorative justice and punishment and the place of proportionality, voluntariness, impartiality and independence within restorative practices. It concludes by asking what the implications of restoring offenders, victims and communities might mean.

In Chapter 4 we provide an overview of the legislation and guidance that saw the introduction of referral orders and youth offender panels, their background and rationale. The chapter goes on to present the design and methods of the research study. As such, it serves as an introduction to the research that informs the subsequent empirical chapters of this book (Chapters 5–11). The chapter concludes with some observations on the research process itself.

Chapter 5 draws upon the findings of the research study and outlines the establishment of referral order teams in the pilot areas, as well as the organisation and delivery of referral orders. It explores the manner in which local youth offending teams put into practice the requirements of the Youth Justice and Criminal Evidence Act 1999. It explores the recruitment and training of community panel members and the management of the referral order process.

In Chapter 6, we explore the relationship between the courts and referral order teams, as well as the views of magistrates, court clerks and youth offending team staff to the implementation of referral orders and the work of youth offender panels. The manner in which the Youth Court has been affected by the new order and some of the legal issues that arose during the course of the pilots are discussed.

In Chapter 7 we discuss the composition, work and dynamics of youth offender panels. We consider the ways in which panel meetings operate and their capacity to meet restorative justice ideals and act as deliberative and inclusive forums. The nature and extent of the contribution of the various parties to the agreements reached are a subject of particular analysis. Chapter 8, by contrast, explores the specific content and nature of youth offender contracts agreed at panel meetings in the pilot sites. The implementation of youth offender contracts and the work done in support of them are discussed.

The next three chapters consider the views and experiences of key participants in the youth offender panel process. Chapter 9 explores the involvement of community panel members, what they bring to the process and their views on the implementation of referral orders. In particular, the nature of relationships which developed between community panel members and youth offending team staff and the way in which they worked together as panel members are discussed. Chapter 10 examines the detailed experiences of young people and their parents who were the subjects of a referral order. It considers their attitudes towards and participation within youth offender panels and the implementation of the subsequent agreements made. Chapter 11 addresses similar issues with regard to the victims of crime. It explores the experiences and views both of victims who had attended a youth offender panel and those who, for whatever reason, had not done so.

Finally, in Chapter 12 we explore some of the important issues raised by the experience of the referral order and youth offender panel pilots. We consider the broader potential implications of referral orders and the manner in which their development is likely to be shaped by wider policy tensions and ongoing preoccupations within contemporary criminal justice policy and practice in England and Wales. The integration of victims within criminal justice and the impact of managerialisation are discussed. We conclude with some observations on the implications of our research findings for evaluation research and criminological analysis of youth justice reforms, as well as the implementation of restorative justice.

Chapter 1

The origins and development of youth justice

Recent years have seen profound changes to the youth justice system in England and Wales. As is the case with much of the penal system, the pace of change has quickened markedly in recent decades. The increasing politicisation of crime has affected all parts of the justice system. In many respects, however, the particular concerns about young people that existed for the whole of the last century, and much of the previous one (Pearson 1983), led to ever more frequent calls for, and attempts to, reform the youth justice system. Our concern in this book is with the most recent and significant reforms of that system – the introduction of a restorative justice-influenced disposal: the referral order. A mandatory order, for first-time offenders pleading guilty in the Youth Court, the referral order involves volunteers from the local community working with offenders, and possibly victims, to construct an appropriate set of activities aimed at combining reparation with punishment. The orders were piloted from 2000 and implemented nationally from 2002.

By the time of the 1997 General Election the Labour Party, having been out of government for almost two decades, had numerous well-developed policies it was ready to implement. Within the Home Affairs brief, reform of the youth justice system was very much top of the agenda. Within a short space of time legislation was introduced and passed – the Crime and Disorder Act 1998 – which made substantial changes to the management, the funding and the organisation of youth justice and the range of penalties available to the Youth Court. So far reaching were these changes that numerous commentators, echoing the emergence of 'New Labour', began referring to this as the 'new youth justice' (see, for example, Goldson 2000 and other contributors to that volume). It is this apparently 'new' youth justice that is the focus of this volume. Before examining the detail of the changes it is necessary to look further back. It is difficult, if not nigh impossible, to understand the contemporary politics and practice of youth justice without first examining its longer-term history. Though its origins go back some way further, this history is one in the main confined to the twentieth century.

Origins

Much of twentieth-century juvenile justice was characterised by a double taxonomy most usually summarised as 'punishment' and 'welfare'. The English (and Welsh) juvenile justice system emerged out of the social reform movements of the nineteenth century, much as the probation service emerged out of the previous century's temperance movement. During the latter half of the nineteenth century the idea was gradually established that young people should be dealt with separately from adults – both in the administration of justice and punishment. During the 1800s numerous reformers sought to establish means by which children might be removed, and kept separate, from the adult prison system. Reformatories and industrial schools were introduced by statute in the 1850s to deal with those convicted of vagrancy. Industrial schools were initially part of the educational system but by the 1860s they, like reformatories, came under the control of the Home Office.

The introduction of the reformatories and industrial schools led to the rapid increase in the number of young people in institutions. By the late 1850s there were over 2,000 young people in reformatories and this had grown to 7,000 by 1870 (Rutherford 1986a). As we shall see, this pattern of development – reform that was broadly welfarist in intention but which had punitive unintended consequences – was not untypical of what was to follow in the following hundred or so years.

In the 1890s two committees – the Gladstone and Lushington Committees – were established by the Home Secretary, Asquith, to examine the penal system. The Gladstone Report advocated 'treatment' alongside punishment in prisons, particularly in the case of young prisoners. The Lushington Committee advocated alternatives to imprisonment, looking in particular to education as one of the remedies for juvenile crime. Both recognised the importance of separate provision for juveniles. By this time juvenile courts were operating in numerous towns, and the advent of a Liberal government in 1906 brought substantial reform.

Borstals, catering for 16–21-year-olds, were also introduced in 1908, though it was some time before any distinctive regime emerged. Just as juvenile courts grew informally prior to the passage of legislation so arrangements for the supervision of offenders also existed before formal legislation was passed. The inter-war years saw a significant increase in recorded juvenile crime and by 1920 the vast majority of people under probation supervision were aged under 21 (Rutherford 1986a). At this period the focus remained firmly upon the 'welfare' of young offenders and the 'treatment' necessary to reclaim or reform them. The subsequent Children and Young Persons Act 1933 reaffirmed both the principle of a separate juvenile justice system and the assumption that the system should work in a way that promoted the welfare of young people.

Though there were shifts in emphasis from time to time, the general topography of juvenile justice continued to be dominated by 'welfarism' for a further 40 years. The Advisory Council on the Treatment of Offenders, established in 1944, 'strongly emphasised the unwisdom of sending young persons to prison' (Bailey 1987: 42) and the subsequent Criminal Justice Act 1948 placed restrictions on the use of imprisonment. One commentator (Stevenson 1989) has suggested that the Ingleby Committee, established in 1956 to inquire into the operation of the juvenile court, actually favoured the development of a local authority-based system of social service based on the existing Children's Departments as a method of decriminalising juvenile justice. The committee recommended the raising of the age of criminal responsibility from 8 to 12 'with the possibility of it becoming 13 or 14' (Morris and Giller 1987), and below that age only welfare proceedings could be brought. The Children and Young Persons Act 1963 raised the age of criminal responsibility to a compromise 10, though Bottoms (1974) suggests that even this was of considerable symbolic importance to later events.

The 'high point' of welfarism in juvenile justice was reached in the late 1960s and, like so much in penal politics, the shift away was rapid. The Ingleby Report was followed first by an inquiry under the chairmanship of Lord Longford which recommended the total abolition of juvenile courts on the basis that 'no child in early adolescence should have to face criminal proceedings', and subsequently by two white papers. *The Child, the Family and the Young Offender* included proposals to establish family councils and family courts, but was undermined by lawyers, magistrates and probation officers. *Children in Trouble*, by contrast, found legislative embodiment in the Children and Young Persons Act 1969. The Act abolished approved schools and the remand homes or centres that existed alongside them. Care was preferred over criminal proceedings; the intention was that the juvenile court should become a welfare-providing agency but also 'an agency of last resort' (Rutter and Giller 1983).

It was also intended that detention centres and borstals for juveniles would be phased out and replaced by a new form of intervention – intermediate treatment. 'This [though] was less a policy of decarceration than a reiteration of the traditional welfare abhorrence of the prison system' (Rutherford 1986b: 57). Between the passage of the Act and the expected date for its implementation there was a change of government and the new Conservative administration announced that it would not be implementing significant sections of the legislation. Rather than a sea-change in juvenile justice, the juvenile courts continued to operate largely as before. In fact, the welfare-oriented care proceedings were initially used very sparingly, and the more punitive disposals were used increasingly in the 1970s. The number of custodial sentences, for example, rose from 3,000 in 1970 to over 7,000 in 1978 (Cavadino and Dignan 1992).

By contrast, in Scotland a very significant set of changes to the juvenile justice system were set in train. Juvenile courts were abolished and replaced with welfare tribunals staffed with lay people. The Social Work (Scotland) Act 1968 gave local authorities considerable powers over, and responsibility for, young people's welfare and, in the form of these new tribunals, established what has become known as the Children's Hearings system. The system came into operation in 1971 implementing the bulk of the recommendations of the Kilbrandon Report (1964). Under the 1968 Act, a new official, known as a reporter, was appointed within the local authority to receive referrals relating to children in difficulty. A child or young person can be referred to a reporter by anybody, but in practice referrals are primarily from the police. The role of the reporter is then to determine what initial action is to be taken in response to the referral. The main courses of action are to:

- take no further action
- refer the case to the local authority for advice, guidance and assistance, or
- arrange a Children's Hearing.

The decision to refer a child to a hearing is generally made where it appears that the child was in need of compulsory measures of care or supervision (Hallett et al. 1998). The hearing is a lay tribunal comprising three panel members. In addition to the panel, also present will be the reporter, the child or young person, at least one parent or carer and a social worker. Others – teachers, family representatives – may attend occasionally. The system is founded on the idea that the promotion of the welfare of the young person is paramount and that decisions taken should be based on 'need' rather than 'deed'. The forum is intended to be non-adversarial and relatively informal. Both the child or young person and his or her parent/guardian should have an opportunity to participate. The purpose of the hearing is not to determine the facts but to decide upon a disposal. Where there is dispute or denial of the reasons for the referral then the panel is able either to discharge the case or to refer it to the Sheriff for adjudication. The Sheriff, where the case is found to be proven, may return it to the hearing for further consideration and the determination of a disposal. The three major disposals are discharge, a supervision order or a residential supervision order. As a welfare-based system the Scottish Children's Hearings have, from time to time, been the focus of attention among those that would seek reform youth justice in England and Wales. Some of the more recent reforms, particularly the referral order, are indeed resonant of aspects of the hearings system – in an amalgam with restorative justice-based initiatives from other systems (Crawford 2003). Why the Scots were able to implement the hearings system whilst England and Wales quickly retreated from the 1969 Act is beyond the scope of this chapter (though see Morris and Giller 1987).

Notwithstanding the fact that its implementation was very partial, the 1969 Act became the scapegoat for all the perceived ills of juvenile crime and juvenile justice in the 1970s in England and Wales. Rutherford (1986a: 59) suggested that it was 'the ideas and attitudes ... culminating in the 1969 Act ... on which the campaign for counter-reform was mounted'. The Act was attacked from all sides, not just those critical of its 'welfare' elements and it is hard not to agree with Morris and Giller's (1987: 111) conclusion that juvenile justice policy at the end of the 1970s 'bore little resemblance to that proposed in the 1969 Act'. As Jones (1984) notes, the 'new orthodoxy' of the 'justice model' began to take hold from the early to mid-1970s onward.

Pratt (1989) suggests there were four major sets of criticisms of the 'welfare' model. First, the treatment-oriented interventions encouraged by the welfare model were perceived to be ineffective. Second, evidence suggested that care could, intentionally or otherwise, become more coercive (and less just) than punishment. Third, professional expertise (that was assumed to underpin welfare approaches) was seen to be less important than hitherto believed. Finally, the welfare approach was alleged to be ineffective in controlling delinquency (referred to sometimes as the 'decline of the rehabilitative ideal'). At the heart of the emergent 'justice model' was a retributive requirement to impose punishment, though this was to be 'in a precise and restrictive form'.

The election of a Conservative government with a 'law and order' agenda seemed likely to reinforce and perhaps further fuel such developments. The reality is more complex however. In practice there was a significant and sustained decline in the use of custody for juveniles during the 1980s. The paradox was that 'the decade of "law and order" was also the decade of what has been called "the successful revolution" in juvenile justice' (Jones 1984). Underpinning this 'revolution' were the practices of multi-agency working and diversion that saw a huge expansion in the use of (informal and formal) cautioning, and an increasingly bifurcated system that sought to distinguish the serious, the dangerous and the persistent from the rest. How was this emergent system to be understood? Writing at the end of the 1980s, Pratt (1989) argued that the debate about justice and welfare was something of a 'sideshow', and that a new form of penological discourse and practice – corporatism – was emerging in juvenile justice. Efficient and effective 'management' of the offending population was now to the fore. This was legitimated by the rediscovery that 'something works'; namely the infliction of a 'just measure of (community based) pain'. For Pratt (1989), corporatism involved a set of strategies based on centralised managerial control with the aim of efficiently managing the offending population. As such it presaged the slightly later emergence of what Feeley and Simon (1994) have termed the 'new penology' in which actuarial techniques of risk assessment and classification come to dominate much penal decision-making and administration. The emergent managerialist and actuarialist discourses of the late 1980s were joined in the early 1990s by the embracing of 'populist punitiveness' by politicians of all hues. Bottoms (1995) suggests three reasons for the attractiveness of this new 'disciplinary common-sense' (Hall, 1980). First, its populist appeal derives from the belief that increased punitiveness may be effective in reducing crime through general deterrence and/or incapacitation. Second, there is a desired belief that it will help foster a sense of moral consensus around issues where currently dissensus or moral pluralism exists. Third, politicians believe that it will be a vote-winner. Rising levels of juvenile crime, a increasing popular and political belief that the youth justice system was ineffective, and widespread concern about the moral health of contemporary youth inspired by a number of high-profile cases involving young offenders – most spectacularly and influentially the Bulger case – provided the backdrop against which New Labour sought to redefine itself in the law and order landscape. In opposition, New Labour drew on the managerialism of the justice model, and added its own potent blend of communitarianism and populism (Newburn 1998). The consequence is, we are told, the emergence of a 'new youth justice' (Goldson 2000), the 'broad contours' of which 'are easily described' (Pitts 2000).

New Labour, New Youth Justice?

In reality, New Labour's youth justice is somewhat more tricky to characterise than some commentators would have us believe. In part this is a result of the sheer volume of activity that the Labour government has undertaken in this area. At least as importantly, much of the governmental 'style' has been to 'talk tough' whilst behind the scenes enabling sometimes more enlightened practices to be developed and promulgated (Savage and Nash 2001). The consequence is a very broad and far-reaching set of changes that are not easily characterised or, indeed, summarised.

In early 1997 six consultation documents on the subject of youth crime were published (Home Office 1997a; 1997b; 1997c; 1997d; 1997e; 1997f), each of which contained considerable discussion of various proposals that had first been outlined in the Labour Party's pre-election discussion paper, *Tackling Youth Crime, Reforming Youth Justice* (Labour Party 1996). The proposals in that document had been heavily influenced by the Audit Commission's coruscating critique of the youth justice system in *Misspent Youth* (Audit Commission 1996). Its view was that the system in England and Wales was uneconomic, inefficient and ineffective. The emphasis in the commission's report was on clarity of objectives, consistency of approach and targeting of resources. Central to this was the aim that resources be shifted from processing to prevention. Its central recommendations emphasised the need for consistency of aims and objectives in youth justice; improved inter-agency co-operation in meeting these aims and objectives; the creation of appropriate performance indicators for all agencies involved in youth justice; and the monitoring of performance so as to improve the functioning of the system.

The major proposals in *Tackling Youth Crime, Reforming Youth Justice* eventually found their way, largely unchanged, into the government's flagship legislation, the Crime and Disorder Act 1998. This Act, though followed by others, contains the key elements of Labour's 'new youth justice': the establishment of the Youth Justice Board (YJB), the creation of Youth Offending Teams (YOTs), and the restructuring of the non-custodial penalties available to the Youth Court. In its white paper, *No More Excuses*, the government had said that there was:

Confusion about the purpose of the youth justice system and principles that should govern the way in which young people are dealt with by youth justice agencies. Concerns about the welfare of young people have too often been seen as in conflict with the aims of protecting the public, punishing offences and preventing offending. (Home Office 1997d: 7)

In response the Crime and Disorder Act contained, for the first time, an overarching mission for the whole youth justice system. Section 37 establishes that: 'It shall be the principal aim of the youth justice system to prevent offending by children and young persons.' New Labour sought, as in so many areas, to impose order from the centre. It established a Youth Justice Task Force in June 1997 under the chairmanship of Norman (now Lord) Warner. This eventually transformed, following the passage of the Crime and Disorder Act, into a non-departmental public body – the Youth Justice Board (YJB) – sponsored by the Home Office.

Its principal function was to monitor the operation of the youth justice system and the provision of youth justice services, together with monitoring national standards, and establishing appropriate performance measures. The 1998 Act also allowed the Home Secretary to expand the board's role and, from April 2000 following highly critical comments in the Comprehensive Spending Review (Home Office 1998) on the current arrangements, the YJB also became the commissioning body for all placements of under-18s in secure establishments on remand or sentence from a criminal court.

The most far-reaching reform brought about by the Act was the creation of Youth Offending Teams (YOTs). Prior to the 1998 Act, youth justice teams, comprising mainly social workers, had had primary responsibility for working with young offenders subject to non-custodial penalties, and for liaising with other criminal justice and treatment agencies in connection with that work. Stimulated by a concern with efficiency and consistency on the one hand, and by a pragmatic belief in multi-agency working on the other, New Labour's new model YOTs had to include a probation officer, a local authority social worker, a police officer, a representative of the local health authority, and someone nominated by the chief education officer. YOTs have been in operation in all 154 local authority areas since April 2000. Social Services remain the major player in local youth justice, contributing 55% of the YOT's resources. They are followed by the police (13%), probation (10%), local authority chief executives (9%), education (7%) and health (6%) (Renshaw and Powell 2001).

The constitution of these new teams echoes and resembles the multi-agency Diversion Panels and in particular the Northamptonshire Diversion Units of the 1980s (Pitts 2001); the latter having been the subject of particularly good press by the Audit Commission (1996). There is one absolutely crucial distinction however. Whereas the diversion schemes were the child of an earlier era – a product of the 1980s 'corporatism' in juvenile justice (Pratt 1989) – YOTs were established not to divert but to intervene. The two primary functions of YOTs are to co-ordinate the provision of youth justice services for all those in the local authority's area who need them, and to carry out such functions as are assigned to the team in the youth justice plan formulated by the local authority.

The Crime and Disorder Act places a duty on local authorities to formulate and implement annual youth justice plans. In doing this, the authority must consult with the senior officers of the major agencies (police, probation, health) that make up YOTs. Such reports are published and submitted to the YJB which monitors local provision and advises the Home Secretary. It was originally suggested that there be some further inspection of YOTs, either jointly by the Inspectorates of Constabulary, Probation and Social Services along with Ofsted, or by the YJB itself (Leng et al. 1998). This was resisted for some time; joint inspection only beginning in late 2002.

In addition to central oversight, new forms of performance management and multi- and inter-agency working, New Labour also promised increased, and earlier, interventions in the lives of young offenders (and those 'at risk' of becoming young offenders). One of the clearest illustrations of the influence of the Audit Commission was New Labour's critique and reform of the cautioning system. The Crime and Disorder Act scrapped the caution (informal and formal) and replaced it with a 'reprimand' (for less serious offences) and a 'final warning'. As the name implies, one of the crucial characteristics of the final warning is that, except in unusual circumstances, it may only be used once. In addition to the change of nomenclature, and the more sparing manner of usage, the new system of reprimands and final warnings also set in motion a set of other activities – such as those previously associated with 'caution plus' – more frequently, and often earlier, than previously had been the case. Under the Act, all young offenders receiving a final warning are referred to a YOT. Offenders are then expected, 'unless they consider it inappropriate to do so' to participate in a rehabilitation programme (in which reparation is expected generally to be present). According to one informed commentator, 'this new approach represents a considerable improvement on Michael Howard's much more restrictive plans simply to crack down on repeat cautioning' (Dignan 1999a: 52).

The Criminal Justice and Court Services Act 2000 removed the requirement that a police reprimand or final warning be given to a young offender only at a police station. This introduced the possibility of 'conferences' at which parents, victims and other adults could be present – sometimes referred to as 'restorative cautioning' (Young and Goold 1999). Though one of the intentions behind the new warnings system may have been to encourage more restorative practices with young offenders, to date there is little evidence that the new system is experienced as a more participative one by young people (cf. Hoyle *et al*. 2002). Indeed, the Home Office evaluation of the Crime and Disorder Pilots (Holdaway *et al*. 2001) raised questions about the appropriateness of some of the change pro- grammes attached to warnings, and the most recent research, conducted in the North West of England, concluded that many young offenders and YOT workers saw 'the warning system as arbitrary, unfair and dis- proportionate' (Evans and Puech 2001: 804).

Labour criminal justice policy generally, and its youth justice reforms in particular, were much influenced by the 'what works' paradigm and the language of risk factors. It introduced a range of new orders, covering both criminal and civil penalties that focused not only on criminal activity but also on 'anti-social behaviour' and 'poor parenting'. Thus, in the child safety order, the anti-social behaviour order, the local child curfew and the sex offender order, for example, there was no necessity for either the prosecution or the commission of a criminal offence. Predictably, such reforms drew considerable criticism in some quarters, as did the often floated abolition of *doli incapax* (*inter alia* Wilkinson 1995; Penal Affairs Consortium 1995). This principle involved the presumption, rebuttable in court, that a child aged over 10 and under 14 is incapable of committing a criminal offence. As such it brought the UK closer to many of its continental European counterparts in terms of the effective age of criminal responsibility. The principle had been under pressure for much of the 1990s and was very nearly abolished in 1996. New Labour, with its focus on individual and parental responsibility (Muncie 2000), and its desire to cement its position on the law and order high ground, was fiercely critical of the doctrine, arguing that it was archaic, illogical and unfair (Leng *et al*. 1998).

Many of the orders introduced by the Crime and Disorder Act illustrated the influence of Wilson and Kelling's (1982) 'Broken Windows' thesis and the importance given to tackling 'low-level disorder' or 'anti- social behaviour'. One of these, the child safety order, relates to children under 10 (i.e. below the age of criminal responsibility). In fact the order, made in a family proceedings court, is aimed at controlling anti-social behaviour rather than protecting a child's welfare and involves placing a child under supervision usually for a period of three months, though up to a maximum of 12 months. Though the child safety order was subject to criticism in some quarters (Family Policy Studies Centre 1998) it was the anti-social behaviour order which drew the greatest ire. The order was designed specifically to tackle 'anti-social behaviour' defined as 'a matter that caused or was likely to cause harassment, alarm or distress to one or more persons not of the same household'. Applications for an ASBO can be made by the police or the local authority. The orders are formally civil – requiring a civil burden of proof.[1] The order itself consists of prohibitions deemed necessary to protect people – within the relevant local authority area – from further anti-social conduct. What is most controversial about the order, however, is that non-compliance is a criminal matter, triable either way and carrying a maximum sentence in the magistrates' court of six months' imprisonment or five years' imprisonment plus a fine in the Crown Court. This led some of the most distinguished critics of the new order to observe that it was strange 'that a government which purports to be interested in tackling social exclusion at the same time promotes a legislative measure destined to create a whole new breed of outcasts' (Gardner *et al.* 1998: 32).

Another provision, the introduction of 'local child curfew schemes', was also subject to considerable criticism. An early consultation paper, *Tackling Youth Crime* (Home Office 1997f), suggested that such curfews might combat the problem of: 'unsupervised children gathered in public places [who] can cause real alarm and misery to local communities and can encourage one another into anti-social and criminal habits' (1997f: para. 114). The provisions in the Crime and Disorder Act enabled local authorities, after consultation with the police and with support of the Home Secretary, to introduce a ban on children of specified ages (though under 10) in specified places for a period of up to 90 days. Children breaking the curfew were to be taken home by the police, and breach of the curfew constitutes sufficient grounds for the imposition of a child safety order. Despite reluctance by local authorities to introduce curfews, and sustained criticism of the provision from some quarters, government has remained keen on the idea. New legislation, the Criminal Justice and Police Act 2001, extends the maximum age at which children can be subject to a curfew up from 10 to 'under 16', and also makes provision for a local authority or the police to make a curfew on an area and not just an individual.

In the custodial arena, New Labour has also drawn criticism, particularly given the fact that the custodial population has continued to rise over the past five years. In its first term, Labour continued with the previous administration's Secure Training Centre building programme – even arguing that they might be expanded – and introduced a new, generic custodial sentence: the Detention and Training Order (DTO). Available to the courts from April 2000, in a DTO half of the sentence is served in custody and half in the community. The intention behind the DTO was to create a more 'constructive sentence' (Home Office 1997d) in which a training plan would be drawn up for the custodial phase and where the subsequent period of supervision in the community would be considered an integral part of the sentence.

As such the DTO represents something of an increase in the powers of the Youth Court to impose custodial sentences. Whereas the maximum period of detention in a YOI for 15–17-year-olds had been six months for a single offence, the DTO has a maximum of two years. Similarly, although the STO for 12–14-year-olds already provided for a 24-month maximum, the DTO has the potential to be extended to young offenders below the age of 12. In practice, the introduction of the DTO has if anything heightened the existing trend towards increased use of custodial penalties for young offenders. In the first year over 6,000 DTOs were made of which 10% involved 12–14-year-olds. The numbers increased steadily during the first year of operation during which time the juvenile sentenced population in secure establishments rose by 15% though the remand population fell by 21% (Renshaw and Powell 2001).

The other significant change in this period, affecting criminal justice as a whole, was the passage of the Human Rights Act 1998 (the HRA) which introduced the European Convention on Human Rights into English law. The HRA focuses particular attention on the safeguards afforded young offenders subject to criminal sanctions. Article 6, for example, guarantees the right to a fair and impartial hearing, adequate notice of the time and place of the proceedings, and a realistic opportunity to prepare and present a case. Linked with this, the UN Standard Minimum Rules for the Administration of Juvenile Justice (Beijing Rules) include:

- the best interests of the child are paramount;
- judicial proceedings should be avoided where possible;
- any intervention should be kept to a minimum;
- police, prosecution or other agencies should be able to dispose of cases at their discretion;
- criminalising and penalising young people should be avoided unless there is serious damage or harm to them or others;
- legal assistance should be prompt and free of charge.

The implementation of the HRA – which came into force in October 2000 – coincided with the referral orders pilots, causing practitioners to consider the implications of the two. The mandatory nature of referral orders, and the restrictions of the possibility of diversion that result from this, clearly raise potential questions about human rights compliance. Similarly, concerns over the proportionality of contracts in relation to the offence committed were sharpened by human rights debates. To date, however, there have been no formal challenges to referral orders or youth offender panels.

Nevertheless, there remains a broader philosophical tension between the individual rights discourse of the human rights agenda and the communitarian appeal to collective responsibilities that informs key aspects of the Crime and Disorder Act, such as ASBOs, curfew orders, youth justice reforms and community safety initiatives generally. Much of the legislation of New Labour has sought to engender a greater emphasis upon individuals' responsibilities towards, rather than rights over, their communities. Moreover, the HRA initiative in 'bringing rights home' (Straw and Boateng 1997) has ambiguous implications for restorative justice, given its emphasis upon formal legal rights over and above interest-based and party-centred negotiation.

Restorative Justice and New Labour

The influence of communitarian thinking was very visible in the Home Office's consultation documents published immediately after the 1997 General Election. Restorative justice, it appeared, was an idea whose time had come. Initially it was most visible in the place given to reparation in the Crime and Disorder Act, and to the support given to experiments such as that with restorative cautioning in Thames Valley (Young and Goold 1999).

The elements of the Crime and Disorder Act that were most obviously based, at least in part, on ideas influenced by restorative justice were the reformed cautioning system, action plan orders and reparation orders. All these sought to promote the idea of reparation and, wherever possible, to include a requirement to seek victims' views. The action plan order was designed to be the first option for young offenders whose offending is serious enough to warrant a community sentence. *No More Excuses* (Home Office 1997d: 7) described the order as 'a short, intensive programme of community intervention combining punishment, rehabilitation and reparation to change offending behaviour and prevent further crime'. The evaluation of the crime and disorder pilots found that many YOTs developed standard programmes in order to meet the reparative requirements of the order and that 'it is common for the same reparative activity to be built in final warning programmes, reparation orders, action plan orders and supervision orders' (Holdaway *et al.* 2001: 42).

The 'reparation order' requires young offenders to make reparation – specified in the order – either to an identified person, or persons, or 'to the community at large'. The language of responsibilisation was once again central to the underlying rationale. According to the Minister of State at the time: 'With the restorative approach there is no way for youngsters – or their parents – to hide from their personal responsibilities' (Michael 1998). The white paper explained the order in the following terms:

> Courts will have to consider imposing [this penalty] on young offenders in all cases where they do not impose a compensation order. The order will require reparation to be made in kind, up to a maximum of 24 hours work within a period of three months ... Of course not all victims would want reparation. The government's proposals will ensure that the victim's views will be sought before an order is made. Where a victim does not want direct reparation, the reparation may be made to the community at large. (Home Office 1997d: 14)

There can be little doubt that there was a concerted effort by New Labour to make both victims' views and reparation more central aspects of youth justice than previously had been the case. However, Dignan was undoubtedly correct when he argued that these 'reforms hardly amount to a "restorative justice revolution", let alone the "paradigm shift" that some restorative justice advocates have called for' (1999a: 58). Following the implementation of the Crime and Disorder Act, the YJB also committed considerable funds to the stimulation of restorative justice projects for young offenders and, together with Crime Concern, issued guidance on the establishment of victim–offender mediation and family group conferencing programmes. Of all New Labour's restorative youth justice initiatives, arguably the most significant, however, has been the creation of referral orders as part of the Youth Justice and Criminal Evidence Act 1999. Before moving on to consider that order in greater detail, we turn next to an examination of the idea and practice of restorative justice.

Note

1 This was confirmed by the Court of Appeal in R. *v.* Manchester Crown Court, *ex parte* McCann (2001).

Chapter 2

Restorative justice: practices and ideals

Restorative justice has been one of the most significant developments in criminal justice and criminological practice and thinking over the past two decades. According to some commentators restorative justice has become *the* social movement for criminal justice reform of the 1990s and into the new millennium (Braithwaite 1998: 324). Restorative justice also offers itself as a philosophy of conflict resolution and a model of justice. Furthermore, this reform movement has established itself at an international level, witnessed by the growth of restorative justice debates within different national jurisdictions and within international treaties and protocols. As such, it has spawned particular academic interest (Johnstone 2002). Yet, in large part it constitutes a practice in search of a theory.

The term 'restorative justice' has come to mean different things to different people. Its popularity has seen it being pulled in divergent and often competing directions as it is shaped to meet the interests and ideologies of different groups, professions and organisations. This appeal is both a source of strength and a weakness. As such, restorative justice has become an ambitious but ambiguous project. This chapter will provide a brief overview of restorative justice practices and the ideals that inform them. In so doing, it begins with an outline of the meaning and international growth of restorative justice. It then goes on to outline lessons and experiences from notable restorative practices from around the world. This overview is not intended to be comprehensive, but rather affords an insight into examples of different models of restorative justice, their commonalities and points of difference.

For some commentators restorative justice is not a 'new' form of justice at all, but rather one that harks back, and returns us, to premodern forms of justice (Zehr 1990: 99). These are to be found both in 'ancient forms of justice' (Weitekamp 1999: 93) and in modern-day indigenous justice (Consedine 1995: 12). Here, restorative justice is seen as timeless. In this large history, it is the modern criminal justice system that is seen as an aberrant development in need of explanation. It is the modern state that has appropriated conflict resolution from communities, victims and offenders and in the process trampled and buried longstanding traditions of restorative justice.[1] Braithwaite goes so far as to suggest that 'restorative justice has been *the dominant model* of criminal justice throughout most of human history for all the world's people' (1998: 323, emphasis added). Nevertheless, restorative justice is also timely as it connects with a number of broader contemporary socio-political and cultural changes: notably the rearticulation of rights and responsibilities across and between state and civil society, particularly inspired by neo-liberal assaults upon the welfare state, and the increasing salience given to victims of crime. The revival of restorative justice, therefore, is borne out of both a critique of traditional criminal justice and an appeal to some notion of the 'good society'. The critique of criminal justice tends to focus upon:

- Its ineffectiveness and failure to deliver on its own aims of offender reform and crime prevention.

- Its marginal role in responding to crime, in that only ever a tiny minority of known offences ever result in a criminal sanction.

- Its 'theft of conflicts' from the central parties to a dispute (Christie 1977), notably the victim who is largely marginalised from the criminal justice process but also the offender who is rarely called upon to play a meaningful active role, as legal professionals and court officials take centre-stage.

- Its failure to hold offenders to account in meaningful ways or to respond adequately to the needs of victims.

- Its reliance upon punishment as a response to harm: with the result that one harm is met by another harm, thus increasing the overall level of harm in society rather than reducing it.

- Its remoteness in time, space and social relations from crimes and the problems and people which influence their occurrence.

- Its reliance upon formal rather than informal social control.

- Its insensitivity to cultural and ethnic diversity.

- Its inefficiency, particularly with regard to time delays in processing cases.

- Its cost in both social and economic terms.

All these constitute the 'negative attraction' of restorative justice (Crawford 1996) borne of a 'failure model' of criminal justice (Garland 2001: 61–3). This pervasive sense of failure that spread throughout the 1970s and 1980s was fuelled by dramatically increasing crime rates. In this context, there was considerable questioning of the state's capacity to control crime and of the role and ambitions of criminal justice. This led to the development of new or alternative practices, discourses and ideas concerning the role of state and non-state actors in crime control. The broad umbrella movement for alternative dispute resolution (ADR), mediation and restorative justice was one of the most influential of such developments.[2]

On the other hand, notions of the 'good society' that inform restorative justice (its 'positive attraction') tend to be drawn from either religiously inspired ideas such as those held by Mennonites (notably in the USA – see Zehr 1990) and Quakers (particularly in the UK – see Wright 1991) or secular philosophies of republicanism and communitarianism (Braithwaite 1995; Braithwaite and Pettit 1990; 2000). Religion and moral theory have provided a strong background for emergent forms of restorative justice (Daly and Immarigeon 1998). In these there lies a humanistic vision of an inclusive, interpersonal and problem-solving alternative to the traditional adversarial system of justice (Van Ness and Strong 1997). These all hold out some notion of justice in keeping with and promoting wider social values of doing good to fellow humans, either premised upon a belief in human nature informing a faith of civic life or a belief in the importance of communal bonds as 'social capital' (Putnam 2000), 'collective efficacy' (Sampson et al. 1997) or moral worth (Etzioni 1993).

Defining Restorative Justice

Given the diversity of practices subsumed under the restorative justice umbrella it is notoriously difficult to define. As already noted, restorative justice emerged as a critique of traditional forms of justice and, as such, is often defined in terms of what it is not rather than what it is.[3] Not only does this oppositional understanding tend to oversimplify traditional justice – largely within a failure model – but subsequently, also over-simplifies restorative justice. One well-established definition of restorative justice is of a 'process whereby the parties with a stake in a particular offence come together to resolve collectively how to deal with the aftermath of the offence and its implications for the future' (Marshall 1996: 37). This definition identifies three central elements in restorative justice: the notion of stakeholder inclusion, the importance of participatory and deliberative processes and the emphasis upon restorative outcomes. We will consider each of these in a little more detail.

First, the notion of 'stakeholders' seeks to recognise that crime is more than an offence against the state. These 'parties with a stake in an offence' include not only the victim and the offender, but also the families and supporters of each and other members of their respective communities who may be affected or who may be able to contribute to the prevention of future offending. Practical expressions of restorative justice aim to consider the impact on victims and others involved, be they family, friends, peers or members of broader networks of interdependencies. These stakeholders are believed to be more directly affected by given acts of harm than is the state. Restorative justice also endeavours to explore the impact upon the community more broadly defined. Implicitly, it seeks to curtail and limit the role of criminal justice professionals. According to Christie's carrion call, 'let's have as few experts as we dare' (1977: 12). In its place, restorative justice prefers to empower victims, offenders, family members and others as partners in the justice process. These are the new stakeholders of a revised vision of justice, which seeks to recognise and bring into play, through their active involvement, a broader con-ceptualisation of the appropriate key actors in dispute processing and resolution. These stakeholders are to be afforded a maximum degree of agency and voice, whilst the power of professionals is to be held in check. The principal decision-makers should be the parties themselves. As such, restorative justice entails a relocation of authority in responses to crime away from the state.

Second is the importance of participatory and deliberative processes. This emphasises the value of participation, empowerment, com-munication, dialogue and negotiated agreements. Good communication requires particular contexts and settings conducive to such exchanges. These will usually be informal environments in which the parties feel comfortable and able to speak for themselves. At the heart of a restorative justice philosophy lies a concern with a particular mode of participatory conflict resolution. This is concerned with consensus-building through a problem-solving approach to crime, grounded in local knowledge and local capacity. Building consensus usually requires that before the process begins offenders accept their involvement in and responsibility for the offence. This may take the form of a guilty plea or some other acceptance of guilt. Restorative processes emphasise the importance of offender and victim participation – choice and control – in the process of face-to-face encounters and decision-making. Restoring a sense of control to the central parties is a key aspect of the restorative process. One intended consequence of party-centred control and participation is to restore responsibility to the participants, in the belief that this will encourage offenders to be more accountable for their actions and to encourage others to take responsibility for ensuring the successful implementation of any agreement reached. Discussion of the consequences of offences is seen as a more powerful way of communicating their gravity to offenders in a way that brings home their impact on victims (Morris 2002: 599). A process that treats people with respect and encourages their empowerment, it is believed, will be more legitimate in the eyes of those participating, encourage a more general respect for the law and understanding of the consequences of individual actions upon others.

Third, restorative justice holds out for, and appeals to, particular restorative outcomes or resolutions. Repairing the harm caused by the crime to all those directly and indirectly affected is an ultimate aim of restorative interventions. Reparation may be symbolic as well as material. The intention is that outcomes should seek to heal relationships. In practice, restorative outcomes often include apologies, compensation or direct reparation to the victim for the harm and indirect reparation to the wider community, all of which may take a variety of forms. It is suggested that restorative outcomes should be flexible and party-centred as well as problem-oriented. As such, restorative justice embraces a creative range of potential solutions (as opposed to a list of presumptive sanctions). One of the hopes of restorative justice is that there will be some reconciliation, rapprochement or greater mutual understanding between the parties. The reintegration of offenders into the broader community is also a desired outcome. In response to the question 'what is to be restored?', Braithwaite offers, 'whatever dimensions matter to the victims, offenders and communities affected by the crime' (1999: 6).

The Growing Interest in Restorative Justice

Restorative justice has tended to focus upon young people. As a mode of conflict resolution, which seeks to impart social and cultural messages and symbols and seeks to operate through informal social control mechanisms, restorative justice has particular implications for responding to youthful offending. Unsurprisingly, therefore, it is in the field of youth justice that notions of restoration have had greatest impact. From the ground-breaking development of family group conferences in New Zealand a variety of restorative justice practices for young people has been spawned across the world (Bazemore and Walgrave 1999; Morris and Maxwell 2001a). This is true of England and Wales as elsewhere.

In recent policy debates in the UK, restorative justice has been distilled into the so-called '3Rs' of restoration, reintegration and responsibility (Home Office 1997d; Dignan 1999a). This is defined in the *No More Excuses* White Paper as:

> *restoration*: young offenders apologising to their victims and making amends for the harm they have done;
>
> *reintegration*: young offenders paying their debt to society, putting their crime behind them and rejoining the law abiding community; and
>
> *responsibility*: young offenders – and their parents – facing the consequences of their offending behaviour and taking responsibility for preventing further offending. (Home Office 1997d: para. 9.21)

In addition to its popularity with government, restorative justice has recently been endorsed as a legitimate pursuit of criminal justice by independent commissions. Lord Justice Auld, for example, in his recent review of criminal justice, recommended the development of a national strategy for including restorative justice within criminal matters with a view to ensuring its 'consistent, appropriate and effective use' (2001: 391, para. 69).

Restorative justice has also secured a significant place at the level of international protocols and instruments. In 1999 the United Nation's Economic and Social Council adopted a resolution encouraging member states to use mediation and restorative justice in appropriate cases. Furthermore, it called on the Commission on Crime Prevention and Criminal Justice to consider the development of guidelines on the use of mediation and restorative justice programmes. The declaration arising from the Tenth UN Congress on the Prevention of Crime and Treatment of Offenders, held in May 2000 in Vienna, called on governments to expand their use of restorative justice. Immediately after the congress, the UN Commission on Crime Prevention and Criminal Justice approved a resolution calling for comment from member states on its own draft *Basic Principles on the Use of Restorative Justice Programmes in Criminal Justice Matters* (United Nations 2000).

Restorative Practices

Despite the fact that some commentators suggest that restorative justice is a set of principles, values or a philosophy rather than a practice (Marshall 1999: 1), it is through practice developments around the world that restorative justice has come to be known and in relation to which theories have emerged.[4]

Victim–offender mediation

The revival of restorative justice has its roots in victim–offender mediation and reconciliation programmes. It is widely recognised that in the English-speaking world, the first vicim–offender programme was established in Kitchener, Ontario, by Mennonite Central Committee workers in 1974. The model spread to the USA and UK throughout the ensuing decade and was particularly developed with regard to young offenders.[5] It involves bringing together a victim and his or her offender at a meeting facilitated by a mediator, the aim of which is to discuss the crime and the harm caused as well as how this might be put right. Mediation is a method of communication by which negotiations between the opposing parties are brought about by a third party who attempts to help the parties reach their own solutions to their problems. The mediator acts as an intermediary – a conduit in communication – but has no authority to make a decision or force a settlement.

In some instances, this does not involve face-to-face encounters but rather the mediator acts as an intermediary, engaging in shuttle negotiation between the victim and offender. Historically, English schemes have relied more heavily upon this 'indirect' or 'go-between' approach as opposed to 'face-to-face' mediation than their North American counterparts (Umbreit and Roberts 1996). A further difference arises from the more comprehensive health coverage and compensation laws in England which provide considerably more financial assistance to victims of crime than is common in the USA. This means that financial restitution is less a concern of victims in England than in the USA (Umbreit et al. 2001: 128).

The first systematic use of victim–offender mediation in Britain was that introduced by the Exeter Youth Support Team, established in 1979 (Marshall 1996). Like many of the later developments, it was established as a supplement to a caution in cases where this was considered too limited a response. This and the other small number of victim–offender mediation and reparation schemes were established as a result of concern and awareness that the victim was denied any basic rights of involvement – to have a say or to be listened to – in his or her own criminal dispute. However, many of these early victim–offender mediation and reparation schemes were set up with the explicit aim of diversion from the courts as part of 'caution plus' schemes. The Forum for Initiatives in Reparation and Mediation (FIRM) was established in 1984 to act as an umbrella organisation (later renamed Mediation UK). In 1985 the Home Office funded four pilot victim–offender mediation and reparation projects in Coventry, Leeds, Wolverhampton and Cumbria. These schemes were the subject of considerable evaluation and scrutiny, an important element of which was commissioned by the Home Office. However, the Home Office's enthusiasm for the idea of reparation was short-lived. Funding for the initial schemes was withdrawn at the end of the two-year pilot period and the publication of the 'official' research report, which was sympathetic to the ideal of mediation and reparation whilst acknowledging some of its shortfalls in practice, was significantly delayed (Marshall and Merry 1990).

Despite some promising findings, the research in these early developments was critical of the way in which, in practice, the needs of victims were often subordinated to the aims of diverting offenders from custody or mitigating their subsequent court sentence (Davis *et al.* 1988; Davis 1992a). In addition, it was found that there was often little or no interest in effecting material reparation (Davis 1992b). Researchers also noted the danger of 'net widening', particularly given the emphasis upon referrals at the cautioning stage.

In their struggle for legitimacy these early local schemes suffered from a deliberate arm's length approach adopted by Victim Support (Reeves 1984) as well as difficulties in securing co-operation with the police. With the withdrawal of support by the Home Office an unofficial orthodoxy in policy-making and academic circles began to take hold. This ran along the lines that the 'new deal for victims' launched with great publicity by the Home Office in 1985 – of which victim–offender mediation and reparation had been seen as a key element – had become a 'new deal for offenders'.

In the intervening years, and on the back of more favourable research findings (Dignan 1992), the schemes that survived and weathered the changing winds of policy have done much to respond to their critics. They became more acutely aware of, and attempted to meet, the needs of victims, developed better links with Victim Support (Reeves and Mulley 2000) and set up advisory or management committees which drew together the involvement and support of relevant agencies. Moreover, they placed greater emphasis on mediation as a process rather than the attainment of specific outcomes (be they reparation, diversion or mitigation) and sought to establish and develop guidelines for ethical practice (see Quill and Wynne 1993). In this regard, Mediation UK did much to co-ordinate practice principally through guidelines on training and standards and the dissemination of 'good practice'.

The referral points and the aims of the schemes continue to differ widely but prior to the introduction of the Crime and Disorder Act 1998, most schemes operated at the cautioning stage or after conviction but prior to sentencing. However, some schemes, such as the Leeds initiative, continued to work with serious offences around the Crown Court and post sentence (Wynne 1996). Nevertheless, many schemes suffered from the policy shift away from diversion and the multiple use of cautions in the early and mid-1990s. By and large, victim–offender mediation in the UK has remained small scale and limited to a narrow range of relatively minor offences.

In a number of ways, victim–offender mediation has been eclipsed by the growth of conferencing as an alternative approach to dispute processing. In recent years many victim–offender mediation schemes have been redefined or re-branded as restorative justice initiatives (Marshall 1999; Miers *et al.* 2001). This is in part due to the political currency of restorative justice in the current policy context but also due to the perceived limitations of the victim–offender mediation model which have been exposed by wider restorative justice debates.

Conferencing

The New Zealand experience

Family group conferences have been one of the most important practice contributions to restorative justice in recent years. Family group conferences were first institutionalised in New Zealand by the Children, Young Persons and their Families Act 1989. Since then, family group conferencing in New Zealand has acted as a catalyst for, and beacon of, the international restorative justice 'movement' informing both theory (Braithwaite and Mugford 1994) and practice (Hudson *et al.* 1996). Interestingly, however, as a reform strategy the New Zealand developments were not originally conceived of or framed in explicitly 'restorative justice' terms. The New Zealand reforms had their origin in political concerns about the appropriateness of responses to Maori youth against a background of a growing Maori political voice. It was felt that processes by which decisions were made about their children were alien to their values and traditions (Hassall 1996: 22). This quest for a culturally sensitive process drew upon Maori traditions of involving extended family and community members in conflict resolution. The passage of the 1989 Act was also influenced by the growing victims' movement in New Zealand.

The 1989 Act introduced a statutory framework for the referral of young offenders (14–17 years) to a conference at the pre-trial stage. It is used for all medium and serious offending (except murder and manslaughter) and operates both as a barrier to court processing and as a mechanism for making recommendations to judges pre-sentence (Morris and Maxwell 2000: 208). The conference is convened and facilitated by a youth justice co-ordinator to mediate the conflict at which offenders, their extended family, victims, their supports, police, social worker (in certain cases) and significant others if requested, are all brought together to meet. As such, conferences aim to incorporate a broader range of 'stakeholders' than victim–offender mediation, notably family and extended family members. Judicial oversight is retained over conference agreements where a young person has been arrested (McElrea 1996).

Conferences are held in relatively informal settings. They may begin with a prayer, blessing or formal welcome, depending on the culture and customs of the parties. The proceedings are reasonably flexible, although they usually commence with the police representative reading out a summary of the offence. The aim then is to involve all those present in determining appropriate responses to the offence; to encourage acceptance of responsibility by the offender for his or her actions and their consequences; and to make amends to the victim. This latter stage may involve the young person, his or her family and supporters in some 'private planning time' away from the rest of the conference (including the facilitator) during which they consider the future plan of action to be brought back and discussed by the conference as a whole. For some commentators, this aspect of the New Zealand model marks it out as distinct and indicates that family empowerment is a primary aim of the process (Masters 2002).

Importantly, in New Zealand family group conferences are used not for relatively minor offenders or trivial offences but for the more serious and persistent offenders in the youth justice system. Conferences are not used in place of cautions or police-based diversion. Morris suggests that conferences are held for about 15–20% of young offenders, the rest are simply cautioned or diverted by the police (2002: 602). Early research into family group conferences in New Zealand indicated that victims attended around half of conferences (Morris *et al*. 1993). However, the researchers suggested that this was largely due to 'poor practice' and a failure on the part of professionals to arrange conferences in the interests of victims or even to invite them at all. The researchers found that only 6% of victims said that they did not want to meet their offender. Victims of more serious offences were more likely to want to attend. Of those victims who did attend conferences, the research found relatively high levels of satisfaction with the process.

Australian experiments

Conferencing in Australia has taken diverse forms with different purposes. In part this is due to the federal constitutional legal structure which devolves criminal matters to the state-level jurisdiction. Whilst all but two jurisdictions (ACT and Victoria) have some form of statutory basis for conferencing, it is to be found in some form in all jurisdictions across Australia. Daly suggests that unlike New Zealand there was not the same commitment to, or engagement with, a constructive racial politics in Australia and that the idea of conferencing 'moved into the policy and legislative process almost entirely via mid-level administrators and professionals, including the police' (2001: 61). There are significant differences in the types and numbers of offences referred to conferences in different Australian States (Daly and Hayes 2001). For example, whilst all jurisdictions prefer that outcomes be reached by consensus they differ on which parties, at a minimum, must agree to it. Interestingly, conferencing in Queensland permits victims a right of veto over conference referrals and outcomes.

One of the most notable Australian developments, largely due to its significant departure from the New Zealand model but also due to the publicity it attracted, was the approach developed in Wagga Wagga in 1991 (Moore and O'Connell 1994), although no longer in operation there. The model has a number of key attributes. First, cases are diverted by the police, as a form of 'effective cautioning' and, as a consequence, are largely less serious than those that go to conferences in New Zealand. Second, the conferences are police-led, in that the facilitators are serving police officers – which has led to considerable criticism in some quarters. Third, conferences follow a 'scripted' format. Fourth, this script is heavily influenced by Braithwaite's (1989) theory of 'reintegrative shaming'. Here, family, friends and other members of the offender's 'community of care' are figures in offender reintegration. They are seen to be the most potent shaming agents in denouncing the wrongfulness of the act but also the most important reintegrating agents in supporting and assisting the offender as a worthy and valuable person, beyond his or her momentary status as 'offender' (Braithwaite and Mugford 1994). It would appear that the model – notably through the scripted approach – appears to prompt the shaming of the offender's behaviour in ways that the New Zealand model does not (Young 2001: 201).

The Reintegrative Shaming Experiment (RISE) in Canberra sought to test a version of the police-led (Wagga) model by comparing it with similar experiences of court processing. The hypothesis drawn from Braithwaite's theory of 'reintegrative shaming' was that whereas formal courts stigmatise offenders and make it difficult for them to lead lives as responsible members of the community, the shame and mobilisation of a 'community of care' engendered by a restorative conference should provide an opportunity for offenders to confront the consequences of their actions and allow the harm caused to be repaired. The belief is that the best way to control crime is to induce in offenders a sense of shame for the wrongfulness and harm caused by their actions, but to maintain dignity and respect for them as a people whilst reintegrating them into the law-abiding community.

The evaluation of RISE found that conferences may have different impacts on different forms of offending (finding greater impact on violent offenders, for example). Subsequent analysis suggests that the legitimacy of the victim in the eyes of the offender may have an important bearing upon reconviction rates (Sherman 2002). The research also found that conferences, more than courts, increase offenders' respect for the police and the law. The findings indicated a higher level of satisfaction on the part of offenders assigned to a conference as compared to court with procedural fairness of their treatment (Sherman *et al.* 2000b). The research also found a significant level of victim satisfaction, although in line with the New Zealand research they identified a degree of victim dis-satisfaction. Also, echoing the New Zealand findings, the RISE results suggest that victims of more serious offences are more likely to attend, but also be dissatisfied with it. The desire for an apology was nearly universal among the crime victims surveyed (Strang *et al.* 1999).

Conferencing in England and Wales
Conferencing in England and Wales has developed ad hoc outside any statutory framework. Whilst the Crime and Disorder Act 1998 established certain elements of a restorative justice approach as part of a mainstream response to juvenile offending, the space for conferencing is largely as an 'add-on' or supplement to specific orders, such as a reparation order or final warning. As a consequence, family group conferencing, along the lines of the New Zealand model, has been restricted to a small number of initiatives working in both the criminal justice and youth welfare contexts (Dignan and Marsh 2001: 87–90).[6] More recently, the Youth Justice Board through its development fund has funded a number of family group conferencing projects.

By contrast, the police-led (Wagga) model of restorative cautioning has found far greater impact in England and Wales, notably through the

Thames Valley Police cautioning scheme. Thames Valley Police and in particular its previous Chief Constable, Charles Pollard (2000; 2001), have actively championed the use of restorative cautioning in place of the traditional caution since 1998 (both prior to and since the implementation of the Crime and Disorder Act changes to the cautioning system for juveniles). Police officers administering a caution were trained to use a script to facilitate a structured discussion of the harm caused by the offence and how this might be repaired. Under this model the police were supposed to invite all those affected by the offence, including any victims, to the cautioning session (Young 2000). In the first three years of the initiative nearly 2,000 restorative conferences took place with a victim and in a further 12,000 the views of any absent victims were relayed by the cautioning officer (Hoyle *et al.* 2002).

Whilst adopting the same broad model, the Thames Valley initiative departs from the RISE programme (and a similar programme in Bethlehem, Pennsylvania (McCold and Wachtel 1998)) in that it takes less serious offenders and operates at a lower point on the tariff. It constitutes a transformation in the established cautioning process rather than an alternative to court processing (Young 2001: 218). Hence, it is exposed to greater concerns over 'net widening'. The outcomes typically involved only a written or oral apology, with little use of monetary payments or community service.

Research found that despite examples of 'deficient implementation' (particularly in the early years) most participants reported that they were satisfied with various aspects of the restorative process. In particular, they felt that the process was fair because they were given the opportunity to say what they wanted to say (Hoyle *et al.* 2002: 26). A large majority of participants felt that the meeting helped offenders to understand the effects of the offence and induce a sense of shame in them (*ibid.*: 30–1). In most cases, symbolic reparation by way of an apology (either offered or arranged) was the outcome. These gestures were mostly seen as a manifestation of genuine remorse. However, in a small number of cases, apologies had to be 'coerced' in that: 'when this does not flow naturally from the process, facilitators often pressure offenders into apologising' (*ibid.*: 35). In addition, nearly two fifths of offenders experienced a form of stigmatisation, saying that they felt the meeting made them 'feel like a bad person', which the process was designed to avoid. The researchers suggest that the quality of the facilitation had significant impact upon the parties' experience of the process and on the restorativeness of outcomes. They conclude that restorative cautioning appears to be significantly more effective than traditional cautioning in reducing the risk of reoffending.

The perceived success of the Thames Valley initiative has encouraged many other police forces to follow this lead, stimulated by the changes to the cautioning system for young people by the Crime and Disorder Act 1998. Government has encouraged police and YOTs to use the final warning as an appropriate referral point for restorative conferences.

Conferencing has become a central mode of implementing restorative justice ideals, some might say it is *the* pre-eminent form of restorative justice. But as we have seen there are a variety of ways of implementing it as a model, all of which raise different broader implications. Variations largely revolve around the following inter-related elements:

- Form of referral – associated with caution; diversion from court; court referral pre-sentence or sentencing option.

- Seriousness of offences: serious; mid-range or minor offences.

- Volume of cases: high or low volume.

- Organisational leadership/facilitation of conference: police-led; youth justice-led or trained volunteer-led.

- Which parties, if any, are accorded a veto right over the referral and/or the outcome.

- The amount of time allowed to complete outcomes and any upper limit on outcomes.

- Legal framework: either statutory or non-statutory basis.

There is much debate within the literature and among practitioners as to the merits and disadvantages of each variation upon the conferencing model, which we will not rehearse here (see Alder and Wundersitz 1994; Morris and Maxwell 2001b). However, it is worth noting the irony to which Daly alludes, that whilst in Australia all but one of the six statutory schemes rejected the police-led Wagga model in favour of the New Zealand model, in other parts of the world where conferencing has been introduced (notably the USA, Canada and England and Wales) the opposite has occurred (2001: 64).

Healing and sentencing circles

Circles were first adapted from indigenous practices of First Nation people in Canada (Stuart 1994). The expansion of circles owes much to the re-emergence of tribal sovereignty on North American reservations. It has also been encouraged by the desire to keep down the numbers of aboriginal young men in prison. Circles are similar in many ways to conferences in that they seek to include the participation of affected parties beyond the victim and offender. However, they tend to incorporate a broader notion of community participation than do most conferences (LaPrairie 1995a). A common aim is to draw extended family and community members into the process of finding resolutions and redress to crimes. They seek forms of consensus decision-making. As such, circles offer a process and structure to enhance local community involvement in matters of justice.

The idea is to assemble actors with the closest relations and social interdependencies to the principal disputants, most notably with a view to bringing together those people with the best chance of persuading the offender of the irresponsibility of a criminal act. There is also an emphasis upon ritual within circles. There is a 'keeper of the circle' whose purpose (like a mediator or facilitator) is to ensure inclusive dialogue and the integrity of the process. There is usually a 'talking piece' – which will often take the form of a feather – that is passed around the circle, only permitting the person holding it to speak. Circles seek to connect with, and allow space for, the spiritual and emotional aspect of aboriginal and indigenous cultures.

Circles may involve multiple meetings in relation to a particular offender. In essence, they are concerned with community capacity building and community empowerment. As Stuart states, the value of circles 'derives not as much from its impact upon the offender, or upon the victim, but from its impact on the community' (1996: 203). Circles tend to take one of two forms: either 'healing circles' that have as their focus the disposition of situations and 'sentencing circles' that have a quasi-judicial capacity in that they make recommendations to judicial authorities for actual case disposition (McCold 2001: 49).

Healing circles

Healing circles have been used to deal with particular problems within specific indigenous communities, most notably incest, sexual assault and domestic violence by addressing both the harm caused and the social and cultural arrangements that allow these forms of violence to persist. Offenders are encouraged to admit responsibility and seek support in changing their behaviour and communities are encouraged to take responsibility for preventing the reoccurrence of similar offences in the future.

Very little research has been conducted to support the claims of circle proponents (LaPrairie 1995b). The most extensive evaluation of circles was conducted in Manitoba, where healing circles were used to work with sexual abuse victims, their offenders, their respective families and the community at large.[7] The research found that the relative isolation and homogeneity of the Hollow Water First Nation community where the circles were held both enhanced and impaired the work of circles (Lajeunesse & Associates 1996, cited in Coates *et al.* 2000: 6). Some participants reported benefiting considerably from the circle process. However, lack of privacy, difficulty of working with family and close friends, embarrassment, unprofessionalism and religious conflict were cited by others as negative aspects of the circle process.

Sentencing circles
Unlike some other restorative justice practices, sentencing circles are part of and replace sentencing in the criminal justice system. They are not a form of diversion but result in convictions and criminal records for offenders. Sentencing circles have not been authorised by statute but exist solely as a result of, and rely upon, judicial discretion. Sentencing circles are community-directed processes – in partnership with the criminal justice system – which seek to develop consensus on appropriate sentencing plans that address the concerns of all the parties. Sentencing circles tend to be used in relation to serious offences that warrant the significant investment of effort they entail. Circles may take a number of hours and may be spread over a number of days. In addition to the parties affected by the crime, the judge, prosecutor, defence counsel, police and court workers may participate. Circles are sometimes held in courtrooms and may split into an inner and outer circle with the direct participants – victim, offender and their families as well as justice professionals usually involved in the court – in the inner circle and professionals who may be called upon to provide information in the outer circle (Stuart 1996: 194). As a circle is held as part of the sentencing process it may occur without a victim present. Furthermore, the central focus is clearly upon the offender and his or her sentencing or rehabilitation. The precise role of the judge in the proceedings is flexible (Lilles 2001: 175). Ultimately, the judge imposes the agreed sentence. If a consensus is not reached the judge can adjourn the case in order to obtain further information or allow the parties to consider other options. The extent to which the circle provides information for a judge's decision or is itself a decision-making forum remains a vexed question.

Most of the reported cases have involved aboriginals living on reserves or small communities in largely rural locations. Here an offender's community is largely a static, geographic one. The application beyond these tight communities is questioned by some commentators who also note that the majority of Canada's aboriginal people live in urban areas. Given the tight-knit nature of some aboriginal communities there are concerns about the potential exercise of power by dominant family groups within a community (LaPrairie 1995b). According to Lilles, circle sentencing is a unique model of restorative justice in that 'it requires a partnership between the community and the criminal justice system', as a result of which 'each gives needed legitimacy to the other' (2001: 177). Moreover, offenders retain their due process protections, victims are given a voice and communities can call on resources available in the criminal justice system as well as those in their community. He suggests that circles are adaptable to urban centres and to all cultures. Nevertheless, he goes on to caution that the use of circle sentencing 'should be restricted to motivated offenders who have the support of their community' (*ibid.*: 161).

Citizens' panels and community boards

Community peace committees in South Africa

There are certain clear similarities between healing circles and the peace committees established by the Community Peace Programme in South African townships, in operation since 1997 in Zwelethemba, north of Cape Town (Shearing 2001a). The Zwelethemba model has two central aspects. The first is problem-solving which entails both peace-making and peace-building. These terms are used to refer to responding to a particular dispute and problem-solving with regard to more generic issues. The second aspect is concerned with sustaining the process of peace-making and peace-building over time. A central element is the importance of local capacity and knowledge within which problem-solving is situated. The principles of the model are set down in a *Code of Good Practice* (*ibid.*: 21), which constitutes the ground rules and ethics governing committees. One particularly novel factor is the independence of peace committees from the formal criminal justice system that marks them out as a distinct model of restorative justice. They seek to handle a wide variety of offences and, like healing circles, they attempt to address the structural conditions that underlie offending (Roche 2002).

Peace committees are usually convened at a victim's request and consequently victim participation is a central theme. They bring together the extended parties to a dispute, their immediate community of care and wider community members. Peace committee members act as facilitators with no specific authority to resolve the dispute. Upon becoming a 'peacemaker', community members are given a six-month renewable licence. Unlike some restorative justice interventions these 'peacemakers' come from the same township as the victims and offenders. The number of 'peacemakers' who attend a committee varies between 2 and 10. Failure to follow the *Code of Good Practice* is a ground for not renewing a peacemaker's licence.[8]

35

Vermont reparative boards

The mission of community boards, as epitomised by the model developed in Vermont, is to enhance social control at the local level and develop a community's capacity to resolve local problems by involving citizens in the justice process. The Vermont Reparative Probation programme has been in operation since 1996. It is currently available across the state in relation to both adults and juveniles, where cases are referred to boards by judges upon conviction of the offender. Attendance at a reparative board represents a condition attached to probation by the court sentence. Therefore, it is not the task of the board to determine guilt. Rather the board convenes with the offender and attempts to work out a solution to the problems caused by the offence. Victims and other affected parties (such as parents) are invited to attend. Unlike other restorative justice initiatives, boards are not facilitated by professionally trained mediator. Boards are composed of citizen volunteers whose aim is to negotiate reparative agreements with offenders. According to Karp and Walther, under the sentencing guidelines available to Vermont judges, community boards are a sentencing option 'for offenders convicted of minor offences who would have otherwise received more traditional probation or short-term custodial sentences' (2001: 200). Offenders who refuse to sign the agreement or who fail to comply with its terms are returned to the court. Typically, offenders return to the board for a mid-term review (after 45 days, half the probationary period) and a final closure meeting before being discharged upon completion of the agreement.

Boards cannot agree a contract that continues beyond the 90-day probationary period, nor can they stipulate any formal terms of super-vision or incarceration. In addition, only the court can order the terms of restitution or financial compensation (in so doing, the court is required to consider the offender's ability to pay). Consequently, the board typically provides oversight of the court's terms of restitution. Nevertheless, boards do have considerable latitude in negotiating a contract that is tailored to the particular case. In so doing, board members have four goals that they seek to accomplish with the offender (Karp 2000). To:

- engage the offender in ways that will help him or her better understand the harmful consequences of the offence on the victim and wider community;
- identify ways that the offender can repair the harm to victims;
- engage the offender in making amends to the community; and
- work with the offender to find a strategy to reduce the likelihood of reoffending.

The Vermont Department of Corrections employs trained probation staff who manage reparative caseloads and work closely with community volunteers. All Vermont residents that live within the particular jurisdiction of a community board are eligible to serve on it, except current offenders and youths under 18. Somewhat contentiously, local people working in criminal justice agencies may be board members. Volunteers undergo training and are expected to observe boards in action before completing their orientation. However, board members are dis-proportionately 'middle-class and well-educated' (Karp and Walther 2001: 203).

Research has shown that in practice victim participation has been 'infrequent and inconsistent' (*ibid.*: 211). In 1998 only 15% of victims attended a board meeting. Nevertheless, in the same year 52% of offenders successfully completed the terms of the probation, including all reparative tasks. Karp (2000) found that in a sample of cases, most contracts (72%) contained restorative elements that were linked to the harm suffered, but few of them (15%) focused strictly upon repairing specified harms. He identifies a number of reasons why restorative outcomes were not negotiated by boards in some cases: first, because the board discovered that no contract could be negotiated; second, due to simple oversight, possibly because the board forgot to address the issue; third, because the board questioned or challenged the responsibility of the offender (such as when the board disagreed with the conclusions of the court or saw the offender as the 'victim'); fourth, due to a failure of the board to define the nature of the harm caused by the offence; and fifth, as a result of practical difficulties in developing or failure to identify strategies to repair harm (if board members focused upon reintegration rather than reparation). More generally, the lack of victim involvement renders the definition of harm inherently speculative and may bias the board's understanding of the crime in favour of the offender's perspective. Some of these reasons raise questions about the appropriate training of community volunteers.

Research found considerable variation between boards in terms of both process and outcome raising concerns about inconsistent justice. Karp and Walther concluded noting that 'community volunteers involved in the boards often appear amateurish, undiplomatic, and less knowledgeable about restorative principles than trained mediators' (2001: 215). They also raised concerns that boards may have an imbalance of power between older, middle-class, well-educated board members and more youthful, working-class, less educated offenders. These raise issues both about restorative values and the structures of particular models as well as the appropriate implementation of restorative initiatives.

Conclusion

Restorative justice has possibly been the most influential development in 'crime control' in the past decade. Practices and policies influenced by restorative justice ideas and ideals are now to be found in every major continent of the world, and have a statutory basis in many. And yet, restorative justice remains particularly difficult to define. Arguably perhaps, the rapid spread and significant influence of restorative justice practices have been facilitated by this absence of clarity. Restorative justice remains a broad rubric encompassing diverse practices and policies – from victim–offender mediation and conferencing, to sentencing circles and citizens' boards. If clarity is not to be found at a practical level, then perhaps it exists at a philosophical level, for all restorative justice initiatives operate, explicitly or otherwise, as a challenge or counterpoint to more formal or traditional systems of justice. Restorative justice appeals to the potential for a stronger and more participatory civil society and challenges many of the modernist assumptions about professional expertise, specialisation, state paternalism and monopoly. Furthermore, it prompts and allows for a re-examination of the appropriate place of the victim and 'communities of care' in responses to crime. It is to these issues and the relationship between restorative justice and other philosophies of punishment that we turn next.

Notes

1 See Crawford (2002), Daly (2002) and Johnstone (2002: Ch. 3) for critiques of this interpretation of history.
2 Others include the growing emphasis upon crime prevention, particularly of a situational type, and appeals to partnerships across the state/non-state divide (Crawford 1997).
3 Rather like its precursors 'informal justice' and 'alternative dispute resolution' (Cain 1985; Matthews 1988).
4 What follows is not a comprehensive review but an introduction to some of the practices that have shaped the unfolding landscape of restorative justice within which referral orders have been introduced. For more extensive reviews, see Braithwaite (1998); Dignan and Lowey (2000); Kurki (2000) and Miers (2001).
5 Variations of victim–offender mediation have a slightly different recent history across Europe, but have been influenced by developments in the English-speaking world (Weitekamp 2001). Criminal law in Austria and Germany, for instance, recognises various forms of restorative actions for juveniles and adults (see Kilchling and Loschnig-Gspandl 2000). France also has seen the significant growth of penal mediation since the early 1990s (see Wyvekens 1997; Crawford 2000).

6 In the criminal justice context, the best known and most well established of these are the Hampshire Youth Justice Family Group Conference Pilot project (Jackson 1998) and the Kent Intensive Support and Supervision Programme.

7 See McCold (2001: 52–3) for an overview of a particular example of healing circles as developed in Hollow Water, Manitoba.

8 A variety of other innovations under the restorative justice rubric have emerged out of the South African transition to democracy. Probably the most notable has been that associated with the resolution of political conflicts at a societal level, in the form of South Africa's Truth and Reconciliation Commission (see Cohen 2001; Skelton and Frank 2001).

Chapter 3

Implementing restorative justice initiatives

In the light of the survey of restorative justice practices and the ideals that inform them provided in the previous chapter, this chapter explores a number of critical issues concerning restorative values and debates regarding the implementation of restorative justice ideas.

The fit between restorative justice and the wider criminal justice system remains a central issue in implementing restorative practices. Securing sufficient referrals has been an enduring problem for many new restorative justice initiatives. It constitutes something of an Achilles heel. As a consequence, many initiatives have remained peripheral to criminal justice, both in terms of low referrals and the relatively minor nature of cases referred to them (Miers *et al.* 2001). This has often left restorative justice as a marginal, irregular and highly localised activity (Dignan and Lowey 2000).

It also means that schemes are reliant upon other criminal justice organisations – police, prosecution service, courts or probation and prison services – making appropriate referrals. These organisations may not share a restorative justice philosophy, may have different organisational priorities or cultural approaches to case management or simply may not appreciate the criteria upon which schemes work. Moreover, there may be no direct consequences for not referring cases. The referral problem also raises difficulties for the evaluation of the effectiveness of restorative interventions as it introduces elements of bias and self-selection. Schemes that rely upon voluntary selection by offenders will always run the risk that those who choose to enter them would be most likely not to reoffend anyway. A common experience is that the criminal justice system presents major structural, organisational and cultural barriers to the implementation of restorative justice.

There is much debate as to the relative merit of different models of restorative justice, albeit that our understanding of the connectedness between the implementation of different models and the cultural and socio-political environments in which they are located is poorly developed. We know very little about the transferability of different models to different contexts. Whilst we are beginning to see the emergence of rigorous and extensive research studies of restorative programmes, the evaluation of restorative justice remains firmly in its infancy. As a consequence, debates over restorative values and principles constitute an important framework within which to understand practice developments.

Debating 'Restorativeness'

In seeking to highlight and advance restorative values, commentators have sought to distinguish, and place emphasis upon, different salient aspects of restorative justice ideals. Many of these debates have been concerned with either defining what should be the boundaries of restorative justice (its internal versus external attributes and characteristics) and the relative restorativeness of different practices (the relative worth of specific internal attributes and characteristics). This effort has dovetailed energies put into developing standards and ethics of restorative justice (Restorative Justice Consortium 1998; Youth Justice Board 2001). The implicit concern is to produce as robust a definition of restorative justice and its central components as possible, in order to render restorative interventions and their impacts empirically measurable, and to clarify the central values underlying restorative practices against counter-claims. In order to know the impact of restorative justice we need to know what practices and mechanisms are designed to produce which outcomes, in what context these might operate and theories that inform why specific outcomes may result. For example, Braithwaite (1998) in his 'optimistic' account of restorative justice outlines 15 theoretically informed explanations for why restorative justice might outperform traditional criminal justice. The outcome criteria used include not only crime reduction, offender rehabilitation and deterrence (individual and general) but also: victim satisfaction, offender satisfaction, community satisfaction, cost effectiveness, securing justice and enriching freedom and democracy.

In this vein, Van Ness and Strong (1997) identify four core elements of restorative justice that, they argue, can lend themselves to empirical investigation: encounter, reparation, reintegration and participation. These are defined broadly as follows:

- *Encounter* entails some form of meeting or series of meetings usually face-to-face between the parties. The meeting will usually be characterised by a combination of 'narrative' whereby each of the parties tells their story from their own perspective, 'expression of emotion', growing 'understanding' of the others, and a concluding 'agreement' that is particular to the situation and achievable by the parties (*ibid.*: 76–8).

- *Reparation* is the process whereby the responsible party makes amends for, or repairs, the harm caused. Reparation should be made first to the parties directly injured and reflect the seriousness of the injury and the seriousness of the offence as well as the capacity of the offender, so that reparation can be made in a timely and feasible manner (*ibid.*: 91–2).

- *Reintegration* is the re-entry of each party into community life as 'whole, contributing, productive persons'. It involves the creation of relationships that are characterised by 'mutual respect', 'mutual commitment' and 'shared values' that lead to an understanding of intolerance for deviant behaviour. Reintegration requires action on the part of the community, offender and/or victim involved (*ibid.*: 116).

- *Participation* means the opportunity for direct and full involvement of each party in the encounter, reparation and reintegration. It necessitates processes that make the involvement of each of the parties 'relevant' and 'voluntary'.

The implication of Van Ness and Strong's arguments is that the more that specific restorative practices conform to the criteria set out, the greater the impact of the interventions is likely to be. The difficulty for evaluations of restorative justice is that it not only reconfigures notions of justice, but also displaces traditional notions of 'success'. The diverse aims of restorative justice introduce new criteria of success which extend far beyond the traditional emphasis upon offender reform to include the satisfaction of the various parties involved with regard to both procedural and substantive justice, the impact upon the various parties, the nature of restoration and reintegration, and so on.

Inclusiveness, Involvement and Participation

Stakeholder participation is a central restorative justice value and one of Van Ness and Strong's four core elements. In specifying this further, McCold (2000) has sought to classify various different restorative justice practices according to the degree to which the direct stakeholders are involved in the process. For the purpose of this 'involvement model', three broad types of stakeholder are identified: victim, offender and community. The extent to which each of these stakeholders is involved is deemed to constitute the essential criteria of 'restorativeness' (see Figure 3.1). For this model, the most restorative processes are those that involve the active participation of all three sets of direct stakeholders. According to McCold, only where all the stakeholders are actively involved can a practice be considered 'fully restorative'. Where one of the stakeholders is missing from a practice this can only ever be 'mostly restorative', whilst where only one set of stakeholders is present this is, at best, 'partly restorative'.

Figure 3.1 McCold's restorative practices typology

Consequently, victim–offender mediation, given the lack of extended community involvement, is only 'mostly restorative', as are conferences, sentencing circles, citizens' panels or reparative boards where there is no direct victim involvement. Compensation schemes, under this typology, are only 'partly restorative', as are reparative boards.

Process Versus Outcome

The relative emphasis placed upon restorative justice processes as opposed to restorative outcomes is a major issue distinguishing both divergent theories and practices. Some suggest that restorative outcomes regardless of process may be sufficient for restorative justice, whilst others maintain that process is everything. Advocates of restorative circles and community boards, for example, highlight the importance of process regardless of outcome:

> It is the bringing together of knowledge and capacity to seek a solution, rather than any particular desired form of outcome (for example, 'restoration as a healing component' for victims, 'restoration as accepting responsibility' for offenders and restoration as 'denouncing wrongful behaviour' for communities (Law Commission of Canada 1999: 27)), that is at the heart of the model. (Shearing 2001a: 20)

Braithwaite likewise leans towards prioritising the deliberative processes over outcomes, albeit from a less extreme position, in his contention that 'stakeholder deliberation determines what restoration means in a specific context' (1999: 6). Morris reinforces this view: '*any* outcome – including a prison sentence – can be restorative if it is an outcome agreed to and considered appropriate by the key parties' (2002: 599). She goes on to suggest that what differentiates restorative from non-restorative outcomes 'is that the offender, victim and their communities of care have had some input in to the sentence, some increased understanding of the circumstances and consequences of the offence and, perhaps, some increased satisfaction in their dealings with the criminal justice system' (*ibid.*).

Bazemore and Walgrave, however, lean towards the alternative position in asserting that restorative justice is 'every action that is primarily oriented towards doing justice by restoring the harm that has been caused by a crime' (1999: 48). Here, restorative justice is consequentialist in its aim to do justice through restoration. This allows them to include within their definition court-based sanctions, such as compensation orders or reparation orders for victims and community service orders (as reparation to the wider community), where these have not arisen out of, or been proceeded by, a restorative process.

Restorative Justice and Punishment

This opens up debates about the difference or similarity between restorative justice and traditional or established forms of justice. Much of the literature prefers to avoid this shared territory by sharply juxtaposing restorative justice as the opposite or antithesis of retributive justice (see, for example, Zehr 1990: 211–14).[1] This is problematic as some restorative outcomes may result in forms of pain, loss or deprivation – despite the fact that this may be voluntarily agreed to by the offender – such as the payment of reparation, work for the victim/community or even a letter of apology. Moreover, these may in actual fact be experienced or interpreted as 'punishments' by the offender and/or other parties to the restorative justice process. For example, victims may desire the reparation to be a punishment and articulate it as such. Some theorists have sought to integrate or accommodate restorative models of justice within a punishment philosophy (Daly 2000; Duff 2002), whilst others have highlighted the commonalities between the two (Zedner 1994). Duff advances his arguments from a normative or philosophical point of view, whereas Daly's starting point is the empirical experience of restorative interventions. Duff (1992) argues that restorative justice interventions are not 'alternatives to punishment' but 'alternative punishments'. Daly (2000) suggests that restorative justice not only allows the expression of a variety of principles of justice, but also leads to obligations for the offender which are unpleasant. For neither Duff nor Daly is this connection with punishment a reason to reject restorative justice, but rather to consider it alongside, and as part of, a much wider set of responses to crime. Others, like Wright (1991) and McCold (2000), however, reject the possibility of punitive sanctions ever falling within the restorative justice frame.

In part, this debate depends upon how punishment and restoration are defined. Punishment is usually understood as requiring coerciveness, the infliction of pain, deprivation or loss, the intention to cause suffering, and the link between the deprivation and the wrong committed. The absence of any one, according to some commentators, denies the act the essential characteristics of punishment (Walgrave 2001: 19). Coerciveness itself is insufficient. Obligations or deprivations that are not linked with a prior wrong are not considered to be punishments. For some theorists it is the *intention* of the 'punisher' that separates punishment from reparation

(Wright 1991; Walgrave 2003): 'It is the punisher who considers a certain action to be wrong and who wants the wrongdoer to suffer for it ... the key to punishment lies in the head of the punisher, not the punished' (Walgrave 2001: 22). According to this argument, the infliction of pain and suffering is only ever a possible side-effect of restorative interventions. This enables Walgrave to counter Daly's claim that restorative justice is experienced as punishment: 'To put it bluntly, restorative justice in its purist form does not care about what offenders feel, as long as their rights as citizens are respected and a reasonable contribution is made to the restoration of the harm, suffering and social unrest caused by the offence' (*ibid.*: 23). However, this rather flies in the face of the restorative need to connect outcomes with the harm caused by the offence in a manner that is meaningful to, and understandable for, the offender. Moreover, it rather simplifies both the notions of intention and of who constitutes the punisher, particularly within restorative interventions. Multiple intentions may co-exist inside the heads of punishers. Who is privileged as interpreting the intention? Is it to be found residing in the declared purpose of legislation, court reasoning or the heads of individual sentencers? Years of socio-legal research have revealed divergent approaches and disjunctures between them (Carlen 1976; McConville *et al.* 1994).

Here it is instructive to consider what the differences are between financial penalties such as a fine or court-ordered compensation and financial reparation as a result of a restorative intervention. All involve the exchange of money in the aftermath of, and as a response to, a crime. Furthermore, all involve what may be regarded as painful obligations. All acknowledge the loss suffered by the victim and attempt to address or redress the harm done. In this regard, they are all victim-centred. In the case of the fine, and arguably the compensation order, there is an intention to punish. In this vein, Walklate contends that compensation orders have become a 'serious contender in the "punishment tariff" ' (1989: 118).

Those advocates who wish to preserve a clear distinction between punishment and restoration envisage restorative justice as a trans-formative logic and ultimately as a replacement discourse for the 'punishment paradigm'. They fear the corruption of restorative justice's potential by the destructive logic of punishment. For different reasons, critics of restorative justice also seek to preserve this distinction as, for them, it marks out the limits of victims' involvement within criminal justice matters. Ashworth, for example, argues that victims may have a legitimate interest in compensation and/or reparation but 'not in the form or quantum of the offender's punishment' (2002: 584). In contrast to this attempt to cleanse restorative justice of any punitive elements we need to recognise that however well intentioned and benevolent they may appear, or intended by some to be, restorative justice interventions constitute a form of punishment (Zedner 1994; Dignan 2002).

The belief, expressed earlier, that any outcomes which are agreed to by the parties in a restorative process will themselves be restorative raises two crucial points. First, it presupposes and necessitates the voluntary and informed consent of the parties. Second, it raises questions and concerns, at least in the minds of some, over proportionality between the seriousness of the harm caused and any agreed outcome.

Voluntariness and the Question of Consent

Many restorative justice proponents consider voluntariness as a key value in restorative justice (Marshall 1996; McCold 2000). Others see voluntariness as improving the effectiveness of restorative outcomes but not as a prerequisite for restoration. For example, Walgrave whilst noting that 'the quality of restoration will decisively improve if the offender co-operates freely', goes on to state 'voluntariness is not a value on its own, but a tool only, to enhance the quality of possible restoration' (2003: 62). The argument here is that imposed restoration is nevertheless restorative justice. This returns us to the relative emphasis upon process and outcome. Those who hold the view that process is more important must by necessity hold more dear the question of consent. In some senses, Walgrave's position is a more honest recognition that: first, criminal justice inevitably involves coercion in some form or other; and second, voluntariness is not an absolute. Freedom of choice within restorative justice will always be qualified by enticements, perceived threats, the limited comprehension of the parties, the availability of suitable information and of alternative courses of action. All restorative processes in and around criminal justice embody 'incentives' and subtle 'inducements' (Silbey and Merry 1986), as well as outright 'coercive sticks' which undermine absolutist notions of 'voluntariness'. Concerns about the reality of choice and voluntariness are particularly acute with regard to young people who may be more vulnerable to persuasion against their will. The dangers of young people being marginalised in a roomful of adults is a legitimate concern (Haines 2000).

Choice, in reality, will often only mean the opportunity to turn down the offer of a restorative intervention or walk out of one to which referral has been made and consequently, return to the conventional criminal justice process. This we might call choice as an ultimate right of exit. This is often true for the parents of offenders and victims, but is particularly salient in the case of offenders themselves who are caught up in, and the subject of, the machinations of a coercive criminal justice process. Within the criminal justice context there will always be (perceived) incentives not to exit (or turn down) restorative justice interventions. The nature of these will depend upon the stage in the criminal justice process at which referrals are drawn and the criminal justice system within which these are based. However, the point is that these 'sticks and carrots' are intrinsic to any system of referral out of, and in some way connected to, criminal justice processes.[2]

Yet, the limited reality of choice relies upon, as a prerequisite, the existence of criminal justice as a 'background system' (Braithwaite 1999) to offer something to exit into and to deal with cases where participants refuse to participate, for whatever reason. As unpalatable as it may seem for some restorative justice proponents, the efficacy of restorative justice may depend upon a coercive, punitive system *as alternative*. There is also a pragmatic point here, if interventions were seriously to hold the question of consent and voluntariness as a sacred value to restorative justice practices, the likelihood is that these would remain peripheral to the criminal justice system, which is by necessity coercive. This certainly was the dominant experience of victim–offender mediation in the UK in the 1980s and 1990s (Marshall 1996).

Proportionality

To desert theorists it is imperative that punishment should always be proportionate to the offence, bearing in mind the seriousness of the harm and culpability (von Hirsch 1993). Despite the way it has been couched in some of the debates between retributivists and restorative justice proponents, proportionality is not 'all or nothing'. Even systems that adhere to rigid 'just deserts' models are unlikely to be able to deliver absolute proportionality in practice. Not only is this because different sentencers may operate different standards, as is the case in England and Wales where variations between sentences are apparent, but also because the same punishment may mean different things or have different consequences for different offenders.

Desert theorists such as Ashworth (2002) acknowledge the problematic realisation of proportionality in practice. Nevertheless, he argues for the importance of 'principles of proportionality' as goals that systems of justice should continually strive to fulfil (even if never being able to do so absolutely). These include: limiting the quantum of punishment that may be imposed upon offenders; ensuring consistency of treatment of offenders; and protecting against discrimination by attempting to rule out certain factors from sentencing calculations (*ibid.*: 586). These may be principles that restorative justice can accommodate. However, Ashworth goes on to state that the

> principle of proportionality goes against victim involvement in sentencing decisions because the views of victims may vary. Some victims will be forgiving, others will not; some shops will have one policy in relation to thieves, others may have a different policy. If victim satisfaction is one of the aims of circles and conferences, then proportionate sentencing cannot be assured and may be overtaken in some cases by deterrent or risk-based sentencing. (*Ibid.*)

And yet, here, Ashworth asserts an absolutist notion of proportionality – to the exclusion of victim involvement in almost any form sentencing. Whilst he notes that 'existing sentencing systems' do not always pursue principles successfully, resulting in variation and inconsistency, he then finds restorative justice wanting with regard to precisely these standards. However, proportionality may be better conceived as a form of bounding mechanism that limits the scope of restorative outcomes, through 'maximum' or 'upper' limits. Notions of 'limiting retributivism' (Morris and Tonry 1990) may be developed in relation to restorative justice programmes, in a way that addresses the legitimate question posed by just deserts theorists, as to the quantum of punishment or intervention.

Precisely because restorative justice interventions may involve some form of punishment they require certain principled constraints as to their nature and intensity. The fear for some commentators is that the diminished or secondary emphasis on offenders' rights within restorative justice, in the current punitive climate, may see 'the corruption of benevolence', which has been a recurring theme within criminal justice (Levrant *et al.* 1999). The 'return of the victim' in particular and the associated discourse of 'public protection' paradoxically may allow for a 'getting tough through restorative justice', whereby victims are drawn into 'the service of severity' (Ashworth 2000). Restorative values are no less susceptible to manipulation in the pursuit of harsher punishments than 'just deserts' approaches that preceded them (Roach 2000).

Impartiality and Independence

The role of community in restorative justice raises important questions about the nature, place and role of third-party facilitators in the processes of justice (Walgrave 2000). If the facilitator is a representative of the community rather than the state – as is the case in referral orders as we shall see, as well as community peace committees, citizens' panels and reparative boards – then upon what notion of legitimacy does their involvement rest? Clearly, it is not founded upon impartiality and independence. It may appeal to greater local capacity and knowledge. However, this confronts a troublesome contradiction in that the more attached to the community facilitators are, the less likely they are to hold the required 'detached stance' which constitutes a central value in establishing facilitator neutrality and legitimacy. The more that facilitators or mediators represent particular interests or value systems the greater the danger that the interests of one of the principal parties may become sidelined or lost altogether. Ironically, of course, it is exactly this pressure to provide neutral and detached facilitators that increases the likelihood of professionalisation of third parties and the formalisation of otherwise fluid and open restorative processes (Sarat 1988).

The involvement of lay people within the processes of justice necessitates that due concern is given to any conflict of interests that they may bring to their participation, particularly where they are cast in a decision-making role (Doran and Glen 2000: 12; Crawford 2001a). Private and parochial interests should not be allowed to affect public decisions. Furthermore, such conflicts may also place community representatives involved in a restorative process at risk of retaliation from any aggrieved party. At a practical level, this fear may put lay people off getting involved in the first place.

Restorative justice proponents consequently still need to confront the connection between facilitator neutrality, independence, impartiality and procedural justice. For as Tyler (1990) suggests, people are more likely to comply with a regulatory order that they perceive to be procedurally just. The more legitimacy through procedural fairness that such facilitators can engender, the more likely they are to impact positively upon the parties and encourage compliance with the law. There is some evidence emerging from the RISE research that citizens' personal judgement that the law is moral may depend upon their judgement that the human agents of the legal system have treated them with respect (Sherman *et al.* 2000b).

Marrying the Past and Future

In an important way, restorative justice departs from the past-focused logic of retributivism, and its preoccupation with matching punishment to the harm done. In this, restorative justice connects with more extensive recent developments in crime management concerned with 'governing the future' through actuarial modes of social control focused around crime prevention and risk minimisation (see Reichman 1986; Feeley and Simon 1994; O'Malley 2003: Ch. 7). Retributivist notions of justice are concerned with the moral dimension to what has happened and the need to make right the violation to the societal order caused by crime. Here, crime itself causes the moral equilibrium to be disturbed requiring that balance be restored by denouncing the wrong through proportionate punishment. This form of justice demands to be done before moving on. By contrast, forms of crime control that have 'security' demands at their core tend to operate around a forward-looking conception, which accords no special privileged place either to the past or to punishment. They do not seek to reorder the past in a moral or symbolic sense. The future-focused logic of crime prevention, risk minimisation and insurance proposes a very different idea of justice, one that is more instrumental than moral, more consequential than symbolic and more utilitarian than retributive.

Some commentators suggest that restorative justice is able to provide an approach to justice that combines both the risk-based and instrumental approach to governing the future with a moral space for confronting the past (Shearing 2001b). This space is particularly associated with the role of the victim within restorative justice, as victims are 'more emotionally involved and less sanguine about the idea of leaving the past to take care of itself'. They require a 'response that acknowledges the importance of symbolically reordering the past' (*ibid*.: 214). As such, restorative justice may offer a resolution to a fundamental schism within penal and criminological theory and practice that lies in the tension between security and justice. And yet, this raises the question to what extent restorative justice processes in practice are able to juggle these potentially tense demands. Can restorative justice manage to look simultaneously to the past and the future, whilst accommodating both the expressive and morally toned elements of justice together with the instrumental demands for future security? Can the demands of future problem-solving adequately address the need (particularly that held by the victims) to reorder the past? Contrary to Shearing's assertion that 'this tension is being lessened where the mentality and practice of restorative justice is taking hold within criminal justice' (*ibid*.: 217), what may be interesting about restorative justice is that its practices express this tension in both visible and tangible ways.

What Does Reintegrating Offenders Mean?

Restorative justice is premised upon the assumption that offender reintegration is both a desirable and feasible aim. The validity of reintegration rests importantly upon the legitimacy of justice and the legitimacy of the community itself. Why might a young offender want to be restored to, or reintegrated within, a moral community that has abused, marginalised or merely not valued him or her? Many offenders live peripatetic lives on the margins of communities. They may experience community, not in its benign form, but as one of alienation and sometimes hostility. For them the community may suffer from significant and important empathy deficits. If we accept the empirical reality that thin and frayed lines exist between offending and victimisation, offenders may themselves have been the victims of crimes against which the community has failed to act or respond (particularly given the high levels of non-reporting and non-recording revealed by victim surveys). This has implications for legitimacy in restorative justice, which calls out for a mutuality of respect. Responsibilities work both ways. This raises questions about the feasibility of community reintegration.

In this light some commentators are sceptical that a limited (one-off) intervention – such as that envisaged by family group conferences – can really resolve the complex problems in young people's lives so as to address their offending behaviour and the source of their social exclusion (Levrant *et al.* 1999). Conferences and other restorative justice interventions place a heavy onus upon, what is after all, a short meeting, even where this is supported by good preparation and follow-up work (which research suggests is not always apparent). This is particularly problematic where there are extensive or structural problems in offenders' lives that cannot be easily be remedied by participants at a conference. Offender reintegration, if taken seriously, may necessitate considerable social intervention on the part of diverse agencies. This, however, contradicts and offends the diversionary, non-interventionist or minimal interventionist ideology of many restorative justice proponents. In addition, it raises questions of cost and the availability of adequate resources that also often hamper restorative justice initiatives.

What Does Restoring Victims Mean?

From the victims' perspective, there are also concerns as to the feasibility of restoration. Victims need recompense for their harm. This is a goal to which restorative justice appeals. And yet, most young people who have offended may not necessarily be able to make sufficient reparation either financially or in kind. In this context, the public interest lies in public restoration to victims of crime through schemes of compensation. Under the benevolent veil of restorative justice the state should not be allowed to abandon its responsibility to compensate victims. Only state compensation schemes and nationwide victim support schemes can seek to address the harm experienced by victims regardless of whether their offender is apprehended, prosecuted or happens to be a juvenile in regard to whom restorative options may be available. Not only may restorative youth justice initiatives be experienced by victims as a lottery, in that victims are only offered involvement if their offender meets certain criteria related to age, previous convictions, seriousness and whether the offender accepts responsibility for the harm, but also because victims' involvement is dependent upon the effectiveness of the criminal justice process in successfully detecting, apprehending and prosecuting the offender(s).

The vexed place of victims within criminal justice raises a number of broader issues (Crawford and Goodey 2000). Even the New Zealand experience of conferencing demonstrates that prioritising victim work within youth justice reforms can demand a significant shift in culture and practice (Morris et al. 1993). In a British context, this may be even more the case. Some time ago, Shapland (1988) likened the integration of victims into criminal justice to a feudal system, whereby each independent fiefdom jealously guards its piece of criminal justice processing, only negotiating reluctantly with others. Moreover, the difficulty for victims is that their needs span several fiefdoms who rarely communicate with each other. She highlighted the difficulty of producing change in such an 'unwilling system': 'a system which is unwilling both because parts of it do not appreciate the need for change and because it is insufficiently coherent to be able to produce change between its separate fiefs' (ibid.: 193). In such a context, effecting significant reform, even with regard to simple and uncontroversial needs of victims, can be highly problematic.

The victim movement has been a significant spur to restorative interventions and the benefits for victims are often promoted as at the forefront of programme intentions. However, as we have seen, these are often difficult to realise in practice. Some of the sternest critics of restorative justice, in the UK in particular, have come from within the victim movement. The danger is that victim's expectations can be raised only to be dashed through the experience of practice delivery. The involvement of the victim in restorative justice prompts a tension between the 'generalised victim' – often evoked in policy discourses associated with public protection – and the 'individual victim'. On the one hand, policy demands uniform rights, recognition and accommodation of victims, whilst, on the other hand, practice necessitates the 'individualisation of the victim' (Sebba 2000), by providing testimonies of *individual* victims, their personalities and/or circumstances through victim depositions, victim reports and victim impact statements. Not only is this individualisation of the victim ambiguous, but the integration of a victim perspective within an offender-oriented system is uncertain, sometimes half-hearted and often riven with contradictions. In addition, critics suggest that victims have subjective and emotional needs that may fundamentally conflict with the universal and reasoned aims of justice (Sarat 1997).

The significant dissonance between policy assertions and practice leaves practitioners – the human face of the criminal justice system – either in a position slavishly to follow policy guidance or to exploit the tensions within policy to fit their own commitments and cultural values. Within the 'unwilling system', the scope for adaptation is likely to be greater where new demands are seen to be a challenge not only to the authority and autonomy of the organisation but also to the cultural values and institutional practices of those inside it. Here lies the space for victim policies to be transformed 'in the service of offenders' (Ashworth 2000: 186), their rehabilitation or management. This is a real concern for many victim advocates.

In the UK, Victim Support has traditionally held a sceptical and arm's length approach to restorative justice reforms in the UK (Reeves 1984; Victim Support 1995). Mediation and reparation were not listed amongst the five key principles in Victim Support's policy paper entitled *The Rights of Victims of Crime* (1995). The reason for this was mainly 'because they were not regarded as a priority' (Reeves and Mulley 2000: 138). Victim Support believes that the five principles that they did identify – information; protection; services; compensation; and freedom from the burden of decisions relating to the offender – are all more fundamental. These are all things that could, or should, be provided for *all* victims. Mediation and restoration can only ever be available to a small minority of victims, those whose offender has been apprehended, charged and admits his or her offence. For Victim Support, therefore, restorative justice is a marginal side-show and peripheral issue to the main demands and needs of victims.

One major concern is that restorative justice imposes new pressures, obligations and responsibilities upon victims. Victims 'may feel guilty if they choose not to participate and yet anxious if they do' (*ibid.*: 139). Approaching victims to participate in restorative justice, it is feared, could also be experienced as an additional burden in the form of unwanted contact with, or even responsibility for, the offender. Furthermore, victims may feel that they ought to participate in the new reforms particularly if asked to do so by a police officer. Consequently, 'Victim Support firmly believes that victims should be free of the burden of decisions relating to the offender. This responsibility lies with the state and should not be placed on the victim' (*ibid*.: 130). As such, addressing victims' needs and interests in ways that do not simultaneously undermine the rights of offenders constitutes major challenges for restorative justice practices.

What Does Restoring the Community Mean?

At one level, all restorative interventions require a minimum conception of 'community', in that the victim and offender must share a 'minimum common interest in settling together the aftermath of the crime constructively' (Walgrave 2003: 68). At another level, most restorative interventions depart from victim–offender mediation in that they seek to incorporate wider relations of care and to work through networks of interdependencies, less prevalent in (but not absent from) traditional criminal justice. These levers of social control beyond the immediate family are usually referred to as communal forms of regulation. Thus, 'community' constitutes an essential element of, and occupies a central position within, restorative rhetoric and ideals (Kurki 2000: 267; Bazemore and Schiff 2001). Some commentators go as far as to suggest that 'community strength is the ultimate outcome measure for [restorative] interventions' (Pranis 1998: 3). Reference to communities in restorative justice generally alludes to some form of regulatory authority or moral value system with powers to induce conformity beyond the family and below the state (the political community). These communities are often differently conceived in different restorative justice contexts. Nevertheless, most restorative justice practices hold a particular place for some community involvement. In family group conferencing, this notion of community may be drawn narrowly and restricted to kinship networks within and beyond the immediate family and friends or supporters of the offender or victim. In New Zealand and South Australia, for example, members of the wider community do not have a right to participate in conferences. To do otherwise, according to Morris and Maxwell 'would be at odds with the principles underlying conferencing' (2000: 215). However, in other jurisdictions conferences may involve a more extended notion of community representatives in a capacity as facilitator, surrogate victim or merely contributor to proceedings, such as local representatives at community conferences in parts of Australia, community members in peacemaking and sentencing circles and community board members in the Vermont Reparative Probation Programme. However, it is rarely clear exactly what the purpose of community involvement is or ought to be, or what the lines of legitimacy, accountability or representation that particular community members have.

The limitations on the role of, and impact on, the wider community in many restorative justice initiatives have led some to posit a vision of 'community justice' as a more embracing and broad-ranging strategy to that of restorative justice (Clear and Karp 1999; Nellis 2002). Often, these two concepts have been used interchangeably, but it is worth highlighting important distinctions between them. The community justice critique of restorative justice is that the latter is inherently reactive and individualistic. Restorative interventions define the problem of justice as lying within the processes and outcomes attached to the management of specific 'cases' of crime. In this regard, it mimics traditional forms of justice. As a reform, some suggest, restorative justice is profoundly traditional in the location of its efforts (Crawford and Clear 2001: 128). It works at the level of particular criminal cases, seeking to alter how they are handled and how they are resolved. When the case is satisfactorily concluded, restorative justice may be seen as having achieved its objectives. However, this leaves most criminal disputes untouched. This is not merely due to the difficulties attached to referrals (discussed earlier) but more profoundly by the fact that most crimes are never reported to criminal justice agencies and, of those that are, most offenders are never apprehended. As a consequence, restorative justice within criminal matters only responds to a small minority of crimes and is therefore of little relevance to the vast numbers of victims.

Furthermore, it is argued that restorative justice initiatives often fail to address the wider social factors, especially structural inequalities, that produce crime and conflict within communities and which may under-mine their resolution. Restorative justice may end up reinforcing existing inequalities. It looks to individuals to solve 'their' problems and as such conforms with what Beck (1992) refers to as the search for 'biographical solutions to systemic problems'. As Abel (1981) noted with regard to earlier forms of alternative dispute resolution, these may end up being rather conservative institutions due to their individualistic and reactive focus.

However, within both restorative and community justice there is a tendency to view community as an homogeneous and cohesive entity, whether community is conceived of as place-based or not. There is little acknowledgement of intra-community diversity and conflict. Com-munities are not always the havens of reciprocity and mutuality nor are they the utopias of egalitarianism that some might wish. Rather, they are hierarchical formations, structured upon lines of differential power relations. Thus, the 'moral voice of a community' and the interests and values for which it speaks, may be both parochial and exclusive. Appeals to community within restorative and community justice often fail to address the relations that connect local institutions to the wider civil society and political economy of which the community is a part or the manner in which local justice may impact upon neighbouring areas (Crawford 1999). Local restorative justice initiatives are unlikely to be capable of reversing structural inequalities that both divide societies and foster crime.

Much restorative justice over-exaggerates the role that communities can play in responses to, and preventing, crime. Restorative justice holds out the promise that communities can give redress to victims for what has been taken from them and to reintegrate offenders within the community. And yet, not all communities share the same access to resources nor can they feasibly restore victims or reintegrate offenders in the same ways or to the same extent. Communities are marked by different capacities to mobilise internally on the basis of mutual trust combined with a willingness to intervene on behalf of the common good as well as differential relations that connect local institutions to sources of power and resources in the wider civil society in which they are located.

The central lessons from research into community crime prevention are: first, that it is difficult to mobilise and sustain community interest and participation in matters of crime, alone, over long periods of time; and second, that there tends to be an inverse relationship between activity and need (see Rosenbaum 1988). Given that participation (and volunteering in particular) is more likely to prosper in low-crime, well-organised and affluent communities, what are the implications of community-based restorative justice for equity? Neither restorative justice nor community justice should be allowed to become a byword for geographic (in)justice. Rather, these conceptualisations of justice need to be housed within an understanding of social justice and a concern for political economy which links notions of restoration with wider social and economic relations and connects a concern for intra-community attributes with the relations that a community has with the wider social framework in which it is set.

Conclusion

Restorative justice ideas present major challenges to our traditional ways of thinking about, and seeking to deliver appropriate responses to, crime and doing justice. It raises some fundamental questions about the appropriate role of the state and civil society in the regulation of dispute processing, as well as the role of professional expertise in managing disputes. It prompts a rethinking of the aims and functions of crime control and the relative balance between criminal and civil ways of working (Sparks and Spencer 2002).

Yet restorative justice remains in its infancy, both in terms of its implementation and an understanding of its effects. There remains a considerable 'gap' between theory and practice: between what is claimed to occur and what takes place in the name of restorative justice as well as between its supposed and actual effects (Daly 2003). Research evaluations of the complex dynamics, relationships, processes and outcomes that structure different restorative interventions are only just beginning. As we have seen, restorative justice provokes considerable debate over its core values and principles as well as the best ways of delivering these. The experiences outlined in this chapter demonstrate some of the challenges confronted in translating restorative ideals into practice. Restorative justice occupies an awkward relationship to the existing system of criminal justice, seeking both to fit with and simultaneously transform it. As such, notions of reparation and restoration constitute a 'conceptual cuckoo' in the criminal justice nest (Zedner 1994: 234). But as well as seeking to change criminal justice, restorative justice ideals are themselves influenced and sometimes undermined by the complex interface of agencies and procedures that make up criminal justice. It is against this background that the recent reforms in England and Wales sought to introduce restorative justice ideals into the heart of the youth justice system. It is the implementation of these reforms to which we now turn.

Notes

1 According to Daly (2002: 58) this oppositional construct constitutes an 'origin myth' of restorative justice and often serves as a shorthand for allusion to the idea of restorative justice as 'good' and punitive justice as 'bad'.
2 The United Nations' draft document on the basic principles on the use of restorative justice programmes in criminal matters recognises this dilemma and seeks to ensure that the 'ultimate right of exit' is not itself undermined by further 'coercive sticks'. The document declares that both where no agreement can be made between the parties and where there is failure to implement an agreement, these factors 'may not be used as justification for a more severe sentence in subsequent criminal justice proceedings' (United Nations 2000: paras 15 and 16).

Chapter 4

Referral orders and youth offender panels

In this chapter we outline the immediate origins and form of the referral order pilots that were initially implemented in 11 areas in England and Wales in 2000. We go on to present the design and methods of the research study that inform the subsequent empirical chapters of this book and conclude with some observations on the research process itself.

Referral Orders: Origin and Intention

The referral order was introduced by the Youth Justice and Criminal Evidence Act 1999.[1] This new primary sentencing disposal applies to 10–17-year-olds pleading guilty and convicted for the first time by the courts. The disposal involves referring the young offender to a youth offender panel. The intention is that the panel will provide a forum away from the formality of the court where the young offender, his or her family and, where appropriate, the victim can consider the circumstances surrounding the offence(s) and the effect on the victim. The panel will agree a 'contract' with the young offender. The work of youth offender panels is governed by the principles 'underlying the concept of restorative justice': defined as 'restoration, reintegration and responsibility' (Home Office 1997d: 31–2). Along with other major reforms to the youth justice system in recent years, the changes fall within the overarching aim of the youth justice system 'to prevent offending by young people' as set out in s. 37 of the Crime and Disorder Act 1998.

The referral order is available in the Youth Court and adult magistrates' courts. It is not available for juveniles with previous convictions. A referral order should not be made where the court considers custody or a hospital order appropriate. Nor will it be given where an absolute discharge is the appropriate disposal. However, in all other cases where the juvenile is convicted for the first time and pleads guilty, a referral order will be the compulsory sentence. There is a discretionary power for the court to make a referral order if a young person pleads guilty to one or more offences and not guilty to other associated offence(s) of which he or she is convicted. The court is required to explain to the offender 'in ordinary language' the effect of the order and the consequences that may follow failure to agree a contract with the panel or a breach of any terms of the contract. Courts may make referral orders for a minimum of three and a maximum of 12 months depending on the seriousness of the crime (as determined by the court) and must specify the length for which any contract will have effect. Where a referral is ordered for two or more offences, the court will make a referral order for each offence. However, each order will be supervised by the same panel and there can only be one contract. When a referral order is made it constitutes the entire sentence for the offence with which the court is dealing and is not treated as an additional sentence to run alongside others, although the referral order may be accompanied by certain ancillary orders such as orders for costs, compensation, forfeiture of items used in committing an offence and exclusion from football matches. As such, referral orders substitute for action plan orders, reparation orders and supervision orders.

The legislation extends the statutory responsibility of YOTs to include the recruitment and training of community panel members, administering panel meetings and implementing referral orders. Panels consist of one YOT member and (at least) two community panel members. In January 2000 the Home Office published draft *Guidance* on the recruitment and training of community panel members as well as the implementation of referral orders more generally, which supplements the statutory framework. According to the *Guidance*, youth offender panels are to be chaired by one of the community members. Moreover, one of the stated purposes of having (at least) two community members as part of the panel is to engage local communities in dealing with young offenders. Selection of community panel members is to be based on personal qualities rather than relevant experience and, consequently, the provision of appropriate training is vital. The intention is that panel meetings should be held in locations as close as possible to where the young person lives and from which the panel members are drawn. It is also intended that the venue should be as informal and non-institutional as possible.

According to the original national standards, the initial panel meeting needed to be held within 15 working days of a referral order being made in court. YOTs are responsible for the preparation of panel meetings. They must contact the young offender to conduct or update a risk assessment. They should prepare background reports, obtain court papers and obtain the previous offending history. In cases where there are identifiable victims, they should contact victims to find out whether they want to be involved in the youth offender panel meeting, whether they are prepared to accept any form of reparation and whether they wish to receive feedback. Victims may bring a friend or supporter to panel meetings.

A parent or both parents of a young offender aged under 16 are expected to attend all panel meetings in all but exceptional cases.[2] The failure of parents or guardians to attend without reasonable excuse may result in contempt proceedings under the Magistrates' Court Act 1980 (s. 63). The court will normally order them to appear. The offender can also nominate an adult to support him or her. It is not intended that legal representatives acting in a professional capacity be included in panel meetings either directly or as an offender's supporter.

The purpose of the panel is 'to provide a constructive forum for the young offender to confront the consequences of the crime and agree a programme of meaningful activity to prevent any further offending'. To encourage the restorative nature of the process a variety of other people may be invited to attend given panel meetings (any participation is strictly voluntary). Those who may attend include:

- the victim or a representative of the community at large – young victims (under 16) should be involved only with the agreement of their parents or primary carer, who should be given the opportunity to accompany them;

- a victim supporter – the victim may be accompanied by a supporter (chosen by the victim and agreed by the panel);

- a supporter of the young person – the offender may be accompanied by an adult supporter (invited by the offender with the panel's agreement);

- anyone else that the panel considers to be capable of having a 'good influence' on the offender; and

- signers and interpreters whom should be provided for any of the participants in the process who require them.

Where there is no direct victim, according to the *Guidance*, the panel may wish to invite 'someone who can bring a victim perspective' to the meeting, 'for example a local business person or an individual who has suffered a similar offence'.

The aim of the initial panel meeting is to devise a contract and, where the victim chooses to attend, for him or her to meet and talk about the offence with the offender. Negotiations between the panel and offender about the content of the contract should be led by the community panel members. The YOT member's role is to advise on potential activities and to ensure proportionality. Where a young offender fails to attend the panel meeting, the YOT member should try to establish the reason and may rearrange the meeting. If no reason is forthcoming, or the reason given is unacceptable, then the offender should return to court for re-sentencing.

The contract should always include reparation to the victim or wider community and a programme of activity designed primarily to prevent further offending. Where possible, it is recommended that reparation should have some relation to the offence itself. According to the *Guidance*, 'contracts should be negotiated with offenders, not imposed on them'.

The YOT member should prepare a written agreement of the contract to be signed by the offender, a panel member and parent if relevant. Contracts are to be written in ordinary language and, where appropriate, to be read aloud to the young person to ensure that the contents are fully understood. A copy of the signed contract should be given to the young person and to parents, guardians, victims or anyone else who will be assisting the young person in complying. The contract is a 'two-way agreement', for which the young person should not be penalised as a result of the YOT's failure to make adequate provisions. The consequences of not complying with the order should also be spelt out to the offender. If a contract cannot be agreed at the first meeting, the panel can hold further meetings. However, if no agreement can be reached, or the offender refuses to sign the contract, then he or she will be referred back to court for re-sentencing. The YOT is responsible for monitoring the contract and is expected to keep a record of the offender's compliance or non-compliance. The panel is expected to hold at least one interim meeting with the offender to discuss progress – the first such review is recommended to be held after one month followed by at least one progress meeting for each three months of the contract. Additional panel meetings will be held if the offender wishes to vary the terms of the contract or seek to revoke the order, or where the YOT feels that the offender has breached the terms of the contract. Towards the end of the order, the panel will meet to review the offender's compliance with the contract. At this stage they may 'sign off' the contract. Once the period of the referral order is successfully completed the offender is no longer considered to have a criminal record under the Rehabilitation of Offenders Act 1974.

Youth offender panels draw eclectically from a variety of prior developments outlined in previous chapters. They borrow explicitly from the experience of the Scottish Children's Hearings system, though unlike Children's Hearings, youth offender panels are located squarely within a penal context as a sentence of the court.[3] They also draw implicitly upon the experience of family group conferencing in New Zealand and Australia and the theoretical literature on 'reintegrative shaming' that accompanied 'conferencing' type developments (Braithwaite 1989). Youth offender panels also draw on the history of victim–offender mediation in England and Wales, notably the development of caution-plus initiatives in the 1980s and the more recent practice of 'restorative cautioning' by the police as well as other developments considered in Chapter 3.

The Pilots

Referral orders were piloted in 11 areas: Blackburn with Darwen, Cardiff, Nottingham, Nottinghamshire, Oxfordshire, Swindon, Suffolk, Wiltshire, and three London boroughs: Hammersmith and Fulham, Kensington and Chelsea and Westminster. The introduction of the referral order pilots was slightly staggered across the pilot areas over the summer 2000. The first referral orders were made in the week beginning 3 July and the first panels met on 24 July 2000.[4] The pilots and their evaluation were overseen by an interagency Referral Order Steering Group chaired by the Youth Justice Board and incorporating representation from the Home Office, Youth Justice Board, Lord Chancellor's Department, Judicial Studies Board, Evaluation Team, police, YOTs, Victim Support, the Magistrates' Association, NACRO and the Restorative Justice Consortium.

Since the completion of the pilot phase, implementation of referral orders in all youth offending teams throughout England and Wales began on 1 April 2002. This national roll-out coincided with the publication of the evaluation final report (Newburn *et al*. 2002).

Research Design

The evaluation began in March 2000 when the pilots set up their operations. In each of the pilot areas the evaluation focused on the recruitment and training of youth offender panel members, the implementation of referral orders and the evaluation of the impact of referral orders. The recruitment and training of youth offender panel members included an analysis of the methods used by YOTs for advertising; the numbers and types of people applying to become community panel members; and the content of training and its perceived effectiveness.

The implementation of referral orders included the examination of the structural arrangements put in place by YOTs for administering and managing, as well as other work in support of youth offender panels; legal issues raised by the introduction of referral orders and related administrative issues such as relationships with the Youth Court and sentencers; the youth offender panel process and the respective roles of those involved, including community panel members, offenders and their parents, victims and YOT staff; and the content of contracts agreed at panel meetings and the nature of the work undertaken with young offenders subject to referral orders.

The evaluation of the impact of referral orders included an analysis of the attitudes of young offenders towards offending and towards victims of crime; the views of victims concerning the offender and the experience of justice; the attitudes of parents or guardians of the young offenders; the views of sentencers and YOT staff involved in implementing referral orders; sentencing patterns; and the workload of YOTs.[5] The impact of referral orders on reoffending is the subject of an ongoing reconviction study.

Methods

Data for the evaluation were of necessity drawn from a broad range of sources. The study included the analysis of various YOT records, observation of training sessions and panel meetings, collection of monitoring data, surveys and interviews with stakeholders involved in the implementation of referral orders and those participating at panel meetings.

Analysis of YOT records

Application forms from the first wave of applicants expressing interest in becoming community panel members were collected and analysed, as were a large sample of 'second wave' applications. Data were also collected on the numbers of referral orders made in each of the pilot areas, the length of the orders, the nature of the offence, details of the offender, the nature of any contract agreed, the number of panels held and, where available, the outcome.

Observation

During the first phase of the pilots, and the first wave of recruitment of community panel members, the evaluation team observed selected examples of all stages of the six-day training programme in each of the pilot sites. In addition, the evaluation team attended a total of 163 panel meetings for observation purposes, although in 33 cases the young person did not attend. Data were collected on the 130 panels that proceeded using standardised observation forms.

Monitoring

In order to collect data on those youth offender panels that the evaluation team did not observe a standardised data panel assessment form was designed for completion by members of the panel themselves.

Surveys

In each of the pilot areas the evaluation team conducted a number of surveys. A first group of surveys was conducted with those involved in sentencing (magistrates and court clerks) and implementing referral orders (YOT staff). One of the purposes behind these surveys was to measure any change in attitudes over the period of the fieldwork. As such, two surveys were conducted with each of these groups. Youth Court magistrates in the pilot areas were surveyed both in July 2000 and September 2001. Surveys with clerks to the Youth Court in the pilot areas were conducted in November 2000 and September 2001. YOT staff were surveyed in January 2001 and again in September 2001. In addition, one survey was conducted in April 2001 of all community panel members who, at that time, had completed their training.

Interviews

In-depth interviews were conducted with a broad range of key groups of people involved in the implementation of referral orders, the running of youth offender panels and those invited to attend panel meetings. Referral order managers were interviewed in relation to the general procedures for administering referral orders and recruiting, training and managing community panel members. In all, 28 interviews with referral order managers were conducted during the fieldwork. Most of the managers were interviewed twice, towards the beginning and the end of the fieldwork. Chief clerks to the justices were interviewed in relation to the impact of referral orders on local sentencing patterns and pleas. In total, nine clerks were interviewed. Some 18 trainers involved in training the community panel members were interviewed in relation to their experience of providing training and using the centrally produced training materials. Referral order administrators were also interviewed (8 in total) in relation to their work administering referral orders and arranging youth offender panels. In addition to the survey of community panel members conducted towards the middle of the fieldwork period, interviews were held with selected community panel members both early in the life of the pilots and towards the end of the fieldwork. Interviews with community panel members covered their reasons for volunteering, their experiences of training and sitting on panels and their working relations with YOT staff. In all, 64 community panel members were interviewed for this purpose, some more than once.

The second group of interviewees included a selection of those who participated in, and/or were the subjects of, youth offender panels. A selected number of offenders were interviewed about their experiences of referral orders and their attitudes to victims and to offending. In all, 90 young offenders were interviewed. A sample of parents and guardians were interviewed in relation to referral orders and their perception of the impact of the process on their child. In total, 75 parents or guardians were interviewed. In addition, two distinct groups of victims were interviewed. The first group of victims was those who had attended a panel meeting. These were interviewed in relation to their experience of the panel process and attitudes towards the young offender and perceptions of justice. The second group of victims were those who, for whatever reason, had not attended a panel meeting. The primary interest here was to ascertain why they had not attended and their potential willingness to have participated. In total, 76 victims were interviewed.

Sentencing and workload data

Finally, data were collected, via the Youth Justice Board, on the types and number of sentences made against young offenders in each of the pilot areas and nine comparator areas for the period July 2000– June 2001.[6] Basic data on numbers of reports (pre-sentence, etc.) prepared by YOTs for the court were also collected for the same period.

The Research Process

The nature of the research design presented a number of challenges for us as researchers. First, the sensitivity to the local setting built into the model of youth offender panels meant that practice would have to adjust to local contexts. The implementation of referral orders, particularly recruiting community panel members, finding local venues at which to hold panel meetings and ensuring that participants represent the communities from which offenders and victims are drawn, presented divergent challenges in the different pilots sites. Hence, systems in place in large rural areas might not have been appropriate for urban areas and cities or vice versa. Given the appeal within referral orders to community involvement, the geographic, ethnic and demographic make-up of specific communities had significant implications for youth offender panels and their management. Hence, the variable nature of different local contexts clearly impinged upon the shape and form of implementation.

Second, the novelty of referral orders and youth offender panels meant that within the confines of the *Guidance* set out, there was a considerable degree of latitude as to how they should be implemented. In practice, this meant that different strategies were adopted in different pilots. Furthermore, even within certain pilot areas, different approaches were embraced within different localities (based around different courts or police divisions). It should also be noted that a number of pilot sites preferred to develop their own ways of implementing referral orders and styles of delivering youth offender panels. Consequently, on occasions they chose to ignore elements of the *Guidance* or to adapt them to local conditions. This creative adaptation was particularly true of the manner in which the official training manual (*Panel Matters*) was used to inform the training of community panel members in a number of areas (see Chapter 5). In some senses, the fact that youth offending teams felt they were part of a 'pilot' for an innovative development within youth justice gave them a certain licence to experiment with diverse ways of working, precisely in order to learn better what might work best within which contexts. Conversely, however, a small number of pilots felt that they were required to stick reasonably rigidly to the letter or spirit of the *Guidance*, precisely because they were the subjects of an evaluation.

Third, not only did practice differ across and within the 11 pilot sites, but strategies and approaches developed and changed over time during the pilot period. The process of 'learning through practice' meant that many of the pilots went through significant shifts in their methods of delivery. Those approaches adopted at the outset invariably had changed by the end of the evaluation period. Moreover, the evolution of referral order management and implementation not always developed in a unilinear direction. Different pilots sometimes moved in different directions. Nevertheless, there were common themes with regard to development. The dissemination of these were facilitated by the formal and informal networks of exchange between staff working in the pilot areas, as they shared their own experiences of implementation. This process was actively encouraged by the Home Office and Youth Justice Board. During the 18 months of the fieldwork for the research – a period in which experimentation and institutional learning were the order of the day – one of the most constant features was change itself.

Finally, as researchers we also added to this shifting landscape in so far as we fed back into the field some of our ongoing findings, notably in the form of two interim reports.[7] By contrast with research studies in which published reports only emerge some time after the end of the programme being studied, these reports were circulated expeditiously and were generally well read and well received within the pilot sites. In some instances, they significantly affected practice. Thus, whilst our role was that of 'external evaluators' (Patton 1986), the evaluation also had a developmental and a managerial role, aiding organisational learning and decision-making (Weiss 1998). Whilst this proved a rewarding aspect of conducting the research, by effecting change in a direct and tangible way, it also served further to muddy the waters of evaluation.

Notes

1 Now consolidated in the Powers of Criminal Courts (Sentencing) Act 2000.
2 The court also has a power to place similar requirements on parents of older offenders where the court deems this appropriate (s.20(1)).
3 The initial training manual (*Panel Matters*), used in the training of community panel members, was prepared by Scottish trainers with experience of training Children's Hearings volunteers.
4 It is worth noting that this came hot on the heels of the implementation of the youth justice changes brought about by the Crime and Disorder Act 1998. On 1 June 2000 all the youth justice activities specified within the Crime and Disorder Act 1998 came into effect and youth offending teams had only been operational since April of the same year, except in a small number of the areas which had been part of the pilots for the earlier reforms (see Hines *et al.* 1999; Holdaway *et al.* 2001).
5 The full evaluation also entailed an assessment of the costs of setting up and running referral orders, which is not covered in this book (see Newburn *et al.* 2002: Ch. 10).
6 The three West London pilots were all in one court area and therefore only one comparator was required.
7 These were conditions of the research contract with the Home Office. The first interim report was circulated within the pilot youth offending teams in

February 2001 and was subsequently published as RDS Occasional Paper No. 70. The second interim report was made available to those working in the pilot areas in July 2001 and was later published as RDS Occasional Paper No. 73. Both interim reports are available on the Home Office Research, Development and Statistics Directorate website (http://www.homeoffice.gov.uk/rds/index.html).

Chapter 5

Organising the delivery of referral orders

A central theme in this book concerns how government policy, in this case in the field of youth justice, is implemented in practice. All government policy, whatever form it takes, from statute to non-statutory guidance, is interpreted and responded to by professionals on the ground. The extent to which local practice reflects central government policy intention depends upon a variety of factors, including the clarity of the policy document, the ease of achievability of its aims, together with numerous local social, cultural, economic and ideological circumstances. Having briefly explored the origins of referral orders we turn now to the pilots themselves. In this chapter we outline the establishment of referral order 'teams', exploring how local YOTs put into practice the requirements of the Youth Justice and Criminal Evidence Act 1999. In the main this chapter is based on data drawn from YOT records, observation of training and from interviews with the YOT managers and staff that managed or otherwise contributed to referral order work.

The Recruitment of Community Panel Members

The Youth Justice and Criminal Evidence Act 1999 stipulates that it is the responsibility of the YOT to recruit and train community panel members, and the *Guidance* provided to YOTs suggests that local recruitment strategies should attempt to attract applicants who are 'properly representative' of the community they represent. The *Guidance* recommends that selection of panel members should be based on personal qualities, such as an interest in citizenship issues, communication skills, good judgement, a clear and firm approach to dealing with offenders and crime, sound temperament, and commitment and reliability, rather than professional qualifications (*Guidance*, Home Office, July 2001: ss. 5.7–5.8).

Advertising and recruitment strategies

When the idea of referral orders and youth offender panels was first mooted there was scepticism in some quarters about how realistic it was to expect YOTs to recruit large numbers of volunteers to play a role in local youth justice. Faced with this task the YOTs in the 11 pilot areas used a broad range of advertising outlets in their attempt to attract community panel members. The response varied considerably between the pilot areas. A number of lessons can be drawn from the experience of the first phase of recruitment:

- Local press appeared to be a particularly effective way of attracting community panel members. In the survey of community panel members, 53% said that they first heard about referral orders through a local newspaper.

- A broad range of advertising appeared to have an impact.

- New forms of communication within the workplace, such as email or internal circulars and newsletters, had some impact.

- An advert in *The Voice*[1] had substantial impact (in the initial set-up phase, it attracted at least eight successful recruits, one from outside London).

- In the initial set-up phase, there was little evidence that the effort that had gone into leafleting had had much success.

A year into the implementation of referral orders, most managers felt that they would continually need to top up their pool of community panel members with (at least) annual recruitment and training programmes. In a number of areas, the community panel members were moving on, many looking to use their experience in a professional capacity. This has been most evident among the younger volunteers. In one pilot area (Blackburn) nearly half the original community panel members who had undertaken the training programme had taken up posts in the YOT or had pursued careers in youth work or in the criminal justice system. One referral order manager believed that if the YOT got 12 months out of them, they were 'doing well'.

As we will describe below, in some areas there were particular concerns about the 'representativeness' of the community panel members recruited in the first phase. Subsequent advertising and recruitment drives undertaken by the YOT pilots tended to be more focused and proactive in an attempt to attract community panel members from specific parts of the local community. All the pilot areas identified an initial lack of ethnic minority representation, problems attracting younger people to the work of the panels and several large rural areas had geographical areas that they felt were under-represented. Nottingham City, in particular, was successful in its second wave of recruitment in targeting minority ethnic communities and younger volunteers (10 of the 39 new community panel members were 'non-white' and 17 were from the 18–29 years' age group). Table 5.1 highlights the specific strategies adopted by the respective pilot sites. The general observations drawn from the second and subsequent phases of recruitment were that:

• Targeted leafleting and promotional literature to specific groups and poster campaigns in local businesses and shops was considered a particularly effective strategy; and

• word of mouth (experienced community panel members speaking to friends and colleagues about the work of the panels) was also regarded as successful, particularly for attracting the interest of ethnic minority groups.

The reality for many of the YOTs was that attracting, recruiting and retaining sufficient numbers of community panel members and getting the range required to demonstrate that they were 'properly representative of the community' was seen as a major issue, particularly as one manager put it, 'you can't force people to volunteer'. Attempting to ensure 'representativeness' is far from straightforward. A potential tension exists between the desire for broad involvement and the necessity of ensuring that community panel members have the requisite skills/qualities for the work. Thus, the active targeting of individuals considered 'ideal' for the work of the panels will have implications for the true representativeness of community panel volunteers as a group. Reliance on, or preference for, 'professional volunteers' may formalise the process and reduce the impact that volunteers are assumed to have. Yet, ensuring broad involvement may bring with it the inclusion of a broader range of attitudes and values than is perhaps anticipated and catered for in the training materials.

Table 5.1 Advertising and recruitment of community panel members after the first phase

Area	Main target groups	Recruitment and advertising strategies
Blackburn	Ethnic minority groups Younger age groups	Advertising in local paper. Sufficient numbers of applicants from previous campaigns on waiting lists
Cardiff	Ethnic minority groups	Flyers. Adverts in local council paper. Advert in local adult education prospectus. Some recruitment through word of mouth. Targeting black and ethnic minorities through outreach project
Nottingham City	Ethnic minority groups Younger age groups	Advertising in local evening newspaper. Community centres, youth clubs. Word of mouth
Nottingham-shire County	Ethnic minority groups Younger age groups Travelling community Geographical areas	Advertisements in local colleges, gym and health centres, Volunteer Fair (CVS Bureau), Rotary Club, local shops and businesses
Oxfordshire	Ethnic minority groups Younger age groups Geographical areas	Distributing leaflets to residential areas. General advertising
Suffolk	Younger age groups	Community groups. Suffolk County Council staff (via email circular). Sessional workers contacting community colleges and clubs. Scheme to persuade the county council to give time off work to employees who work as community panel members
Swindon	Ethnic minority groups	Approaching companies directly and emails to Swindon Borough Council
Wiltshire	Ethnic minority groups	Names kept on file from first round of training. Word of mouth
West London sites	Ethnic minority groups and younger people	Contacting community groups. Promotional literature to churches, trade unions, faith organisations. Poster campaigns. Adverts in *Metro* and *Evening Standard* newspapers. Choice FM radio station. Leaflets in barber shops. Word of mouth

The Training of Community Panel Members

Delivery of the training

The local training of community panel members generally covered six days, with an additional training day for chair panel training and occasionally other training events for community panel members and YOT staff. Three major approaches to training in the pilot sites could be identified:

- *The YOT-led approach* (Blackburn, Nottingham City, Swindon, Wiltshire) saw the training delivered primarily by YOT staff usually supplemented by specialist speakers for particular subjects.

- *The partnership-led approach* (Oxfordshire, West London sites) saw a sharing of the training between YOT staff and independent trainers.

- *The independent trainer-led approach* (Nottinghamshire County, Cardiff) saw an arrangement in which professional independent trainers led the training, often supported by YOT staff.

The advantages and disadvantages of the different approaches were outlined elsewhere (Newburn *et al.* 2001a) and will not detain us here, save to note that the central lesson for YOTs concerned the importance of maintaining clarity in relation to the roles and responsibilities of the different parties involved.

The content of the training

After the first wave of training, and in light of comments made by YOT trainers and the evaluation team, the training programme was amended quite significantly.[2] The revised training programme, *Panel Matters 2,* was generally considered by those most fully involved in delivering the package, particularly referral order managers, to be more varied, easier to deliver and altogether more 'user friendly'. In particular, it was thought that the new programme injected some realism into the nature and expectations of the role of community panel members. Nevertheless, in the light of their experience most referral order managers felt that although they would use *Panel Matters 2* as a base for future training programmes, they would vary the content or provide additional training as deemed appropriate for their locality.

The need to take account of local circumstances in delivering the training was considered very important, particularly in relation to issues such as drug use, minority ethnic communities and diversity issues. Many of the pilot sites had, over the course of the pilot period, provided additional training on human rights, sex offenders, the working of the Youth Court, community reparation schemes and victim issues. However, they were wary of overloading people and also by turning community panel members into 'mini-YOT officers' by encouraging them to become experts on everything. Managers were also aware that making the training too intensive could be counterproductive: 'It's about weighing up the intensity of the training and balancing it with other issues to keep their enthusiasm and commitment.'

In the survey of community panel members conducted midway through the pilots, we asked about the formal training programme and how well it had prepared them for their work as panel members.[3] Three fifths (61%) of respondents said that the formal training was very useful and a further third (35%) said it was reasonably useful. Only a small number (4%) said that the training was not very or not at all useful. When asked to look back in the light of their experience working as a panel member, one fifth (20%) of respondents said that the formal training had prepared them very well for their work as a panel member. The majority (53%) felt that they were reasonably well prepared by the training for their work, whilst a further fifth (19%) felt adequately prepared. Again, only a small proportion (6%) felt either not very or not at all well prepared by the training.[4]

As with the training programme as a whole, when asked how well the training had covered particular issues involved in the work of panel members, responses were generally positive (see Table 5.2). For instance, almost nine tenths (88%) of respondents felt that the principles behind referral orders were covered either well or very well. Respondents were most critical about the coverage of the available local programmes of activity, which the majority 53% said was dealt with poorly or very poorly. There were two other issues upon which more respondents felt had been covered poorly or very poorly than those who felt that it had been covered well or very well. These were mental health issues (for which 42% responded poorly or very poorly) and human rights (37% responded poorly or very poorly).

Trying to equip community panel members with the key skills of communication and questioning techniques and approaches was felt to be crucial. The key skills identified for community panel members can be summarised as:

- group dynamics;
- communication skills;
- mediation/negotiation skills;

- listening skills;
- confidence;
- managing emotion/anger; and
- running/chairing a meeting.

Table 5.2 How well particular issues were covered by the training programme (%)

	Very well	Well	Adequately	Poorly	Very poorly
Principles behind referral orders	51	37	10	1	0
Procedure of initial panel meetings	39	32	22	5	1
Restorative justice	33	34	27	4	1
The work of the YOT	32	36	26	5	1
Procedure of subsequent panel meetings	31	29	29	8	2
Victims	27	35	29	6	3
The youth justice system	26	33	33	6	1
Communication skills	22	38	36	2	1
Proportionality of contracts	20	32	32	12	4
Child development	14	34	41	9	1
Managing conflict	14	31	37	15	2
Drugs and alcohol	13	25	38	22	2
Forms of reparation	12	26	31	25	6
Mental health	7	18	32	34	8
Human rights	5	19	39	30	7
Local programmes of activity available	4	15	27	36	17

Communication skills were felt to be particularly important. This involved encouraging community panel members to move away from simply descriptive 'tell me what happened' line of questioning, and get to grips with the nuanced motivational issues of 'why did you do that?' Maintaining an appropriate balance between a gently interrogatory and an exploratory approach can be challenging. After working with the community panel members for over a year, one referral order manager felt that there was a tendency for the community panel members to ask the question and answer it at the same time without sufficiently challenging the young person. The difficulties of selection and recruitment were widely appreciated, not least because making the training too intensive could be counterproductive.

It was widely acknowledged that if the community panel members are to be representative of the community, and the idea is to value and accept diversity, then the selection and recruitment process should be inclusive in order to reflect that diversity. One manager felt that the training caused people to look at their own values and beliefs and confront their prejudices:

> Diversity is about recognising differences and acknowledging that we all have prejudices. When it comes to the training I'd rather that happens than it is screened out for the sake of a quiet life. We need to engage with it not run away from it.

Demographic background

The timetable for the initial set-up phase, establishing basic arrangements locally for the introduction of referral orders, was very tight. Although YOTs were aware early on in 2000 that they had been selected as one of the pilots for referral orders, in many cases there was then a delay of some months before funding was officially confirmed. This led to some concern in local areas, particularly if it was felt that this delay was not fully taken into account by government when checking on progress. One of the consequences of the tight timetable was that the need to attract a 'representative' group of community panel members generally took second place to the immediate need to recruit sufficient numbers of people to enable the panels to start on time. Table 5.3 provides basic demographic information on the majority of applications received from the start of the recruitment period in April 2000 up to 31 July 2001.[5]

Of the applicants for whom we had information, the vast majority (88%) was white. In terms of ethnic origin it was only in the West London sites where a significantly different pattern prevailed (where two fifths of applicants were non-white). Two thirds of all applications (66%) were from women. Just over one fifth (22%) were aged 18–29. Only one tenth (11%) of applicants were aged 60 or more. In terms of their background, applicants came from a wide range of occupations. The public and private sectors appeared to be equally represented. However, very few were in manual work or unemployed.

Further demographic data were available from a survey of all community panel members who had trained and worked as a panel member. Conducted approximately a year after the implementation of referral orders (summer 2001), the survey had a response rate of nearly 60% and constituted a reasonably comprehensive census of active panel members. The profile of community panel members from the survey confirmed the picture suggested by the profile of applicants. During the pilot period, most community panel members were white (91%), female (69%), over 40 years of age (68%) and were employed in professional or

Table 5.3 Applicants in the 11 pilot areas

	Number of applications received by 31 July 2001	*Male*	*Female*	*Ethnic origin*	*Age range*	*Screening interviews*
Blackburn with Darwen	54	22	32	47 White 4 Pakistani 2 Other 1 Missing	18–29: 18 30–39:17 40–49:10 50–59: 4 60+: 5	Yes
Cardiff	45	11	34	43 White 2 Black African	18–29:14 30–39:12 40–49: 11 50–59: 5 60+: 3	No
Nottingham City	97	32	65	79 White 8 Black Caribbean 3 Black other 3 Pakistani 2 Indian 1 Chinese 1 Other	18–29:28 30–39:22 40–49:26 50–59:15 60+: 6	No
Nottingham-shire County	25	12	13	25 White	18–29: 3 30–39: 8 40–49: 9 50–59: 3 60+: 2	Yes
Oxfordshire	76	27	49	72 White 1 Black Caribbean 2 Indian 1 Other	18–29:10 30–39:10 40–49:18 50–59:21 60+: 17	Yes

Table 5.3 continued

	Number of applications received by 31 July 2001	Male	Female	Ethnic origin	Age range	Screening interviews
Suffolk	23	6	17	23 White	18–29: 5 30–39: 1 40–49: 6 50–59: 9 60+: 2	Yes
Swindon	60	23	37	59 White 1 Other	18–29: 11 30–39: 13 40–49: 21 50–59: 11 60+: 4	Yes
Wiltshire	62	23	39	61 White 1 Mixed heritage	18–29: 7 30–39: 13 40–49: 18 50–59: 18 60+: 6	Partial
West London pilot sites	77	20	57	46 White 7 Black African 15 Black Caribbean 3 Black other 3 Black English 2 Mixed heritage 1 Pakistani	18–29: 17 30–39: 20 40–49: 15 50–59: 14 60+: 11	H & F yes K & C no West- minster no

managerial occupations (50%). Community panel members from black and minority ethnic communities were located primarily in the West London pilots and Nottingham City. In the survey, we asked community panel members how well, as a group, they felt they represented the local community. The majority (53%) replied very well or reasonably well, although a sizeable minority (18%) felt that community panel members did not yet represent the local community particularly well.

Figure 5.1 Reasons for becoming a panel member (%)

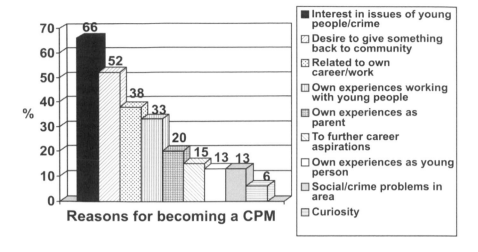

Figure 5.2 The skills that community panel members feel they bring to panel meetings (%)

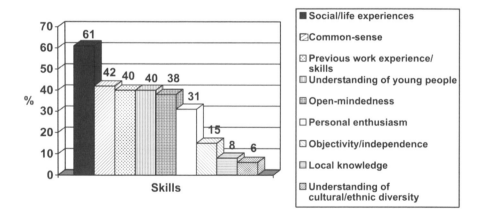

The survey of community panel members explored why people wanted to become a panel member, and what skills they felt they brought to the process. Respondents were asked to identify up to three reasons for becoming a panel member. Figure 5.1 shows that two thirds (66%) of community panel members said that interest in the issues of young people and crime prompted them to apply. The next most popular reason cited by over half of all volunteers was an altruistic desire to give something back to the community.

Respondents were also asked to identify up to three skills they felt that, as a member of the public, they brought to panel meetings. Over three fifths of respondents (61%) felt that a broad range of social and life experiences gave them skills which informed their work as panel members (see Figure 5.2). The second most cited skill was that of 'common-sense' (42%), and a similar proportion of respondents also identified 'previous work experience' and/or 'understanding of young people' as key skills they brought to the role of community panel member. Whilst only 6% of community panel members as a whole responded that an understanding of cultural or ethnic diversity is a key skill, the vast majority of those from ethnic minorities identified this as a key skill that they bring to their work as panel members.

Organisational Issues

In addition to recruiting and training community panel members, YOTs are responsible for administering youth offender panels and for under-taking much of the work agreed as part of the youth offender contract. In what follows, we examine the structures YOTs developed to manage this work, together with some of the staffing and administrative issues that also arose.

Organisation and structure

At the start of the pilot period, the 11 sites adopted different models and operational strategies for implementing the referral order work. These fell into three broad types:

- *The inclusive model:* all YOT staff were involved in every aspect of referral order work (Oxford, Swindon, West London sites).

- *The dedicated model:* discrete referral order teams were established specifically to work on referral orders, for the most part working independently from the rest of the YOT (Blackburn, Nottingham City, Nottinghamshire County, Suffolk, Wiltshire).

- *The partnership model:* operational aspects of referral orders were delivered by the YOT, and the recruitment, training and supervision of community panel members and the administrative co-ordination of panel meetings were undertaken by a contracted service provider (Cardiff Mediation).

Table 5.4 highlights the model originally adopted in each area and notes the change in structure and organisation that took place over the subsequent 12 months. A number of significant changes took place as working practices evolved, workloads increased and a number of staffing issues developed.

Table 5.4 The organisation of referral order work

Area	Model adopted at start of pilot	Model in use 12 months later	Reason for change
Blackburn	Dedicated	Inclusive	Workload
Cardiff	Partnership	Partnership	No change[6]
Nottingham City	Dedicated	Dedicated	No change
Nottinghamshire County	Dedicated	Inclusive	Geographical issues, workload
Oxford	Inclusive	Inclusive	No change (but some staff developing RO specialist skills)
Suffolk	Dedicated	Inclusive	Geographical issues, workload
Swindon	Inclusive	Inclusive	No change
Wiltshire	Dedicated	Dedicated	No change
West London sites	Inclusive	Inclusive	No change

On the whole, those pilot areas that had adopted the inclusive model tended to remain with that form of service delivery.[7] The major advantages of this approach were that it was seen as a way of distributing the workload and ensuring that all YOT staff became familiar with the process and gained some experience of the new sentence. The greatest perceived disadvantage was that it meant that often YOT staff were unable to consolidate their experience of the panel process or get the opportunity to build a working relationship with the community panel members.

Two of the five YOTs with dedicated referral order teams did not make any fundamental changes to operational practices over the course of the year and did not see any reason to do so. One (Nottingham City), despite conceding that at times the volume of work had been 'overwhelming' and 'a bit scary when it had hit a peak', felt it was the most workable and appropriate way of managing the work. The other YOT that maintained a dedicated referral order team throughout the pilot period (Wiltshire) felt that the work needed to be 'driven' and that it would become too disparate if the whole YOT team were to become involved. In addition, they felt that the size of the county meant that both in terms of time and logistics the organisational task would be too difficult without a dedicated team.

However, the most significant changes in working practices came mainly from those areas that had initially adopted the dedicated model. Over the course of the year, in three of the pilot areas (Blackburn, Suffolk and Nottinghamshire County), the referral order work was gradually integrated into the mainstream work of the YOT to include all or most YOT staff. A number of reasons were given for the change. The most frequently expressed concern was the heavy workload for individual case managers, which when combined with the considerable anti-social hours that the work entailed made such a role unsustainable. However, the change of working practice was greeted with mixed views. One manager was concerned that as the work had become generic, there was a lack of control over the decision-making process and a general lack of involvement and responsibility, commenting that 'I don't feel as involved, but because I have had the specialist experience, I sometimes think that I get to mop up and deal with all the difficult or unpopular stuff'. Another believed that the original structure should have been maintained because

At the end of the day, the work is about young people and we should never lose sight of that fact. Working as a separate entity allowed us to focus on the quality of the work we were doing and give it that more personal touch.

Overall, a number of major difficulties were noted with the specialist dedicated model, sometimes referred to as a 'lone ranger' approach. First, concentrating responsibility in one or two hands meant that there was often no one to cover for absences such as attendance at training courses, or periods of annual leave or sickness. At such times, the referral order process was subject to potentially significant delays with cases having to be prioritised according to the risk factor and meetings scheduled to run consecutively in the one venue. Second, 'dedicated teams' tended to work in isolation from the YOT and in some cases this had the effect of lowering the status and importance of the referral order. As a result YOT staff did not prioritise referral order work and were felt to display insufficient commitment to the work specified in the contract. Third, difficulties in communication between YOT staff and referral order staff meant that there was perceived to be a continual need 'to have to try and sell the new orders to try and gain support and trust'.

One YOT (Cardiff) departed from the others in establishing a 'partnership model' in which a voluntary organisation, Cardiff Mediation, was engaged to undertake the recruitment, training and co-ordination of community panel members. One of the advantages of this was that Cardiff Mediation was able to bring experience and expertise in mediation and restorative justice to bear on this work. However, there were difficulties too, relating primarily to differing understandings of the potential of restorative justice in the overall process. This resulted in distinctive operational emphases and priorities that struggled to achieve a benign synthesis. The two respective organisations' contrasting views of the referral order sharpened the distinction between the roles of professional and volunteer, which manifested itself, at times, as a 'them versus us' (statutory versus voluntary) mentality. This somewhat undermined the potential benefits of the partnership. Difficulty in establishing a corporate approach, the lack of rigorous strategic co-ordination and the existence of twin avenues of accountability caused further frustration with the result that there was a lack of ownership of the whole. Occasional communication lapses between teams within the YOT multiplied those between the YOT and Cardiff Mediation:

> As a result we've lost some kids in the system as well. I bet I could go out there and say "what's happening to this kid or that kid?" and they would be somewhere no one would know.

Recruitment and retention of staff

Throughout the pilot period, recruitment to professional posts in the YOT was extremely difficult and most YOTs had several staff shortages. The difficulty in recruiting professionals meant that sessional workers, support workers and casual staff were used with increasing frequency. In one area (Suffolk), the substantive posts for referral order work in the YOT were being formally drawn up for unqualified staff. In a number of the pilot areas reparation workers appeared to be particularly thin on the ground which, given the importance of reparation to the contract conditions, posed some considerable problems and knock-on effects to service delivery.[8]

Mangers felt that it was difficult to attract people for a number of reasons. First, on a general level the pay and conditions of referral order posts were often less favourable than those attached to other YOT posts or projects.[9] One area (Oxfordshire) noted that the high cost of living in some areas was not properly reflected in the salaries that were available. Second, the anti-social hours requirement was a big issue particularly for those with families and child care arrangements to make. Many contracts for referral order staff stipulated an element of evening work. Nonetheless, for many YOT staff there was considerable resistance to significant evening working. In some cases, this meant that areas increasingly had to schedule panel meetings during the day or make substantial overtime payments to staff.

Training

Prior to training community panels members in each of the pilot areas, a national 'training the trainers' event was held in London in March 2000. This event, facilitated by the authors of the training manual, was attended by 21 prospective trainers, with at least one representative from all the 11 pilot sites. The prospective trainers consisted of two broad groups of people: first, those designated YOT members charged with the task of co-ordinating the set-up, selection, training and/or the implementation of referral orders; and second, trainers who had been contracted to perform the training of panel members on behalf of YOTs.

The course facilitators were identified for particular praise as was the quality of the training material. Prospective trainers derived particular benefit from facilitating a task and observing other participants doing so. In addition, the event was seen as a useful opportunity to meet colleagues as well as to share views, skills and experiences with those from other pilot areas.

The surveys of YOT staff indicated that the extent of subsequent training in the pilot YOTs was uneven. More than half the staff responding to the surveys conducted by the evaluation in January and September 2001 indicated that they had not received *any training* in respect of referral orders and panel meetings. Nearly two thirds (62%) of those who had been trained had received one day (8 hours) or less. This was seen as being significant in that only 16% of respondents to surveys conducted with YOT staff indicated that they were not involved, in any capacity, in referral orders.

In particular, the first survey drew attention to the limited extent of training in victim contact work as it related to referral orders. Almost exactly the same pattern emerged in the second survey. Forty respondents (25%) indicated that they were involved in victim contact work and of these, 12 (30%) had received no specific training in the workings of the referral order or youth offender panels; 28 (70%) had received such training but only 11 (28%) of these indicated that the training covered preparing victims and their supporters for panels.

Training appears to have been most consistently delivered in terms of the general operation of the order. Over three quarters of those trained indicated that training had covered the principles behind the legislation, eligibility criteria for a referral order, the procedures to be followed in panel meetings and the role of the YOT officer on the panel. More specific aspects of what happens between an order being made in the court and the first panel meeting appear to have received less attention. Less than half of those trained indicated that training had covered such things as preparing young people and their parents/carers for panel meetings, how to prepare a report for community panel members, or how to prepare victims to attend or contribute to panels. Similarly, the referral order processes that flow from a panel meeting were less consistently covered. Under half the respondents reported that training covered aspects of the order such as monitoring compliance or procedures for breach of the contract agreed at a panel.

Relatively few respondents (20%) indicated that training had covered the impact of the Human Rights Act 1998. For YOT staff whose nominal role in the panel is to ensure proportionality and safeguard the welfare and rights of the child such training could be particularly helpful. That staff appreciate the training that is provided was clear from the fact that in both surveys over 80% indicated that they found the training useful or very useful. That the training was effective is suggested by the finding that 87% of trained YOT staff felt adequately prepared, or better, for undertaking their role in relation to referral orders whilst only 40% of those who had received no training could say the same:

> This YOT has not allowed all members of the team to be trained about referral orders or panels; yet it expects all staff to work with the order. The team is too small and the work is spread to all with little or no training. This gives the distorted impression that we are coping with the workload when in fact we are not.

Administrative issues: record keeping

Arrangements for administering referral orders varied considerably between the 11 pilot sites.[10] However, across all the YOTs, it appeared that the administrative burden had been underestimated, and the overall workload was consistently described as being 'excessive' and 'considerably more resource intensive than first anticipated'. Across all the pilot sites, various systems had been established to collate basic information about referral orders. Whilst some areas (Nottingham City, Suffolk, Oxfordshire) were proactive and sophisticated in their approach to developing manageable, accessible and accountable IT systems, others (Swindon, Wiltshire, West London sites) were less so. Several co-ordinators/managers acknowledged that in hindsight, more attention, thought and resources (in the form of staff) should have been given to the arrangements for collecting and collating basic administrative information. It was recognised that of particular importance was the necessity to be able to produce accurate records for court purposes, the ability to be able to track individual cases, cross-reference to other systems, and also provide accurate feedback and information for external (court personnel) or internal (evaluation and monitoring) purposes.

In general, a number of arrangements were in place for recording information in one form or another:

- Most pilot areas had YOIS or one of several computerised recording systems such as PROTÉGÉ and CAREWORKS for central record-keeping. Many managers indicated teething problems with the introduction of these systems but were keen to develop their use.

- A separate database usually on EXCEL or ACCESS, specifically for referral orders, was developed in a number of areas. This contained details of the offender (gender, ethnicity, age), the offence(s), length of the referral order, date the order was given in court, scheduled date of the panel meeting(s), the allocated community panel members and basic details about victims.

- A database containing names, addresses and contact details of community panel members.

- A database outlining details of venues, such as the contact details of booking staff at the venue, the cost of hiring the venue, suitability, limitation.

- A paper file for each referral order case held by the allocated case worker, containing paper copies of all correspondence and running case notes of the progress of the order.

- A central diary in which all the panel meetings were entered, placed in a central administrative office where it could be accessible to key workers.

In areas where there were several YOT sites, split sites or a wide geographical spread of offices (Suffolk, Nottinghamshire County, Wiltshire, Oxfordshire), the fact that administrative staff were often located in a different office from the operational YOT units led to some problems in communication and record-keeping. One manager (Suffolk) suggested that the reason control and co-ordination of the process had worked so well was in no small measure down to the personalities involved, and in particular the enthusiasm and commitment of the administrator.

Management of community panel members

A number of issues arose in relation to the management of community panel members, covering both how they were allocated to panel meetings and the extent to which panel 'work' was evenly spread among the available community panel members. Two major models of allocating community panel members were in operation in the pilot areas. First, a number of areas (Blackburn, Nottinghamshire County) had adopted, or were considering moving to, a structured approach to both the organisation of youth offender panels and the selection of which community panel members would sit on them. By choosing to operate a rigid rota system for the panel members, limiting the number of venues and standardising the panel meetings to specific times or days, some managers felt that they had more control over the organisation and that it was ultimately less time consuming and vulnerable to delays. It was felt actually to enhance the effectiveness of the panel itself. As one manager commented:

> The panel members know where they are, they know what is expected of them and when. It limits the amount of ringing around trying to get people for individual panels, and it also allows people to get to know each other and build up experience of working with certain people and working together as a team.

A more flexible, personalised approach to scheduling panels and selecting panel members was favoured by a number of other pilot areas (West London, Nottingham City, Oxfordshire, Wiltshire).[11] Several managers felt strongly that a rota system was too simplistic and mechanical to cope with the wider intricacies of the panel process, and that it ran the risk of producing a conveyor belt system of justice. In fact, advocates of this approach were aware that instigating a structured format was not technically in the 'true spirit' of the legislation. However, they took the view that the major advantage of this arrangement outweighed the inconvenience of continually having to reschedule panels, rearrange the community panel members (some of whom have limited availability) and having to rebook the venues.

The second issue concerns the spread of work among community panel members. Responses to the survey suggest that by the time it was conducted in April 2001 a significant number of community panel members had sat on at least a few panels. Nevertheless, the data also indicate that there were a small group of panel members who had sat on a much larger number of panels. By the time of the survey, 21 panel members (10% of the total) had sat on 20 or more panels. Six of these panel members had sat on 40 or more panels each. Moreover, 29 panel members, nearly all of whom had sat on a significant number of panels, always did so in the capacity of leader of the panel meetings. This may point to an early emergence of a core of highly active community panel members upon whom the YOTs rely heavily. By and large, community panel members did not feel that they were being asked to do too much work as a panel member. Seventy one per cent said that they were being given neither too much nor too little work. At the time of the survey, about one quarter of respondents felt somewhat underemployed with 17% replying that they were given too little and 7% far too little work.

The management of community panel members raises important questions about the possible future quasi-professionalisation of panel members and the consequent loss of the particular attributes that their voluntary, community-based participation is felt to bring to youth offender panels. In addition, it is clear that the logistical pressures facing those organising and administering panels may lead to the routinisation of panels and a shift away from the informal, personalised forums intended by the legislation.

Supervision of community panel members

Most areas had monthly, bi-monthly or quarterly supervision meetings for community panel members with the managers or co-ordinators. More regular, informal individual feedback from YOT officers was provided on an ongoing basis usually in the post-panel discussion. Attendance at the supervision meetings was an issue in a number of areas. Community panel members who failed to attend group sessions caused resentment from those who valued the notion of teamwork, and managers who had taken the time to organise events. Lack of attendance was something of a mystery:

> I don't know why they don't come because one of the concerns they raised before was the lack of supervision. That is one of the downsides of working with panel members. They are very needy and expect you to arrange things and run around after them, but then they don't attend for things that you do arrange.

On the whole, confidentiality and attendance at panels were not regarded as a significant problem, as community panel members were felt to be completely reliable. On rare occasions when a panel member had given cause for some concern, he or she was dealt with on a one-to-one basis. Supervision sessions or appraisal sessions tended to include discussions about performance-related issues and was a way of dealing with any problems that had arisen in a sensitive manner. One area had organised individual sessions that lasted about two to three hours. These looked at performance issues and sensitively raised any issues, which may have been mentioned on the feedback forms from the offenders. Generally, for each panel member supervision sessions covered: feedback from the YOT based on their observations at the panel; trying to identify further training needs; group support issues; health and safety issues; victim issues; and any other business.

Conclusion

Realising the implementation of the Youth Justice and Criminal Evidence Act 1999 required a considerable amount of often complicated planning, management and administration. In the event, a significant body of community panel members was recruited in all the pilot areas. They were then trained and, in due course, sat on panels. Local areas experienced difficulty in recruiting a representative body of community panel members, though many have subsequently undertook new recruitment exercises targeting particular groups in the community.

Both this, the organisation of youth offender panels and subsequent work were a particular challenge for YOTs. In the spirit of a pilot phase, different areas adopted different approaches to the management of the work. In the main, those that adopted an 'inclusive' model, in which most or all YOT staff were involved in referral order activity, found that this worked reasonably well and found no reason to change. By contrast, some of those that adopted a 'dedicated' model at the outset, in which particular staff took full responsibility for referral order work, found that it was a source of tension and occasional inefficiency. Hence, some shifted towards a more inclusive model.

Two potential tensions were noted in connection with the management of community panel members. The first concerned the routinisation of panels in response to the logistical pressures of managing a large and complex group of people and interests. The second concerned what was referred to as the potential 'quasi-professionalisation' of community panel members through the use of some with far greater frequency than others. The pressures that led to both of these adaptations are understandable and real. However, they raise the very important issue concerning the appropriate basis for community panel members involvement in panel meetings. That is, should community panel members be involved in a particular meeting because of personal characteristics (gender, ethnicity, age, area of residence, skills, interests, etc.) and their social relationship to the young person? Or should they be involved simply because they happen to be the person that is most obviously available, easy to contact or even next on a rota? These are issues that we return to in Chapter 9.

Notes

1 A national magazine primarily aimed at the black community.
2 The first interim report of the evaluation includes a detailed examination of the content of the training programme and recommendations for possible revision (Newburn *et al*. 2001a). Many of the recommendations were incorporated into a revised version of the training manual.
3 The responses were based on experiences of different waves of training and hence, slightly different training programmes. The form and content of the training were different across the various pilot sites.
4 The remaining 2% did not feel able to comment yet.
5 Not all these applicants proceeded to undertake the training programme.
6 At the end of the fieldwork period this was subject to review by a newly appointed YOT manager.
7 Although there had been some discussions about having specialised referral order workers in Oxfordshire, this was not implemented due to fears that it would restrict individual workers. Nevertheless there was evidence of some unofficial specialisation among YOT staff who particularly liked working on referral orders taking on larger caseloads to leave other work for the remainder of the YOT.
8 Only one area (Blackburn) had a noticeable improvement and felt that there had been an increase in staffing levels and expertise attracted to the YOT with three new members of staff to help the workload. Furthermore, the community panel members had been a lucrative recruitment ground with volunteers moving to become casual workers and becoming heavily involved in the work of the YOT.
9 The Intensive Supervision and Surveillance Programme (ISSP) project in particular caused a flurry of departures from referral order teams across the pilot sites involving managers and other staff.
10 Administrative arrangements established in the set-up phase were covered in detail in the first interim report (Newburn *et al*. 2001a: 33–5).
11 Whilst it needs to be acknowledged that the relatively low number of referral orders in the West London sites may have facilitated the more personalised approach, it should be noted that Nottingham City, with the largest number of referral orders in the pilot period, also favoured the individual case-by-case model.

Chapter 6

Referral orders and the courts

Referral orders represent potentially a significant change to the operation of youth justice, affecting not only the working of Youth Offending Teams, but also that of the Youth Court. In this chapter we examine the views of Youth Court magistrates and clerks to the new order and its operation. We consider the ways in which relationships between YOTs and the Youth Court have been affected by this new development. Finally, we discuss some of the legal issues that arose during the course of the pilots.

Magistrates, Clerks and YOT Staff Members' Views of Referral Orders

As we have outlined referral orders are informed by the principles of restorative justice. Consequently they represent a central aspect of the increased incorporation of restorative justice into the youth justice system. As we saw in Chapters 2 and 3, there is much debate as to the meaning of 'restorative justice'. Of particular interest in relation to the key professionals involved in youth justice is how they viewed the intended operation of referral orders and youth offender panels. Two surveys of magistrates, justices' clerks and YOT staff were conducted as part of the research. Here we focus primarily on data from the second surveys[1] –

conducted in September 2001 – drawing comparison, where appropriate, with the earlier surveys.

The first survey of magistrates found that overwhelmingly they endorsed the restorative justice approach that was assumed to characterise referral orders. This was maintained in the second survey with over 90% of magistrates agreeing with the statement that 'the introduction of a restorative justice approach is a step in the right direction'. Similarly emphatic endorsement of the general intention of the legislation was to be found in the positive responses to statements that referral orders offer 'a new and positive way of responding to youth crime' and help 'render offenders more accountable for their crimes' (85% and 83% respectively agreeing). Magistrates' confidence that the order would 'help address the causes of offending' appeared to have increased with 71% agreeing that it would do so compared to 59% in the first survey. A similar increase, from 68% to 77%, occurred in magistrates' responses to the statement that referral orders would 'encourage offenders to repair the harm or damage they have caused'.

The results of the first survey indicated that justices' clerks were also broadly in favour of the principles behind the legislation, though their enthusiasm was somewhat more muted than that of the magistrates. None the less, the second survey indicated that, in general, their support for referral orders had increased (see Table 6.1).

The generally positive views of referral orders were reinforced by the results of the two surveys of YOT staff. Although YOT staff were slightly less positive in the second survey than the first, none the less their views

Table 6.1 Justices' clerks' views of referral orders and youth offender panels

Referral orders and youth offender panels	1st survey (% agree)	2nd survey (% agree)	1st survey (% disagree)	2nd survey (% disagree)
offer a new and positive way of responding to youth crime	56	66	13	6
help render offenders more accountable for their crimes	48	59	10	9
help address the causes of offending	49	60	7	7
encourage parents and guardians to be more responsible	34	46	20	9

remained strongly in favour of referral orders. Thus, whereas over four fifths of YOT staff in the first survey agreed that 'referral orders and youth offender panels offer a new and positive way of responding to youth crime', this had dropped to three quarters by the time of the second survey. Arguably more important than the slight decline in the proportion agreeing with the statement was the fact that after a year's experience of referral orders three quarters of YOT staff still felt generally positive about referral orders and panels. In particular, this positive view was reflected in the perception among YOT staff that referral orders would have a positive effect on young offenders: four fifths (80%) agreed that they would 'help render offenders more accountable' and over two thirds (69%) said that they would 'help address the causes of offending'. Interestingly in this regard, where in the first survey only 15% of YOT staff thought that referral orders would 'encourage offenders to repair the harm or damage they had caused' (69% didn't express a view), this had risen to 83% by the time of the second survey.

Community involvement

One of the intentions behind referral orders was to broaden the involvement of various groups in the criminal justice system. These groups include the parents and guardians of young offenders, victims and the community in general. Although substantial proportions of magistrates (52%), clerks (46%) and YOT staff (75%) thought that referral orders would 'give victims greater involvement' in youth justice, there was widespread concern among these groups about the level of victim involvement that had been achieved in practice. We deal with the experience of offenders and their parents and with victim involvement in greater detail in Chapters 10 and 11. In relation to the community involvement (see Chapter 9), this was an area where magistrates, clerks and YOT staff were generally positive about the success of this new initiative (see Table 6.2).

The proportion of magistrates who agreed that referral orders 'encourage parents and guardians to be more responsible for those in their care' rose from just under half (48%) in the first survey to over two thirds (67%) in the second. There was a corresponding change in the views of clerks, the proportion agreeing increased from one third (34%) to a little under one half (46%). YOT staff had been very positive in the first survey (68% agreed with the statement) and this remained the case in the second survey (64% agreed). In terms of encouraging community involvement, magistrates and YOT staff were both generally positive (52% and 66% agreeing respectively). By contrast, clerks appeared less impressed, with only one third (34%) agreeing. Similarly, a majority of magistrates (57%) and YOT staff (68%) thought that referral orders would encourage others

Table 6.2 The impact of referral orders on involvement

Referral order and youth offender panels	% magistrates agreeing	% clerks agreeing	% YOT staff agreeing
encourage parents and guardians to be more responsible	67	46	64
encourage community involvement	52	34	66
encourage other people who care about offenders to become involved in responses to crime	57	41	68

to get involved in responses to crime. Again, a significantly smaller proportion of clerks (41%) agreed. The following comments by magistrates illustrate these generally positive views regarding the inclusive nature of youth offender panels:

> Giving the message to young people that the community really does care about what they do.

> Any mechanism that further involves offenders and parents/ guardians in addressing the consequences of their actions and the effect of crime on victims is to be welcomed.

Relationships between YOTs, Panels and the Youth Court

The YOT perspective

Almost all the YOT managers felt that in the early stages of the pilots, engaging with the Youth Courts had been problematic, but that over the course of the year the attitude of both magistrates and clerks appeared to have changed quite significantly with disgruntled voices and initial scepticism gradually giving way to genuine interest and enthusiasm for the process. One manager described engaging with the courts over the pilot period as 'a voyage of learning and discovery', and another emphasised how open-minded they felt the magistrates had been, remarking that they 'have been quite excited about being a pilot and being at the forefront of everything and so have really got into things and become involved'. Some managers were slightly less fulsome and described a 'gradual warming' by magistrates to the referral order process.

According to YOT managers, overcoming initial reservations about the new changes had taken considerable effort. One manager felt that communication was the key to success and had deliberately played the community card, saying: 'I go to meetings to talk about the problems in the various areas and impress on them that the community does have some input – we are all part of the community and should work on this together'. Establishing lines of communication and maintaining regular liaison was seen as *the* vital component to the successful development of the process. All the pilot areas had established regular monthly or bi-monthly meetings between the YOTs and court personnel in some form, including Sentencing Forums, Court User meetings and Court Practitioners Groups (West London, Nottingham City, Swindon, Wiltshire, Suffolk). In addition, some areas had the more formal Steering Group Committees with representatives from the court making a significant contribution to the formulation of policy and protocols (Blackburn, Nottinghamshire County and Nottingham City). One area (Nottinghamshire County) staged a highly successful and well-attended social event in the evening for magistrates, members of the YOT and community panel members with a programme of role-playing scenarios and 'question and answer' sessions enabling the different participants to gain some understanding of each others' role. In a number of areas, magistrates were invited to observe panel meetings (Blackburn, Swindon and Suffolk) to give them first-hand experience of the new process.

The strategy of attempting to keep the courts informed, fostering a good relationship and being extremely proactive in the court enabled any loopholes or lack of clarity on procedural issues to be addressed and tightened up immediately. One referral order manager emphasised the benefit of the 'professional presence of the YOT in court' in being a practical response to magistrates' concerns over the new changes and particularly the loss of control or flexibility in their sentencing powers. Relationships between the courts and YOTs were most harmonious where both parties encouraged the exchange of information and developing rapport. This was often facilitated by the existence of formal steering committees or similar forum for periodic information exchange. In part, some of these strategies have helped magistrates understand the new process and work with it rather than against it. Good working relations required some sensitive handling but appear, according to both parties, to have been largely successful in the pilot areas.

The view from the Youth Court

In the first survey, conducted as the pilots were beginning, over half of magistrates (53%) felt that referral orders and youth offender panels would improve relationships locally between the court and the YOT. In the second survey, conducted after the pilots had been running a year, the proportion was very similar, rising slightly to 56%. In both cases only a very small proportion of magistrates disagreed with the statement (5% and 7% respectively). Clerks had been, and remained, more sceptical in this regard. In the first survey 28% of clerks agreed that the new orders would lead to improved relationships. This rose to 34% in the second survey.

How well informed did magistrates and clerks feel in relation to referral orders and, more particularly, the work of panels? Asked to what extent they felt well informed about the role of community panel members an almost equal proportion of magistrates stated they felt reasonably informed (43%) as not very well informed (44%). Three quarters (75%) of the sample felt that they were reasonably, or better, informed about the workings of panels, but a similar percentage (71%) felt that they had insufficient feedback on the terms of the contract agreed at the panel. A lot of magistrates alluded to this in their comments and highlighted the benefit of communication strategies or procedures:

> I have met some panels' members and would welcome occasional meetings with them to discuss progress and concerns. It is important that there is a partnership and that all parties are aware of each other's role.

> Youth Court members are invited periodically to observe a YOP [youth offender panel] in session which I welcome. A YOP rep has attended our panel meetings for Youth Court Magistrates but otherwise feedback is limited. Perhaps communication could be legislated for at each court to keep magistrates in touch.

In their open comments magistrates frequently complained of inadequate feedback on what happened to the young person once he or she had left court – a point made more generally by the Audit Commission some years previously in relation to the inefficient running of the youth justice system (Audit Commission 1996). This absence of information is reflected in the responses to a series of questions in the survey that sought to establish levels of satisfaction among magistrates on the information they are provided with on aspects of the referral order process (see Table 6.3). Only in relation to the working of the youth offender panel and the reasons for

Table 6.3   Magistrates satisfaction with information provision (%)

How satisfied are you with the information provided on	Satisfied	Neither	Dissatisfied
the working of the youth offender panel	54	22	23
the role of the community panel members	33	37	30
the composition of panels	31	37	31
the terms of the contracts agreed	31	34	34
the reasons for referral back to court	56	26	11
the implementation of contracts	34	34	31

referral back to court did even a small majority of magistrates report being satisfied with the information they had available. In relation to the panel process, magistrates seem to have been somewhat in the dark with, for example, one third reporting being dissatisfied with the information in relation to contracts. In addition, a significant minority clearly wanted more information on the role of community panel members, the composition and workings of panels.

There was, therefore, something of a gap between the views of YOT and referral order managers, on the one hand, and magistrates, on the other hand, in relation to the quality and quantity of information provided to the Youth Court. Consequently, this was an area in which further thought will need to be given to the nature and structure of feedback in relation both to the work of panels and to the nature of contracts agreed. The one area where magistrates appeared relatively satisfied was in relation to information about reasons for referral back to court. Here, one tenth of magistrates described themselves as dissatisfied, compared with between almost one quarter and one third in relation to the other main areas of information provision.

The Impact of Referral Orders

Discretion

The clearest evidence of change – where the experience of referral orders appeared to have prompted magistrates to modify their views – was in relation to the extent of discretion available to them. In the first survey only just over a quarter (26%) of magistrates felt that the order would severely limit their discretion – despite its mandatory nature. By the time of the second survey the proportion had more than doubled to over half (53%). The percentage of those who disagreed with such a view fell from just under two fifths (39%) to just over one fifth (22%). Moreover, it seems clear that these magistrates were also concerned about the likely impact of limited discretion. Thus, almost half (48%) of magistrates felt that the lack of discretion would undermine their authority, as opposed to just over a quarter (27%) in the first survey. The clerks' views were even stronger than those of the magistrates. Over four fifths of clerks (84%) felt that referral orders would 'severely limit discretion of magistrates in the Youth Court' (though they were less concerned than magistrates that this would undermine the authority of the court – only 31% agreed).

Magistrates, clerks and YOT staff were asked a series of further questions about what they thought the implications of reduced discretion would be. Over half of magistrates and clerks felt that the new orders would lead to a transfer of discretion to the YOTs, whereas the proportion of YOT staff agreeing with the statement was closer to one third (36%). In the case of clerks and YOT staff these proportions had declined between the first and second surveys. By contrast, having had experience of referral orders, the proportion of magistrates who agreed with the statement increased from 13% to 55%. Only a minority of all three groups – under one third in all three cases – thought that the mandatory nature of the order would reduce the load of the Youth Court.

One of the concerns expressed at the introduction of a new mandatory sentence was that the reduced discretion available to sentencers would lead to inappropriate use of the order at the bottom end of the scale – in relation to minor offences – and at the top end in relation to the use of custody. Although a majority of clerks (53%) thought that the new orders might lead to 'heavy handedness' among magistrates, only a minority of magistrates (31%) and YOT staff (38%) agreed with the statement. Interestingly, however, whilst the proportion of YOT staff agreeing had declined between the first and second surveys, significantly larger proportions of magistrates and clerks indicated concern about heavy handedness. Such concern was not borne out in responses to the statement that referral orders would 'encourage magistrates to use custodial sentences for more serious crimes'. Less than one tenth of magistrates (9%) and fewer than one in eight clerks (12%) agreed with the statement (and in both cases the proportion declined since the time of the first survey).

Minor offences

The surveys of magistrates, clerks and YOT staff indicate that one of the clearest areas of concern is the use of referral orders for relatively minor offences that might better be dealt with in other ways. Thus, asked to indicate the approximate frequency with which they felt another form of sentence would have been appropriate 50% of magistrates suggested this was sometimes the case, a further 12% indicated this occurred often and 2% very often. A supplementary question asked the magistrates to elaborate, briefly, and specify their preferred sentence. It is clear from their responses that imposing referral orders in respect of minor offences creates the most irritation. Non-serious motoring offences were the largest identified category of offence and magistrates' most frequently cited preferred sentence is that of a fine or conditional discharge. Magistrates' open comments in the survey emphasised their evident frustration at the removal of discretion in this regard. The following comments from magistrates were typical:

> Referral orders for minor motoring offences are not appropriate but there is no alternative.

> Minor offences are a problem, these must be removed from the current system allowing the court to apply less intensive sentences.

> The option to give a conditional discharge rather than a referral order or absolute discharge is needed. There have been several instances when an absolute discharge was far from correct and yet a referral order was far too harsh.

> I now use absolute discharge in those cases which should never come to court as such requirements for a referral order merely clog up the system.

Interestingly, for some magistrates the restriction of sentences (such as a fine or a conditional discharge at first appearance) was seen a positive feature of referral orders, although these sentiments were by no means widespread:

> I consider that this type of sentence allows the offender to look at his offence and address it properly rather than being given a conditional discharge. It allows time to be spent with the offender that the courts are unable to do at the moment.

Concerns about minor offences were shared by clerks and YOT staff. Just under half of YOT staff (48%) indicated that they felt that they sometimes or often felt that a sentence other than a referral order would have been the appropriate sentence in cases resulting in a referral order. A similar proportion (49%) agreed that referral orders would 'lead to in-appropriate use of resources for those committing minor offences'. In their general comments on referral orders YOT staff appeared less preoccupied in the second survey with the mandatory nature of the order than they had in the first. Some were still critical saying, for example, that there needed to be 'a better filter mechanism – too many orders are not worthwhile and a direct punishment could have been applied at court, e.g. a compensation order or conditional discharge'. Similarly, other YOT staff commented:

> Magistrates should be able to decide which offenders should receive a referral order because for some offences they are not necessary or suitable and they take a lot of time and effort to set up.

> People who have few issues which need addressing, who are convicted of driving offences, are having to attend panels when a conditional discharge, disqualification or a fine would be more appropriate.

Though concerns remained, it appeared that they were tempered among YOT staff by a recognition of the creative potential of the referral order. Once again, the strongest views were expressed by clerks. In response to the survey three fifths of clerks (61%) said that they 'sometimes' felt that a different sentence would be appropriate rather than a referral order, one tenth said this occurred often and a further 7% very often. A small minority (17%) of clerks said they experienced this rarely or never. Whilst clerks had expressed concern in the first survey about minor offences, in the second survey it was this issue that was their overwhelming concern about the operation of referral orders. Invited to comment on what they considered to be the most and least successful aspects of referral orders, the overwhelming majority of critical comments by clerks focused on magistrates' loss of discretion and, more particularly, minor offences attracting referral orders. Clerks referred to this as 'a waste of resources', as being disproportionate, and that other sentences, such as a fine or conditional discharge, would be more appropriate: 'The least successful aspect is when it may be clear that no particular intervention is necessary, when a fine or a conditional discharge is an adequate and appropriate penalty but magistrates have no discretion.' The introduction of a statutory minimum level of intervention for all young people entering the criminal justice system is perceived by some clerks as unnecessary: 'Many young offenders never offend again after their first appearance in court so it is hard to comment on whether those referred to panels were prevented from offending by the panel.'

Early Intervention

The opportunity for early intervention was identified by both magistrates and YOT staff as a positive factor. Four fifths of YOT staff agreed with the statement 'early intervention is in the interests of young people'. Similarly, two fifths of YOT staff (41%) agreed that the new orders would 'speed up responses to youth crime'. The following comments by YOT staff are illustrative of a fairly broadly held view:

> The opportunity to catch young offenders early with a relatively heavy first sentence. This gives the young offender the clear signal that their offending is not acceptable and will not be tolerated.

> The principle behind the provision is excellent. [The] young person is given early opportunity to make amends and to address issues of relevance.

Referral orders, being for the most part a mandatory sentence that does not require the court to consider any form of report prior to imposition, might be expected to accelerate decision-making in the court. Just under half of magistrates (45%) responding to the first survey felt that the order would 'speed up the responses to youth crime'. Several magistrates highlighted this as one of the most positive aspects of the changes:

> Speeds up decision-making where the referral order is mandatory.

> It has speeded up youth justice because magistrates' hands are tied in the punishment of the convicted youth.

However, a third (33%) neither agreed or disagreed with the proposition that referral orders had speeded up decision-making. In the second survey just over half (51%) felt that the court was responding more quickly, and the undecided proportion had decreased to less than a quarter (23%). However, the proportion who disagreed with the statement also increased from 13% in the first survey to 19% in the second. This may reflect comments from the open section of the survey which suggested that magistrates identified success in accelerating their decision-making in court but were concerned that delays were occurring afterwards in establishing a contract with the young person:

> Speed at which the panels deal with offenders. This may be due to lack of resources. Court time in dealing with offenders has been greatly reduced but this is being offset by the time taken by the panels to set contracts in train.

It's quick – a case can be completed within 3–4 days of being charged. Young offenders are confronted with the consequences of their action … Setting up panels and drawing up contracts is taking much too long in many cases.

We return to this issue of the time taken to set up panels in the following chapter.

Legal Issues

Finally, there are three other aspects of the referral order that require brief comment. They are, first, the stipulation that the parties that may attend a panel should not include a defence solicitor; second, the issue of 'breach'; and third, the fact that once a contract has been successfully completed by the young offender, the conviction resulting in the referral order is considered 'spent'.

In the surveys, clerks and YOT staff were asked whether young people should be entitled to legal representation in their panel meeting. Approximately one fifth of YOT staff and clerks agreed that such representation should be allowed (20% and 23% respectively). In both cases, the experience of referral orders appears to have led to greater confidence in this regard, as almost one third of YOT staff (30%) and almost half of clerks (48%) had agreed at the time of the first survey. Similarly, by the time of the second survey, less than one fifth of magistrates (17%) agreed that 'certain legal protections offered to vulnerable people may be compromised in panel meetings', a decline from 21% in the first survey.

There were concerns expressed, particularly initially, that the referral order process might be subject to a challenge from defence solicitors under Art. 6 of the European Convention of Human Rights under the Human Rights Act 1998. To date, however, such a challenge has not been made and local referral order managers believed that this was as a result of strict adherence to the principles of drawing up SMART contracts: ones that are specific, measurable, achievable, realistic and timetabled. Certainly the interview data presented in Chapter 10 suggest that young people and parents generally felt that contracts were not overly harsh. Furthermore, young people and parents did not seek legal representation at panel meetings. One pilot area was aware of a major firm of solicitors advising their clients to take the contracts to them immediately following the panel meeting so they could be checked, but there had not been any complaints or problems. As the referral order manager noted: 'The reality is that once they have come out of the panel, the young person and their family are usually just so relieved that it is over with that they just want to get the contract conditions over and done, they don't want to kick up any more fuss.'

Greater concern was expressed in relation to the possible impact of legal advice on pleas. More particularly, some referral order managers were worried about cases in which solicitors advised clients to plead guilty to avoid a more serious charge, or where they advised their client to plead not guilty and opt to go to trial and then if the witnesses attended, recommend that their client change his or her plea. Despite these concerns we found little evidence that the introduction of referral orders had had a significant impact on pleas.

The second issue concerned reoffending by young offenders subject to a referral order. When referral orders were first being considered, some concern was raised about the possibility that offenders returned to court for failure to complete the terms of a contract might find themselves subject to overly severe punishment. At the time of the first survey, between one half and three fifths of magistrates (49%), clerks (56%) and YOT staff (60%) expressed concern about this possibility. Again, experience of referral orders in practice appears to have led to diminished concern. By the time of the second survey, the proportions agreeing with the statement that 'upon referral back to court for re-sentencing magistrates may sentence more harshly offenders who have breached their contract than they would otherwise have done', had diminished to less than half of magistrates (44%) and YOT staff (45%) and less than two fifths of clerks (39%).

On the whole, referral order managers felt that cases that were returned to court were dealt with efficiently, with magistrates generally being willing to extend the referral order if appropriate. However, the issue of young people who reoffended or who were returned to court for sentencing for an offence which may have predated the offence which was the subject of the referral order, was less clear. If the further offence attracted only a conditional discharge, it caused the referral order to be revoked, often mid-contract, which could in itself by seen as an easy option by the offender. Furthermore, in cases where the young person had reoffended, some managers felt it was not clear whether the young person should continue to attend the YOT to comply with the referral order whilst he or she was awaiting sentence, particularly if the referral order was likely to revoked. One manager felt that one problem with 'the speeding up of justice' was that: 'A young person could receive a referral order on a Monday and then receive a fine on the Friday for an offence which predated the referral order, resulting in the order immediately being revoked'.

One potentially positive aspect of the new provisions, and an intended spur to young people to comply, is the cancellation of the criminal record on completion of the referral order. To date, this does not appear to have made a big impact on the main professional participants in the process. Thus, for example, in the 'open' section of the survey only six YOT staff commented on this aspect of the order, though all did so positively. Similarly, only three magistrates from a single pilot site (Oxford) commented on the 'spent conviction' aspect of the referral order. Again, it was viewed positively alongside other perceived advantages of the order, such as: 'The opportunity for first offenders to meet face to face in an informal way fellow members of the community and do reparation work, and that if the contract is successful for the conviction to be spent.'

Comments in this area were made relatively infrequently but were uniformly positive. No magistrates, clerks or YOT staff commented critically on this provision. It is possible that with the relevant legislation, the Rehabilitation of Offenders Act 1974, currently under government review, the implications of a spent conviction are seen as somewhat provisional. More likely, it is, at least for time being, simply seen as a positive and uncontroversial attribute of the new system.

Conclusion

In general the broad welcome extended to referral orders in the lead-up to their implementation in the pilot areas was maintained during their first year of operation. Nonetheless, in this chapter we have discussed two features of the referral order that appear to concern magistrates and court clerks. One of these is integral to the order; the other concerns an aspect of its implementation. The first, and major, concern was the mandatory feature of the order. This was somewhat in contrast to the picture gained from the first survey conducted just prior to implementation. In particular, having no option but to make a referral order in relation to minor offences caused the greatest irritation. The mandatory nature of the order and the fact that on occasions intervention is required by law despite little evidence of need continue to be a source of frustration to YOT staff.

The second main area of concern among those in the Youth Court focused on problems of communication. Magistrates in particular expressed the view that there was insufficient feedback from YOTs in connection with the work of youth offender panels and subsequent activity undertaken in relation to agreed contracts. This perceived absence of information occurred despite the fact that YOT and referral order managers felt that considerable effort had gone into working with their local Youth Courts and indeed felt this to be a successful aspect of their work. By contrast, magistrates and clerks both reported relatively high levels of satisfaction principally with the information provided to the court in connection with cases returned for re-sentencing. Given the extent of change to established sentencing practice required by the referral order, investing resources to enhance communication between the YOT, the panel and the courts is likely to prove fruitful in exploiting the potential of the order.

The concerns of magistrates and clerks need to be understood, however, within the general context of extremely positive views of referral orders. Both they and YOT staff all viewed the emphasis on restorative justice positively, welcomed the broader community involvement intended by the legislation and anticipated that the approach would lead to better working relationships between YOTs and the Youth Court. They approved of the opportunity for early intervention and anticipated that the new orders would lead to some speeding up of the youth justice process. In this connection, however, a further concern was raised. Magistrates and court clerks were on occasion critical of the time taken between the making of the order and the arrangement of the first panel meeting. We explore this in greater detail in the next chapter.

Note

1   A total of 206 magistrates responded, representing a response rate of 36%. Sixty-one clerks responded to the second survey, a response rate of 51%, and 157 YOT members returned questionnaires, representing a response rate of 46%.

Chapter 7

Youth offender panels

Panels are designed to provide a less formal context than court for the offender, his or her parents, the victim, supporters of the victim and/or offender and members of the community to discuss the crime and its consequences. The intention is that panel meetings should be held in locations as close as possible to where the young person lives and from which the community panel members are drawn. Panels adopt a conference-type approach to decision-making that is intended to be both inclusive and party-centred. As such, they mark a significant shift away from a court-based judicial model in which the parties are represented rather than speak for themselves. There is considerable emphasis upon both 'restoration' – which should be a part of all contracts – and 'reintegration' of the offender into the wider community. Not only does the panel have the symbolic power to 'sign off' the referral order once it has been discharged successfully but this also has the effect of purging the offender of the offence (as it is considered spent). The reintegrative element of referral orders is strengthened by the fact that panel meetings are not merely 'one off' events, but in principle entail structured meetings over the lifetime of the referral order. As a result, panels may meet to review developments as well as support, discuss and, where appropriate, congratulate the offender on progress made. Panels must hold at least one interim meeting – the first such review is recommended to be held after one month followed by at least one progress meeting for each three months of the contract. Panels are not only forums for deliberation about the harm and its consequences, but also act as a means of monitoring contract compliance and championing reintegration. According to Dignan and Marsh, as decision-making forums youth offender panels are 'potentially one of the most radical aspects of the entire youth justice reform agenda' (2001: 99). One of the more radical aspects of panels is the manner in which they seek to draw lay volunteers into the decision-making process as community panel members.

In this chapter we discuss the composition, work and dynamics of youth offender panels. We outline some of the quantitative data on panels and their composition during the research fieldwork. We go on to consider the dynamics of panel meetings through an analysis of observation data gathered on a sub-sample of panels. First of all, however, we present some background data on the referral orders made during the period of the research.

Referral Orders: an Overview

Orders

Basic data were collected on *all* referral orders made between the beginning of the pilots (approximately July 2000) and 31 July 2001. In addition, fuller information was collected on those orders which had been *closed* in the same period. In this context, closed orders refers to those where the offender had fulfilled all requirements of the contract or where they had been terminated for another reason such as further offending. The reasons for unsuccessful completion are discussed in more detail in Chapter 10.

There were 1,803 referral orders made in the 11 pilot sites from their outset until 31 July 2001. Table 7.1 shows the distribution of the orders across the 11 pilot sites. One feature worth noting is the small number of orders made in the three West London pilot sites (Hammersmith & Fulham, Kensington & Chelsea and Westminster) compared with sites outside the capital. This apparent shortfall is difficult to explain entirely, but there appear to have been a number of contributory factors. The first was that referral orders became available in London over a month after the majority of other pilot areas. Second, the West London Youth Court ruled, uniquely among the pilot areas, that only offences committed after the commencement date would be considered eligible for referral orders. The effect, in combination with the delayed start, was to reduce the period for valid data collection from approximately a year to something nearer nine

Table 7.1 Overall numbers of referral orders in the pilot sites before August 2001

Area	Frequency	%
Blackburn with Darwen	102	6
Cardiff	223	12
Hammersmith & Fulham	37	2
Kensington & Chelsea	20	1
Nottingham City	350	19
Nottingham County	191	11
Oxfordshire	274	15
Suffolk	292	16
Swindon	123	7
Westminster	28	2
Wiltshire	163	9
Total	1,803	100

months. Third, the numbers of new defendants appearing in the West London Youth Court fell by 60% in the second half of 2000.

Table 7.2 provides information on the length of referral orders. Over four fifths of all the orders made were for six months or less. Relatively few were for the maximum 12 months. The pattern differed somewhat from area to area. Blackburn with Darwen, for example, had a higher proportion of shorter orders (70% being for three or four months and about 30% being for six months or over) than Swindon and Wiltshire (where around 40% of orders were for three or four months and approximately 60% were for six months or over).

Table 7.2 Length of referral orders

Length of order in months	Frequency	%
3 months	785	44
4 months	192	11
5 months	25	1
6 months	482	27
7–9 months	156	9
10–12 months	152	8
Total	1,792 [1]	100

Offenders

As would be expected, the offenders were predominantly male – less than one fifth (17%) of offenders receiving referral orders were female. Data on the ethnicity of offenders were available in 82% of cases. As is shown in Table 7.3 just under 90% of these offenders were white. Only in the West London boroughs, Nottingham City and Blackburn with Darwen were more than one fifth of offenders non-white.

Table 7.3   Ethnicity of offenders

Ethnicity	Frequency	%
White	1,304	88.0
Black	20	1.0
Black British	16	1.0
Black African	9	1.0
Black Caribbean	17	1.0
Indian	8	0.5
Pakistani	14	1.0
Bangladeshi	1	0.1
Other	89	6.0
Total	1,478	100.0

Across all pilot sites, over half of the offenders were over 16 years of age when the order was made. The age profile of offenders was similar across the pilot sites with the exception of Cardiff which had a higher number of 15-year-olds. The age profile of offenders is illustrated in Figure 7.1.

Figure 7.1   Age at date of order

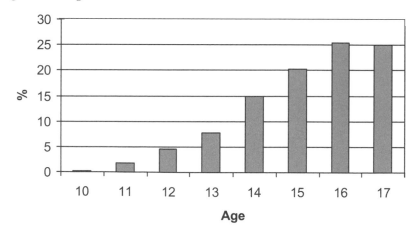

Offences

There were over 150 different types of offence committed by young people in the pilots. Table 7.4 reduces these to eight broad categories. Acquisitive and vehicle crime accounted for almost half (47%) of all offences resulting in a referral order.

Table 7.4 The range of offences resulting in referral orders

Nature of offence	Frequency	%
Acquisitive	454	25
Burglary	156	9
Contact (includes robbery and harassment)	328	18
Vehicle offences	385	21
Public order	177	10
Damage	215	12
Drugs	60	3
Other	14	1
Total	1,789	100

There has been some concern voiced that the mandatory nature of referral orders would result in their being made for minor offences where they are inappropriate as a disposition (Windlesham 2001). One anticipated consequence of this is that lawyers might advise clients to plead not guilty and then offer no defence so as to get a discharge or small fine. An attempt to estimate the extent to which referral orders were being made for minor offences was undertaken by selecting cases in the data set which did not involve dishonesty, burglary or contact and where the order length was the minimum three months. After manually excluding certain other offences such as taking and driving away, this left a group of 289 cases that might arguably have been 'minor'. This was made up of 99 cases of criminal damage, 98 vehicle crimes (of which 76 were 'no insurance'), 62 'minor' public order offences (including 23 drunk and disorderly) and 30 cases of cannabis possession. This upper estimate represents some 16% of the total orders made during the pilot period.

Youth Offender Panels[2]

A distinctive feature of the referral order is that, though the order is made by the court, it has to be 'activated' by a panel meeting in which a contract is signed. It is only at this point that the order can proceed to implementation over the time period set out by the court.

Initial panels

Initial panel meetings were held in 761 of the 874 cases that were closed by 31 July 2001. Thus, in 113 closed cases (13%) the process was aborted before it started. This attrition was attributable to a range of factors including illegal orders being made and previous convictions coming to light. Data were available on 58 such cases. In 26, there was either no response to appointments, failure to co-operate with the preparation of an ASSET report or non-attendance. In 24 cases there were prior offences uncovered or subsequent offences committed prior to the initial panel, or the offender moved out of the area (with referral orders at this stage only being available in selected pilot areas, movement by the offender generally meant he or she had to be dealt with in another way). Where the initial panel was held, it went ahead at the first attempt in 87% of cases and in all except a small handful of instances the panel took place successfully at the second or third attempt.

Review panels

Table 7.5 shows the number of review panels held. It is perhaps an indicator of the minor nature of some of the offences that in 315 cases (43% of those for which we have data), there was no review panel arranged and in 357 cases, no review meeting was in fact held. So, in 50% of the closed cases, for which there was information, no review meetings actually took place. It should be noted that the 'closed' cases covered by this study necessarily under-represent the more serious cases and longer orders as fewer of these would have been completed by 31 July 2001.

Table 7.5   Review panels

No review panels held	357	
1 review panel held	250	(276 arranged)
2 review panels held	78	(98 arranged)
3 review panels held	19	(28 arranged)
4 or more review panels held	3	(11 arranged)
Not applicable	13	
Missing data	41	
Total	761	

Review panels were held in approximately a quarter of cases where the order was for three months and in around half of cases where the order was for six months. Review meetings became rarer in the last three months of the longer orders but the numbers of such orders analysed here are small as few were completed within the time period.

Final panels

A final panel was held in 432 cases, some 71% of valid cases, and no final panel was held in 173 cases. This may have been as a result of the fact that an earlier review panel had agreed that progress was satisfactory and that so long as the young person continued to keep out of trouble during the remainder of the referral order the YOT would 'sign off' the young person without a further panel meeting. In these circumstances, the 'review panel' effectively acts as a final panel. Where a final panel was held, 75% of offenders attended. Successful completion of orders will be discussed in more detail in Chapter 8. Not surprisingly, in 99% of these cases where the young offender attended the final panel, he or she had completed all the elements of the contract successfully.

Number of panels held for each young person

Table 7.6 provides data on the total numbers of panels held for each young person. It shows that in the majority of cases two or three panels were held.

Panel Assessment Data

During the research fieldwork, basic data were gathered on the composition, duration and characteristics of panels. These panel data were collected by panel members completing an assessment form designed by

Table 7.6 Total number of panels held

	Frequency	%
1	118	17
2	341	48
3	179	25
4	54	8
5	12	2
6	5	1
Total	712	100

the research team. Panel assessment forms were completed on a large number of panels in most cases up to the end of September 2001. In all, data were collected on 1,630 panel meetings, including 1,066 different initial panel meetings, forms on 340 review panel meetings, 210 final panel meetings and 14 breach panel meetings.[3] This data set provides useful insights into the composition and timing of panels which supplements the quantitative data from the 'closed cases' and the qualitative data on the sub-sample of panels observed by research team members (to which we return later in this chapter).

Timing and location of panel meetings

Time between sentence and initial panel meeting
For the pilot period a national standard was set in which the initial panel was to take place within 15 working days of the referral order being made in the Youth Court. In estimating the number of 'working days' between these two dates we have always allowed for the greatest number of 'non-working days' between the court date at which the referral order was

Table 7.7 Time between court and initial panel meeting

Working days between court and initial meeting	Number	% of all initial meetings	% of initial meetings with known data	Cumulative percentage
Data missing	184	17	—	
Within 15 working days	275	26	31	31
16–20 working days	187	18	21	52
21–25 working days	129	12	15	67
26–30 working days	99	9	11	78
31–35 working days	59	6	7	85
36–40 working days	40	4	5	90
41–45 working days	29	3	3	93
46–50 working days	12	1	1	94
51–55 working days	17	2	2	96
56–60 working days	7	1	1	97
61–65 working days	10	1	1	98
66–70 working days	3	0	0	98
71–75 working days	4	0	0	98
> 75 working days	13	1	1	100
Total	1,068	100	100	

made and the date of the initial panel. Thus, for example, it is only when 21 or more calendar days have elapsed between the making of the order and the initial panel that we have assumed that this represents more than the national standard of 15 days (i.e. 15 working days plus three weekends). It is also important to bear in mind that some of the panels will appear to fall outside the national standard because they include periods in which at least one panel, and occasionally more, had been scheduled but did not go ahead because of the non-attendance of the young person. We have included these in the analysis as they reflect the reality of convening panels. As shown in Table 7.7, less than one third (31%) of panels took place within the national standard of 15 working days, though almost a further half (47%) occurred in between 16 and 30 working days. This is similar to the early experience of court-referred family group conferences in New Zealand (Maxwell and Morris 1993).

On the basis of the experience of the pilots new guidance to be published prior to national roll out in April 2002 increased the national standard time between court and initial panel meeting to 20 days in cases involving a victim. Table 7.7 shows just over half of initial panels (52%) during the pilot were held within this timeframe.

When do panels take place?
It is clear that panels are predominantly an evening activity, which is consistent with the expectation that most young people attend school and that many community panel members are employed during the day. Table 7.8 shows that the majority of panels were held after 5 p.m. Evening panels were seen to be more accommodating to the various parties, notably community panel members, young offenders, their parents and victims. However, evening panels did have implications for the location of suitable venues and the working arrangements of YOT staff, particularly those staff acting as panel advisers.

Table 7.8   Time of day at which panels were held (%)

Time of day	Initial	Review	Final	Breach	All
Before 12 p.m.	11	8	11	17	10
Between 12 and 5 p.m.	33	30	34	34	33
After 5 p.m.	56	62	55	49	57
Total	100	100	100	100	100

Panel venues

The diversity of locations and venues reflects the aim of locating panels within local communities and the consideration given by most of the YOTs to the needs of prospective participants in the panel process in deciding the most appropriate locality of each individual panel meeting. Despite the declaration in the revised *Guidance* that 'panel meetings should, wherever possible, be held in community venues, not youth offending team offices or police stations' (para. 8.11), YOT offices and police stations were relied upon considerably as venues in the pilots. Table 7.9 outlines the principal locations and venues used across the pilot areas.

In arranging panel meetings, the principal factors for consideration were accessibility and logistics (victim, offender and community panel member locality), venue suitability and community panel member skills and attributes. One of the primary considerations concerned the location and venue of the panel meeting and the issue of whose interests, if any, should take priority. This provoked some mixed views.

Victim attendance: Almost all the managers acknowledged that the needs of the victim (if attending) assumed priority, and that victim attendance largely determined location and venue and the choice of community panel members, some of whom may be more skilled at dealing with victims.

Offenders: In cases with no identifiable victim, managers suggested that the offender's needs would be prioritised. One area determined that the panel should be held no more than three miles from the offender's home.

Community panel members: It was recognised that some community panel members did not feel comfortable sitting on panels in their own community as they felt it potentially made them vulnerable to unwelcome local attention or criticism and in some cases for fear of reprisal or retaliation. A further issue concerned the potential conflict of interest when the community panel member had a personal interest in the case or was known to the young person and his or her family.[5] This issue goes to the heart of a paradox regarding community involvement in panel meetings, namely that, on the one hand, panel members should be *from*, and *of*, the community (i.e. share a social and geographical proximity). On the other hand, the more attached to the community from which the offender comes that panel members are, the less likely they are to hold the required 'detached stance' that constitutes a central value in establishing facilitator neutrality and legitimacy.

YOT officers: In three areas the YOT team operated on a strict rota basis although this was primarily to limit the burden of the amount of anti-social hours and evening work on individual YOT workers. One manager

Table 7.9 Venues and location of panels

Pilot area	Location of panel meetings	Venues at which panel meetings were held
Blackburn with Darwen	Blackburn Darwen	NACRO offices Community centre (rarely used)
Cardiff	Cardiff	Local community venues, such as Salvation Army hall, adult education centre, community arts centres
Nottingham City	Nottingham City centre and around 25 suburbs	57 venues in total ranging from sports centres, leisure centres, community centres and police stations (rarely used) to YOT office (regularly used)[4]
Nottinghamshire County	1 Mansfield/ Ashfield team 2 Newark/ Bassetlaw team (Newark, Ollerton, Worksop, Retford)	Police stations, YOT office, civic centre youth club: community café bar, training centre Library, schools
Oxfordshire	Oxford, Banbury, Bicester, Witney	A variety of leisure centres, family centres and schools. YOT offices were used as a venue of last resort
Suffolk	Ipswich, Lowestoft Bury St Edmunds	YOT offices, Town Hall annex, social services local office, NCH office, family centre, community education establishment and youth club
Swindon	Swindon	YOT office
Wiltshire	Trowbridge, Westbury, Melksham Warminster, Wootton Basset, Chippenham	Court Mills Centre, social services offices, resource centre, community centres
West London sites	Hammersmith & Fulham	YOT office, Community Hall
	Kensington & Chelsea	YOT office
	Westminster	YOT office

whilst acknowledging that young offenders were 'not a nine to five problem' took the view that, at the end of the day, the most important group when considering who should take priority in the organisation of panels were members of the YOT:

> I have to think of the morale of the team … I said very early on that the most important person to consider when arranging the panel is the YOT officer. Someone's got to come first, someone has got to take priority and I've said, rightly or wrongly, that it has to be the YOT officer. They are the major players, it's their job.

Across some of the pilot areas, finding suitable venues to hold the panel meetings in the community was regarded as a continual challenge. The availability of buildings, cost, health and safety factors, and in some cases a resistance from external agencies to become involved, posed a number of difficulties. The logistics of selecting venues, arranging panels and choosing suitable panel members require considerable co-ordination and assessment. Some pilot areas limited the panel meetings to one or two locations largely because it was felt to be convenient and beneficial to have a regular fixed booking and that this strategy also reduced the potential for unforeseeable problems to develop. Two areas adopted a proactive approach and acquired community venues across a wide range of premises such as schools, community centres, youth clubs, leisure centres, sports centres, libraries and resource centres (as well as using YOT offices and police stations).

At least five areas had developed only a limited number of venues in the community and primarily used police stations or YOT premises for panel meetings. This arrangement was seen to have a number of advantages particularly in relation to safety concerns when a victim was likely to be in attendance, and also concerns about the community panel members. Health and safety issues were a principal consideration for most managers. One manager recognised the need to venture out from the familiar, formal security of the YOT office into alternative venues but was concerned about the practicalities and risks this entailed:

> Most panels are in the evening, most of the venues we might use are in risky, unsafe sort of areas, it might be dark … but then we want to make changes. The YOT building is very much an offender's place, it's not a victim's place.

Another manager reiterated this general concern:

I don't agree with having panels out in the sticks, mainly for health and safety reasons. One of the venues we have is a death trap in the winter and the roads out here are hazardous in the winter. People have volunteered to do this, but a couple have had some bad experiences and have said that they will not travel to certain venues and I don't think we can expect them to take risks. We have a responsibility to people. Can we expect community panel members or victims to attend some of these places? I don't think so.

The intention that the panel meetings should be held in locations as close as possible to where the young person lives and from where the panel members are drawn, clearly posed some challenges for a number of the pilot areas. One manager was uncertain about whether the emphasis on creating an informal and non-institutional environment for the panel meeting was actually appropriate as it could undermine the authority of the occasion:

I am concerned that having panels in church halls or youth clubs actually lowers the status of the panels. Low key places means low key status. We need to be impressing upon young people that the panels are important – having them in a village hall or community centre does not give them that impression.

How long do panels last?

The length of a panel meeting varied considerably depending on what type of panel meeting it was. In general, initial meetings tended to be longer in duration than other panel meetings. Nearly three quarters of initial panel meetings (74%) lasted between 20 minutes and an hour (Table 7.10). Nearly a quarter (23%) lasted over one hour (5% of the total lasted over an hour and a half) and only 3% lasted less than 20 minutes. Our data suggest that on average panels lasted for less time than do family group conferences, on the basis of the Australasian experiences at least. The New Zealand research showed that only a third of conferences took less than an hour, whilst almost a third took between an hour and an hour and a half. More than a quarter took between one and a half and two hours and around 10% took more than two hours (Morris and Maxwell 2000: 210). Furthermore, the average length of a conference in RISE in Canberra was 71 minutes compared with an average of 13 minutes for court hearings (Strang et al. 1999). The shorter duration of panels as compared to conferences may be explained, in part, by the relative absence of victims. By contrast, the duration of panels approximates more closely to the length of children's hearings in Scotland, where the available data suggest

Table 7.10 Duration of panels (%)

Duration	Initial	Review	Final	Breach	All
< 20 mins	3	32	62	38	19
20–45 mins	39	55	33	56	42
45–60 mins	35	12	4	3	24
61–90 mins	18	1	1	3	12
> 90 mins	5	0	0	0	3
Total (%)	100	100	100	100	100
n	899	323	230	32	1,484

that the majority of hearings (67%) last between 16 and 45 minutes (Hallett et al. 1998: 42). Most review and final panel meetings took less than three quarters of an hour (88% and 95% respectively).

Panel composition

In only 18 instances did an initial panel involve more than one young offender (less than 2% of the total). Of these, 14 involved two young offenders, three panels involved three young offenders and one panel brought together four offenders. Where possible, involving more than one offender (given a referral order in relation to the same crime) offers particular opportunities to confront the responsibility of the young people in a collective context. It allows panels to address offending behaviour in the context of group behaviour and peer pressures. Furthermore, it removes from young people the scope to deflect their responsibility on to others. If a victim is involved it also offers opportunities to address the victim's feelings without the victim having to attend more than one panel and without potentially having to deal with conflicting accounts by the young people. However, it also presents acute challenges for managing the process and ensuring that the victim does not feel outnumbered.

As expected most panels involved three panel members; 89% of initial panels and 84% of all panels. However, Table 7.11 shows that there was some variation in this, with 9% of initial panels involving four panel members, most usually where inexperienced panel members sat alongside others, primarily to observe the process. In addition, 8% of all panels only had two panel members.

Table 7.12 shows that most panels were made up of a mix of male and female members, albeit that a significant minority of panels were all female (16% of initial panel meetings). From our sample, 115 male

Table 7.11 Number of people on different types of panel

Panel members	Initial	Review	Final	Breach	All	%
1	1	0	1	0	2	0
2	23	58	43	3	127	8
3	906	259	211	38	1,414	84
4	88	30	17	1	136	8
Total	1,018	347	272	42	1,679	100

Table 7.12 Gender composition of panels

	Initial	%	Review	%	Final	%	Breach	%	Total	%
All female	164	16	48	14	36	13	4	10	252	15
All male	45	4	10	3	10	4	3	7	68	4
Mixed	811	80	289	83	226	83	35	83	1,361	81
Total	1,020	100	347	100	272	100	42	100	1,681	100

offenders (15% of the total) attended all-female panels, whilst 6 female offenders (3% of the total) attended all-male panels.

While a quarter of initial panels (26%) had an ethnically mixed panel membership, most were all-white (74%). From our sample, 63% of ethnic minority offenders appeared before an all white initial panel (this comprised of 42% black offenders, 64% Asian offender and 84% offenders from 'other' ethnic minority groups).

Attendance at panel meetings

From the data collected on over one thousand initial panel meetings (1,066), we know that in over two thirds of cases (68%) the young person attended with only one other person. In a further 15% of cases the young person attended alone. This means that in over four fifths of cases (83%) the young person attended either by him or herself or only with one other person. In the 728 initial panels where the young person was accompanied by only one other person, this was usually the young person's mother (68%). In a further 22% it was the young person's father, 7% by another family member, 7% by a non-family appropriate adult and 2% by another non-family supporter. In 14% of all initial panel meetings the young person attended with two other people. Most of these saw the young person accompanied by both his or her parents (61%) or by his or her mother and another family member or supporter (36%). In less than 3% of all initial panels were young people accompanied by three or more other people and never by more than four other people. Unsurprisingly, our data also show that attendance by family members declines at subsequent (both review and final) panel meetings (see Table 7.13).

Table 7.13 Panel attendance – offender's group

Young person attends	Initial	%	Review	%	Final	%	Breach	%	All	%
Alone	158	15	77	23	30	14	4	29	269	17
With one other person	728	68	222	65	157	75	9	64	1,116	68
With two other people	152	14	39	11	23	11	1	7	215	13
With three other people	24	2	1	0	0	0	0	0	25	2
With four or more other people	4	0	1	0	0	0	0	0	5	0
Total	1,066	100	340	100	210	100	14	100	1,630	100

Initial panels

Table 7.14 sets out the attendance of offender's supporters at initial panel meetings on the basis of the panel assessment form data. Despite the aim that panels should invite other supporters or appropriate adults in the young person's life to attend the panel, there is little evidence of this occurring in practice. This suggests that initial panel meetings are generally significantly less inclusive of young offenders' family members and supporters than family group conferences. For example, the data from New Zealand suggest that two fifths of family group conferences were attended not only by members of their immediate family but also their extended family (Morris and Maxwell 2000: 214).

Panel Observations

During the fieldwork members of the research team attended 163 panel meetings for the purpose of observing and recording the panel partici- pants and process. To this end, a series of pre-coded panel observation forms with free text boxes were devised to record panel attendance and key aspects of panel dynamics at the different meetings. A fifth of the panels at which an observer was present did not proceed as the young

Table 7.14 Attendance at initial panel meetings

Young person	Mother	Father	Other family	Non-family appropriate adult	Other supporter	Number of panels	% of known panels
✓						158	15
✓	✓					456	43
✓		✓				163	15
✓			✓			49	5
✓				✓		47	4
✓					✓	13	1
✓	✓	✓				92	9
✓	✓		✓			34	3
✓	✓			✓		8	1
✓	✓				✓	13	1
✓		✓	✓			3	0
✓		✓		✓		1	0
✓		✓			✓	1	0
✓	✓		✓	✓		2	0
✓	✓			✓	✓	1	0
✓	✓	✓	✓			8	1
✓	✓	✓			✓	3	0
✓	✓		✓	✓		3	0
✓	✓		✓		✓	1	0
✓		✓	✓		✓	1	0
✓		✓	✓	✓		1	0
✓	✓			✓	✓	2	0
✓		✓		✓	✓	2	0
✓	✓	✓		✓	✓	3	0
✓	✓	✓	✓	✓		1	0
Total						1,066	100

person failed to attend. As a consequence, we have data on 130 panels that proceeded comprising 92 initial, 21 review and 17 final panel meetings.

The panel observation forms enabled both qualitative comments to be collected about the panel and factual information to be recorded about events that occurred during the panel. They also included rating scales for the observer to judge the general atmosphere and the occurrence of consensus and conflict during the panel. Many of these recordings were made at the beginning and end of panels in order to capture any shift that may have occurred. Six-point Likert (0–5) scales were created to make these recordings. For ease of presentation these have been collapsed into three categories (low, medium and high) in the tables contained in the sections that follow. The mean scores for scales are also reported. We begin, however, by looking at the preparatory work for panel meetings.

Initial Panel Meetings

This section presents the in-depth findings from the observation of 92 initial panel meetings attended by a young person.

The information provided to panel members

Paragraph 3.5 of the original *Guidance* stressed the importance of preparation prior to the panel meeting. As well as receiving information about any contact with victims and their views on reparation, notably if they do not wish to attend the panel, the *Guidance* states that 'information about the young person's past and current offending behaviour and relevant family circumstances and education and health needs will be essential if the programme of activity is to be targeted effectively to prevent reoffending' (para. 3.10). Observation of panels revealed that all panel members received some form of report about the young person: in 93% of panels they received a specially prepared report from the YOT; 5% received the full ASSET report for the young person (the routine practice in one pilot area); and the remaining 2% received some other form of report. As will be discussed in Chapter 10, the community panel members found the timely receipt of this information to be important for their pre-panel preparation. Most community panel members preferred to receive a few days before the panel to assist them in preparing for the meeting. However, some YOT managers were concerned about issues of confidentiality where reports were sent to community panel members' home addresses through the post. Receipt of reports some days before panels were due to meet enabled the relevant community panel members in some areas to have regular discussions among themselves (usually over the phone) about a particular case and prepare for it.

Pre-panel discussions

In almost all pilot areas, the community panel members met prior to the panel (usually 15–30 minutes beforehand) to discuss offence and offender-related issues and procedural matters. Understandably, the timing of receipt of written reports had an important bearing on these pre-panel discussions. In some areas reports were received just 10–30 minutes before the meeting, in others several days in advance of the meeting. In general, the pre-panel discussion was a time for clarifying any uncertainties, supplementing written reports with verbal information from the YOT member, and discussing reparation and possible contract contents. What was clear from the observed panel meetings was that (depending on when they received the report) most community panel members came very well prepared for the meeting, many having made extensive notes and having given considerable thought to each individual case.[6]

Opening a panel

The opening stages of each panel meeting usually began with a welcome and an introduction to the parties, followed by an outline of the ground rules and purpose of panels. Observations suggested that the composition and identity of the panel were clearly explained to those present 'in full' in the vast majority of cases (88%) and in part in the remainder. The purpose of the panel were clearly explained in full in more than three quarters of panels (77%) and in part in a further fifth. Similarly, ground rules, in line with any local guidance, were clearly explained to those present in full in a majority of cases (64%) though not at all (17%) or only in part (18%) in the remainder.

In very few cases (10%) was the young person advised by the panel of any right he or she may have to terminate the meeting at any time during the proceedings or to return to court (5%). Given the possible implications of a human rights agenda, it may become important for panels to examine the way in which they operate in this regard. This has particular implications for the content of locally agreed panel ground rules.

Contribution of Participants

One of the principal tasks of the community panel members at the initial panel meeting is to encourage participatory discussion and provide an environment in which young people and others feel able and willing to communicate. We sought to measure the contribution of the various parties to panel deliberations. Despite some commentators' fears that young people would be marginalised in a roomful of adults at panel meetings (Haines 2000), the observation data (Table 7.15) show that most of the participants (when attending a panel meeting) contributed significantly to proceedings. Merely 11% of young people made only monosyllabic responses or said nothing during their panel meeting, whilst almost half (49%) made lengthy and full contributions. This suggests that

Table 7.15 Contribution to panel by different parties (%, where in attendance)

What was the extent of the overall contribution to the panel by	Nothing	Mono-syllabic responses	Short but several responses	Lengthy and full contribution	Total
the young person	1	10	40	49	100
the young person's father	0	4	40	56	100
the young person's mother	0	7	41	53	100
the young person's (other) supporters	0	22	26	52	100
the victim(s)	0	0	0	100	100
the victim's supporter(s)	0	0	67	33	100

panels were more successful in engaging young people than Scottish children's hearings, where similar observational evidence revealed that over a third of young people (37%) contributed only through mono-syllabic responses, affirmations/negations and non-verbal responses (Hallett *et al.* 1998: 47).

Responsibility, remorse and apology

Along with encouraging the contribution of young people to speak for themselves, it is hoped that within that process, young people acknowledge their offending behaviour and take responsibility for their own actions. Observers of panel meetings categorised the extent to which each young person appeared to acknowledge responsibility for his or her offending behaviour (Figure 7.2).

Figure 7.2 Acceptance of responsibility for offending behaviour

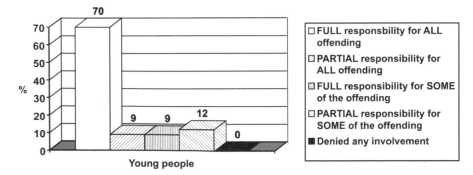

The rate at which young people apologised in panels varied significantly in initial panel meetings according to whether a victim attended. In initial meetings *not* attended by victims only 30% of young offenders apologised to anyone, compared to 77% of panels that were attended by a victim. However, a larger proportion of young offenders expressed remorse in initial panels in some way other than by apologising. Four fifths did this verbally. Of the 56 young people who did not apologise to anyone in the panel, a third also did not show any other sign of remorse.

The Victim Perspective at Initial Panels

The lack of victim presence at most panel meetings left the responsibility on the panel of ensuring that there was a victim perspective at meetings. Figure 7.3 shows that panel members did this in over half (56%) of all panels that were not attended by a victim or a victim representative. However, observers noted no mention of a victim perspective at all in a fifth of panels (21%).[7]

Figure 7.3 The nature of victim input

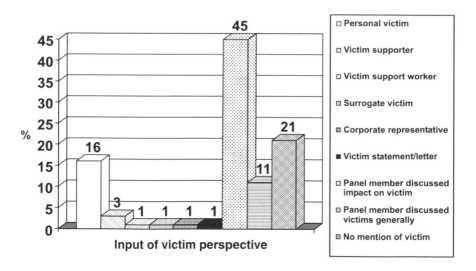

The General Atmosphere of Panels

Our observations indicate that ground rules for panels were observed completely in 90% of panels, most of the time in a further 6% of panels, and rarely only 1%. In 3% of cases this was unclear. There were no threats of violence during any of the panel meetings that were observed. In general, it appears that initial panels were largely successful at achieving a potentially 'restorative atmosphere'. All panel members were predominantly considered to be non-judgemental by observers. As would be expected of someone in their role, panel chairs emerged as the most directive, though as volunteers chairing a meeting containing professional 'experts' this can perhaps be taken as an indication of the success of the youth offender panel model.

The observation schedule measured the possibility that various attitudes might change between the early and later stages of the panel. Thus, for example, the levels of support shown for the young person increased quite substantially between the beginning and end of panels. The number of panels featuring high levels of support *tripled*. A similar pattern is evident for expressions of hope for the young person, and is slightly weaker for expressions of concern. In general, levels of empathy – measured as expressions of support, concern and hope, and the absence of anger or contempt – rose during the course of panel meetings (see Figure 7.4).

Figure 7.4   Shift in expressions by panel members

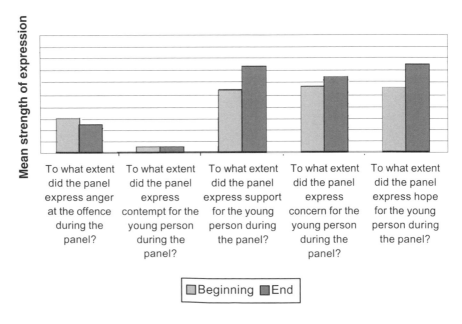

Deliberations over Contracts

The ultimate aim of initial panel meetings is to agree a contract with the young offender through negotiation. The initial *Guidance* noted that 'Contracts should be negotiated with offenders, not imposed on them' (para. 8.16). Furthermore, it states that 'agreeing the contract should be led by the community panel members, who should be encouraged to suggest interventions for inclusion in contracts that draw on community rather than just youth offending team resources' (*ibid.*). Our observations also took account of the process through which contracts were formulated and agreed and sought to assess the extent to which parties contributed to contractual outcomes.

In total, 329 contract elements were proposed during these panels: 256 elements in panels that were not attended by victims and 73 in panels attended by victims. Almost nine tenths of the elements in contracts were suggested by either the community panel members or the YOT panel member. This is perhaps not too surprising. However, it suggests that more latitude could be given to the parties themselves contributing to contract terms.[8] It is noteworthy that victims suggested only 14% of the elements considered for contracts in panels that they attended, though this is still substantially higher than the number of elements suggested by young offenders (5%) or their supporters in all panel meetings (2%) (Table 7.16).

Table 7.16 Contributions to contractual deliberations

Person in panel	Panels without victims		Panels with victims		Combined	
	Number of contract elements	*%*	*Number of contract elements*	*%*	*Number of contract elements*	*%*
Panel member	155	61	37	51	192	58
YOT	77	30	22	30	99	30
Young person	14	5	2	3	16	5
Family of young person	7	3	1	1	8	2
Other supporter	1	0	1	1	2	1
Victim	0	0	10	14	10	3
Unknown	2	1	0	0	2	1
Total	256	100	73	100	329	100

Figure 7.5 Contribution to contractual outcomes

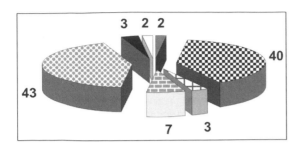

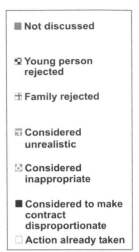

- ■ Not discussed
- ▨ Young person rejected
- ⊞ Family rejected
- ▦ Considered unrealistic
- ▨ Considered inappropriate
- ■ Considered to make contract disproportionate
- ☐ Action already taken

Of the 329 contract elements that were proposed, 82% were accepted and 18% rejected. The main reasons for them being rejected were that they were considered inappropriate by the panel (43%), or the young person did not wish to do them (40%). A small number were rejected as they were considered practically inappropriate (7%) such as the young person being too young to carry out a task, or the making of practical reparation being unfeasible because the victim could not be contacted (Figure 7.5). The negotiation of contract elements is intended to be a 'two-way agreement' that the young person actively agrees to undertake. Encouragingly four fifths (81%) of the 240 elements assessed by observers were 'actively' accepted by young people, whilst the other fifth appeared to be only 'passively' accepted.

Elements suggested by victims were the most likely to be rejected by panels. However, the very low number of suggestions made by victims mean this should be regarded with caution. The majority of suggestions that were made by victims were rejected because they were considered impractical for the young person or because they were disproportionate. There was only a small number of suggestions that were made by 'other' supporters of offenders (such as mentors or youth workers). Those suggestions made by YOT officers, followed by those made by the community panel members were the least likely to be rejected (Table 7.17).

There was no mention of proportionality in almost three fifths (59%) of observed initial panel meetings, and a low level of discussion in a further 5% of panels. There was a medium to high level of mention of the need for proportionality in a third of cases (37%).

Table 7.17 Proposed contractual element and whether they were accepted

Who	Number of elements proposed	% accepted
Panel member	192	82
YOT	99	88
Young person	16	69
Family of young person	8	75
Other offender's supporter	2	100
Victim	10	50
Unknown	2	50
Total	329	

Conclusion

Youth offender panels appeared relatively quickly to have established themselves as deliberative and participatory forums in which to address a young person's offending behaviour. The informal setting appeared to allow young people, their parents/carers, community panel members and YOT advisers opportunities to discuss the nature and consequences of a young person's offending, as well as how to respond to this in ways which seek to repair the harm done and to address the causes of the young person's offending behaviour. The pilots highlight the difficulties faced in finding suitable venues for all the parties. Ideally, venues should be as community based and non-institutional as possible. There should be a separate waiting area for victims and offenders with their family. All venues should be secure and as accessible as possible for all the parties. There are tensions however between these multiple aims of proximity, security and an informal and pleasant ambience.

It is clear that there are a number of barriers that result in delays to the arrangement of initial panels. Although only a minority were held within the extant 15 days' time limit, a half occurred within the revised limit of 20 days, and nearly four fifths within 30 days. Thought needs to be given in a constructive manner to increasing the likelihood of prompt arrangement of panels.

The pilots suggest that those organising panels should be encouraged to facilitate the attendance of a wider group of people who may have a beneficial impact upon the panel process. Most notably this includes people who care about and are capable of having a positive influence on the young person (this may be extended family members or other people that matter in a young person's life), as well as victims and their supporters, or where this is not possible someone else who can bring a victim perspective to the meeting. The presence of a victim at panel meetings appears significantly to alter the dynamics of the process and have a beneficial impact on participants, especially offenders. A noticeable shift was detectable in the 'mood' of panels, in particular towards increased empathy with, and support for, the offender. In a relatively short period of time community panel members appear to have become effective chairs of panels and facilitators of inclusive deliberations. In addition, they appear to have experienced relatively few difficulties in working with professional youth justice staff. Let us now turn to a more detailed analysis of the outcomes of panel meetings, namely the youth offender contracts, their contents and their implementation.

Notes

1 In this and other tables that follow the totals often fall slightly short of the total of 1,803 referral orders made during this period. This is because of missing data in YOT records.
2 The data that follow refer to all panels held from the beginning of the pilots up until 31 July 2001.
3 The data are broadly representative of panels in all the pilot areas except for Hammersmith and Fulham where difficulties in collecting the data were experienced.
4 In Nottingham, police stations and YOT offices were originally favoured as panel venues, particularly for consideration of victim and community panel member safety. Towards the end of the pilot there was a move towards the use of the civic centre and YOT office only for panel meetings due to the adoption of a structured rota system and the unavailability of the police station on regular basis. The police station was the favoured venue when victim attendance was likely.
5 This raises the question as to whose responsibility it is to identify and determine what constitutes a conflict of interests and what actions should follow.
6 A more detailed analysis of the content of pre-panel discussions can be found in the second interim report from the research.
7 It should be noted that only two of the 16 offences considered at these panels could be considered 'victimless'.
8 Furthermore, it suggests that during the fieldwork period panels operated in a somewhat different manner from other restorative processes, notably family group conferencing, where the participants are generally more involved in creating plans.

Chapter 8

Contracts and their implementation

In the previous chapter we explored the process by which contracts were agreed. In this chapter we focus on the nature of the contracts agreed in youth offender panel meetings. We consider their content, the work undertaken in support of them and whether they were successfully completed. Being the principal element on which the potential success or failure of the referral order is built the contract is central to the operation of the order. The youth offender contract should always include some element of reparation to the victim or the wider community together with a programme of activity aimed at preventing reoffending. According to the original draft *Guidance*, the programme of activities 'should be challenging but achievable' (para. 3.56). In this chapter we draw upon two main sources of data: summary data taken from YOT records and further information collected on panel assessment forms completed by community panel members. A total of 1,093 panel assessment forms were completed covering 1,068 separate initial panel meetings. Contracts were agreed in 98% of these initial panels. In half of those cases where a contract was not agreed ($n = 18$) the young person was returned to court. In the remainder, where data were available, a further panel was to be held.

Of the contracts for which we have information, 15% included a single element, 29% included two, and 35% contained three elements. Four fifths of contracts (79%) contained three or fewer elements (see Table 8.1). Of the 934 contracts for which information was collected, 119 (13%) appeared

Table 8.1 Number of elements per contract

	Compulsory elements	%	Voluntary elements	%
0	—	—	808	87
1	139	15	84	9
2	268	29	27	3
3	326	35	6	1
4	136	15	2	—
5	65	7	0	—
Total	934	100	927	100

also to contain voluntary elements in addition to the compulsory elements. Of these, the majority (71%) contained one voluntary element. Only eight contracts contained more than two voluntary elements. The use of voluntary elements is in line with the *Guidance* which suggests that additional activities may be included in the contract 'on an optional basis'.[1] The logic of voluntary elements is not to include too many or intensive interventions as compulsory elements in order that the contract be achievable, but also to allow young people to sign up to broader commitments which may be harder to monitor or measure, but which are desirable none the less.

Table 8.2 summarises the broad categories into which these elements could be divided. The most common compulsory element in all contracts was some form of reparative activity, making up 40% of all contract elements. The next most frequently occurring elements of contracts were offending behaviour work (9%), attending supervision/assessment sessions with a YOT officer (6%), exploring employment and career options (6%), and education (5%) and victims awareness work (5%). Education and reparation also formed the most common voluntary elements in contracts.

That reparative elements dominate contracts is to be expected – such activity being a compulsory element. That this is almost being achieved is illustrated by our two major sources of data on contracts. The data from the panel assessment forms show that there was a clear element of reparation in over four fifths (82%) of contracts. Table 8.3 details the different types of reparation appearing in contracts. It is noteworthy that mediation and direct work with victims are rare, confirming the conclusion that victims are under-represented in both panel meetings and panel outcomes.

Table 8.2 The contents of contracts (panel assessment data)

Elements of contract	Compulsory	%	Voluntary
Reparation	1,008	40	29
Offending behaviour	228	9	4
Employment/careers	161	6	17
YOT supervision	147	6	8
Education	137	5	36
Victim awareness	130	5	—
Drugs work	111	4	5
Anger management	99	4	5
Motoring	92	4	2
Self-esteem	75	3	—
Mentoring	52	2	8
Sports/youth work	42	2	15
Curfews/restrictions	29	1	10
Health, mental health	28	1	5
Supervised activities	26	1	—
Repay parents/fine	27	1	4
Attend further panels	25	1	—
Life skills	20	1	1
Other/unclear	86	4	15

Table 8.3 Types of reparation found in contracts (panel assessment data)

Type of reparation	Number	%
Community reparation	432	42
Written apology	335	32
Job for parents	37	4
Verbal apology	24	2
Pay compensation/money to charity	23	2
Direct reparation	21	2
Mediation	20	2
Apology – unspecified	5	<1
Restorative conference	4	<1
Unspecified reparation	136	13
Total	1,037	100

This broad picture of the content of contracts is confirmed by the data collected from YOT records. These covered a total of 761 'closed' referral orders. The major elements in the contracts agreed in these cases were grouped into five major categories: reparation (76%), YOT activities (64%), education or other courses (27%), contacts with professionals (26%) and other activities (19%). There was some overlap between these categories – for example anger management could be a YOT activity or an educational course. Similarly, a visit to the Educational Welfare Officer could be classified as either contact with a professional adviser or part of an educational element. None the less, the general categories allow a picture of contracts to be developed. We explore each of these briefly in turn.

Reparation

Reparation was specified as part of the contract for 578 young offenders or 76% of all 'closed' cases where there was an initial panel meeting. The most common form was community reparation (42%), followed by written apology (38%), indirect reparation (10%), direct reparation to victim or the payment of compensation (7%) and then various forms of unspecified activity. These figures tie in closely with those derived from panel assessment forms (see Table 8.3). Three quarters of young people (76%) undertook just one element of reparation, and the remainder undertook two (22%) or three (2%). Of 251 young people that undertook one element of reparation and for whom we have data, 70% took 8 hours or less on that element.

Several serious concerns about reparation were raised by referral order managers.[2] Trying to tailor the reparation to the offence, and trying to find suitable reparative activities were regarded as extremely difficult. One manager felt that finding suitable community reparation for people in the younger age groups of 10, 11 and 12 was a 'non-starter', commenting 'what is there that a 10-year-old can usefully do for the community?' In several areas, finding adequate supervision for reparative activities was also problematic. One area admitted to being wary about including reparation in the contract because it could lead to a battle about supervision responsibilities. Persuading people to be involved in community reparation was regarded as a source of major difficulty given some of the challenges that working with young offenders could present. It was recognised that the goodwill that underpinned offers of support could quickly evaporate, particularly in circumstances where young people did not always attend when expected, or behave in ways considered appropriate. Whether through lack of imaginative ideas or lack of resources, there was a growing tendency in all the pilot areas to use the same reparative activities over and over. One of the dangers with this was that it ran the risk of being incommensurate to the offence, thus diminishing its relevance in the eyes of the offender. As a consequence, several areas preferred reparation elements in the contract to be left open ended or unspecific so that YOT staff had the flexibility to organise something at a later stage. A further difficulty here is that too much delay and there is a risk that the reparative activities may not be completed within the lifetime of the order. Such delay will anyway not 'send the right messages' to young offenders.

Specific problems concerning letters of apology were raised by referral order managers. In particular, it was felt that there were situations where the young person might have worked quite hard on writing a letter of apology to the victim on the understanding that it would be given to the victim, when in fact this was not the case (see also Miers *et al.* 2001). This issue was in part attributed to the first *Panel Matters* training manual, which had encouraged community panel members to assume that every victim would want a letter of apology and should have one, even if the victim had actually given no indication that he or she did. In several pilot areas it seemed probable that a high proportion of letters of apology never reached the victims to whom they were addressed because referral order staff had not been given the 'green light' to deliver them, or the police had insufficient time to deliver them. However, where letters of apology were sanctioned, their effect could be useful, particularly if the victim chose to reply:

> It was a nine month order, and six months into the order he [the offender] gets this letter back [from the victim] telling him 'I am still affected by this incident, good luck to you for the future, but I am still affected'. It brought home to him [the offender] that although things were working out quite nicely for him, the victim was still suffering the effects of what happened.

Other Activities

Activities with the YOT were specified in 484 contracts. The most common of these were meetings with a YOT officer (20%), attending offending behaviour sessions (17%), anger management sessions (13%), drugs/alcohol awareness sessions (9%), victim awareness sessions (8%), and attending courses on the consequences of violent behaviour (3%). Again, three quarters (73%) of young people undertook just one YOT activity, 18% undertook two activities and 9% undertook three or four YOT-related activities.

Some form of course or education activities were specified for 206 offenders. In 16 cases, there were two educational elements. The most common of these (approximately one third) were in relation to school or college attendance but there were also requirements to undertake driving awareness courses (15%), to seek careers advice (18), to attend a local Young Offender Institution (4%), participate in mentoring schemes, anger management courses and imaginatively to work with a park ranger, at a dog pound or with a rugby club. Contracts required that young offenders saw a professional in 198 cases. These included careers advisers (36%), drugs/alcohol workers (20%), Community psychiatric nurses (10%), education welfare officers (9%) and health workers (6%). Of these, 160 young people saw just one professional whilst 32 saw two and 6 saw three. Slightly under three quarters (71%) of those young persons who saw a professional adviser as part of the contract completed their contract successfully.

Other elements were specified in the contract for 144 young people. Many of these elements have reparation or education overtones (for example, 16 offenders were contracted to undertake jobs for parents). But there are elements that fall outside these other categories – although they appear more exhortatory than substantial. Most common were that the young person should abide by parental rules, keep parents informed of whereabouts, keep out of trouble, observe curfews, avoid certain peers and stay away from particular areas. Of those young persons who had these other elements included as part of the contract, two thirds (67%) completed that contract successfully.

Variation and Completion of Contract

Finally in this regard, of the 761 'closed' referral orders on which we collected data, there was variation in the terms of the initial contract in only 40 cases (5%). These variations were all specific to individual cases with no obvious linking theme – reparation activity was added or reduced, apology letters were included or excluded and so on. Examples involved attending family therapy, attending driving offences group or delivering letter of apology personally.

Outcome: Completion, Breach or Reconviction?

A key issue in relation to the 'success' of youth offender panels is whether the referral order was completed and the contract fulfilled. Did the order run for the allotted time, did the young person attend the panel meetings and did he or she comply with the elements agreed in the contract? By 31 July 2001 as noted above, 1,803 orders had been made by the courts in the 11 pilot sites. At that date, 874 (48%) were regarded as closed and of these there had been an initial panel meeting in 761 cases. In discussing the possible success or failure of referral orders we focus only on these 761 cases.

Young people completed the contract successfully in 539 cases – or three quarters (75%) of cases where a panel had met and where only one offence was being considered. This success rate dropped to just under two thirds (64%) where the panel was dealing with more than one offence, and to half (50%) where the panel was dealing with more than one count of the main offence.

The chances of the young person completing the contract successfully differed little between male and female offenders – approximately 75% of males and 72% of females completed the contract successfully. Rates of completion by age revealed no particularly significant pattern, though the younger and older age groups appeared to have the highest completion rates, with over four fifths (81%) of 17-year-olds successfully completing the contract.

The timescale of the research study meant that comparatively few of the longer orders had been completed during the period of the study. Thus, of 69 orders over six months only 14 or approximately 20% had been completed successfully. For three-month orders the success rate was over 85% and for six-month orders it was 67%. There are a number of reasons why different orders might have different completion rates. First, the longer orders are likely to be for more serious offences. Second, the longer the order the longer the period in which reoffending can take place. Of the 69 completed orders over six months, 46 offenders committed further offences subsequent to the contract being agreed.

Given the apparent relationship between order length and completion rate, one might expect also to find some connection between the nature of the offence for which the order was made and completion rate. The highest rates of completion were for drugs offences (87%), vehicle crime (80%) and criminal damage (77%). The lowest completion rates were in connection with burglary (61%) and contact crime (68%). Assuming that the majority of drugs offences were non-Class A possession offences, then the above pattern tends to confirm the picture that the less serious offences, and therefore shorter orders, will tend to have the highest completion rates.

Finally, in this regard we consider whether the number of elements in a contract had an impact on completion rate. On one level, this might be expected for it was those categories of offence that attract the longer orders which were also those that had the greatest number of discrete elements in the contract. Thus, for example, over a third of orders made for burglary had four or more elements in the contract, whereas overall under one quarter of offenders agreed to contracts with that number of elements. As we noted earlier, three elements in the contract was the most common disposition. The completion rate for contracts with only one element was 89%. It dropped to between three quarters and four fifths for contracts with two (76%) and three (79%) elements. Overall, as we have seen, three quarters (75%) of offenders completed their contract successfully. However, where contracts had four or more elements the completion rate declined to under 70%.

In just under a quarter of those closed cases where there had been an initial panel meeting the young person was convicted of a further offence. In three quarters of such cases, the order was revoked and the offender was re-sentenced. Of the 88 such cases for which information was available, 27 resulted in an action plan order, 21 in a supervision order (in some cases with a fine and/or costs) and 13 in a conditional discharge. The remainder was made up of a broad range of other disposals including reparation orders (5), attendance centre orders (4), fines (3), combination orders (3) and community service orders (3). Six cases ended with custodial sentences. However in about 40 cases, the young person was ordered to continue with the referral order. In 32 of these cases, the order was extended. Half (16) were extended for a further three months, and eleven for longer periods; one for nine further months. One half (50%) of offenders whose order was extended went on successfully to complete the contract.

In 51 cases (7% of the closed cases), the young person failed to comply with the terms of the contract agreed with the panel and was returned to court for re-sentencing. We were able to collect data on 47 such cases. In seven cases the Youth Court either rejected the breach and ordered the offender to continue with the panel or extended the order. In the other 40 cases, the referral order was revoked.

Conclusion

The centrality of reparation and related activities to contracts agreed in youth offender panels appears to be very much in line with the intention of the legislation. However, as indicated above, it is community reparation that predominates and this reflects, at least in part, some of the difficulties that were encountered in the pilots in engaging with victims. That processes of reparation pose a distinct challenge for YOTs has been noted before (Dignan 2000). As we shall see in the next chapter, community panel members were somewhat critical of the range of options open to panels for consideration for inclusion in contracts. Clearly, the anticipated community-based nature of many contract elements only partially materialised in many of the pilot areas and panels were often limited primarily to YOT-based activities for inclusion in contracts. The danger here is that the work done as part of a contract may come increasingly to resemble the activities that might be found in many other community penalties. None the less, it is clear that the contracts agreed as part of referral orders contain considerable scope for creativity, even if much of the potential remains to be fully realised.

Notes

1 The *Guidance* goes on to suggest that such voluntary elements should be 'listed on the same piece of paper as the contract, but clearly distinguished from it' (para. 8.24).
2 Several managers voiced concern that there was a danger that the referral order would be turned into a community service order, particularly with the new emphasis on Community Payback, feeling that issues around reparation would have to be reviewed in light of this.

Chapter 9

Community panel members

One of the more radical aspects of youth offender panels is the manner in which they seek to draw lay volunteers into the decision-making process as panel members. In this chapter we explore the involvement of community panel members in the implementation of referral orders. We do so, through an analysis of the experiences and views of community panel members working in the pilot sites, their attitudes to the work and operations of panels and relationships with youth offending team staff.

Interestingly, it was not the government's original intention to involve lay members of the community in the youth offender panel process. Initially, the intention had been that panels 'would contain a mix of youth justice practitioners – a magistrate (if possible, one of the magistrates responsible for the referral), a YOT member, and perhaps a police officer' (Home Office 1997d: 33, para. 9.35). The idea of 'ordinary' community volunteers making up the majority on panels did not appear as part of the original philosophy or ideology of referral orders.[1] The government appears to have opted for this approach rather late in the day and more by accident than by design. Nevertheless, this begs the question: what precisely do lay members of the public contribute or add to the panel process? According to the *Guidance*, it is intended that panel members constitute people who are 'properly representative of the community they intend to serve and who have the appropriate personal characteristics for the challenging task of dealing effectively with young offenders, and their victims, in a restorative justice context' (Home Office 2000: para. 1.4). Panel members must be 18 years of age or over. However, above that minimum age young panel members are particularly encouraged as, according to the *Guidance*, they 'may be particularly well equipped to engage and communicate with young offenders, and to understand their needs and motivation' (*ibid*.: para. 1.16). A criminal conviction is not a bar to panel membership, where the applicant can demonstrate that he or she does not present any risk of reoffending. The recruitment criteria are to be 'based on personal qualities rather than professional qualifications'.

Contrary to the government's original intention to include criminal justice professionals among panel members, it now suggests that such people should only be recruited 'in a personal, volunteer capacity, rather than as representatives of any group or profession' (*ibid*.: para 1.19). Moreover, the *Guidance* goes on to state that 'it will always be inappropriate for those involved in the youth justice system to sit as community panel members where they have been previously involved as sentencers or in a capacity in the young offender's case' (*ibid*.: para. 1.20). The *Guidance* also asserts that 'it will be inappropriate for panel members to be involved in any case concerning a young offender who is a family member or close acquaintance' (*ibid*.: para. 1.21). However, it is unclear at what point 'acquaintance' presents a potential conflict of interests. Herein lies an inherent tension, for whilst, on the one hand, the intention is to reduce the social distance between panel members and participants, on the other hand, it is undesirable for justice to be compromised by prior personal relations.[2]

Youth Offender Panels: Administrative and Procedural Issues

Preparation for panel meetings

It is to the credit of the training programme that, according to the survey conducted mid-way through the research, a majority of community panel members (57%) felt at least reasonably confident when sitting on their first panel. However, it is also clear that confidence tended to increase with experience. By the time they had sat on a few panels, a third of all respondents said that they were very confident and a further 57% were reasonably confident. On average, most panel members indicated that they spent between 15 minutes and an hour in preparation for each panel, excluding pre-panel meetings with the YOT panel member. Generally, when asked whether they felt that there was sufficient preparation before panel meetings 72% said that there was, while 23% said that there was not enough.

Thirty per cent of respondents agreed with the statement that 'panels tended to be arranged for the convenience of YOT staff'. However, a greater number thought that the convenience of the young person was a more over-riding consideration. A majority (56%) agreed with the statement that 'panels tended to be arranged for the convenience of young offenders', and two thirds of respondents (67%) felt that 'the venues are generally appropriate to the needs of panels'. The sufficiency and timeliness of the information provided to community panel members about the young person and the offence are crucial if community panel members are to exert a significant influence over panel proceedings. Approximately half (49%) of community panel members said that they were usually provided with a report more than two days before the panel. However, over a quarter (28%) received reports on the day of the panel, most between 15 minutes and an hour before the panel began. This reflected different practices in different pilots. In several areas respondents commented that reports were usually received on the day of the panel, sometimes less than 15 minutes before a meeting. Where panel members did not get information until the day of the panel meeting they tended to feel that this restricted the input they could have on panel proceedings, especially in relation to deciding the contents of the contract.

The vast majority of community panel members (86%) felt that they were provided with sufficient information about the offence and the young person (77%). A majority felt that where relevant they received sufficient information on the victims (54%), though a sizeable minority (40%) felt that the information they received in this area was not enough. However, the main areas in which respondents felt that they did not receive enough information were:

- the views of the magistrates who gave the referral order (74%);
- the programmes of activity available (62%); and
- the forms of reparation available locally (55%).

Youth Offender Panels: Relationships, Ownership and Control

Working relationships

The research suggests that working relationships – which might have been anticipated to be problematic – were generally positive. Community panel members were overwhelmingly positive, with over three fifths (62%) saying their relationship was very good and a further third (32%) reasonably good. One third (32%) said that they worked well with all the other community panel members in their pilot area and a further 61% said that they worked well with most of them. Ninety three per cent of respondents agreed with the statement that 'generally panel members work together well as a team'. Four fifths of community panel members felt either very (51%) or reasonably (29%) valued by YOT staff. A similar proportion felt either very (55%) or reasonably (25%) supported by YOT staff.

Managers appeared to take a slightly different view of the nature of the relationships between YOT staff and community volunteers. On the whole, managers felt that their YOT staff were not keen on working with community panel members, though most recognised that adapting to the new way of working had been problematic, several describing it variously as a 'culture shock', 'challenging' and 'really hard to shift to the new ideology'. YOT managers recognised that YOT staff had found it very difficult to open up their practice to outsiders and that there was deep suspicion and resentment about volunteers from the community coming in and telling them what to do, as illustrated by the following comment from a manager:

> A lot of people in the YOT were very suspicious about opening up their practice … some people really didn't like their decisions, practices and professional expertise being questioned. We have only got round it by a lot of negotiation with YOT staff and saying 'this is the way of the world now – get used to it'.

One of the concerns in the running of panels was the extent to which community panel members felt able to influence the meetings or, conversely, felt dependent on, or dominated by, the YOT panel members' expertise. Interestingly, three fifths of panel members (59%) did not agree that 'YOT panel members tend to direct the proceedings', albeit that 20% agreed to some extent. By contrast, three quarters (76%) agreed with the statement that 'community panel members determine the direction of meetings'. This would seem to be an indication that, despite managers' impressions, community panel members were becoming more confident and assertive of their central role and position in steering panels, particularly in relation to the role of the YOT panel member. More specifically, when asked about their own contribution to panel meetings most community panel members felt content with their level of participation. As an indication of this, two thirds (67%) said that they disagreed with the statement 'I do not contribute as much as I would like to panels'.

Nonetheless, tension could arise between individual YOT officers and panel members partly due to conflicting understandings of the roles each should play at the panel. One issue that was particularly difficult was 'giving over' the panels to volunteers and ensuring that they were not YOT led. The shifting responsibility and blurring of boundaries – respecting a lay person's views and being directed by them and being subject to their decisions – was a difficult role for many YOT officers to handle. Several managers not only expressed reservations about this issue but also some strategies for dealing with it:

> I actually prefer to drop some hefty hints to the panel about what we want to do in the young person's interests. It's about control of the thing [the panel] and I do have some concerns about the inconsistency of the decisions made by the volunteers.

Several managers felt that in areas of risk assessment and proportionality, the YOT staff needed to direct the proceedings and also felt the community panel members needed to respect the experience and expertise of the YOT officer:

> The volunteers would often have their own ideas about reparation … the volunteers might say to the YOT officers 'I want him to do this and I want him to do that' … and that caused a bit of conflict to begin with, and this may sound a bit strong, but we've stamped that out. I don't think we've had any panels where the YOT worker has been surprised by the local knowledge of the panel as I think was intended in the legislation.

The issue of the YOT officer trying to dominate the panel meeting was acknowledged as a challenging problem which did not appear to have been addressed on a formal basis across the pilot sites, but rather was negotiated on a one-to-one basis with individual YOT officers. There was a lack of clarity in role expectations and the decision-making process, in particular what the community panel members should expect from the YOT officer, and what YOT staff needed to appreciate about the role of volunteers. Trying to get YOT staff to work out a balance between the two was difficult with some YOT staff struggling to come to terms with a new way of working:

> The YOT do not like working with the volunteers. It is a big issue for them and has also contributed to the whole resistance to referral orders generally. Some of the workers in the YOT have really struggled and feel that when it comes to the panels, deciding what should be in the contract is no business of the public.

Whilst one manager recognised that it could be quite difficult for volunteers to be assertive in the face of 'someone throwing their professional weight around', another said that many of his YOT staff felt that the community panel members were just there to 'rubber stamp' YOT proposals:

> Most of the people in the YOT really don't need a volunteer telling them what to do or advocating a certain programme of activity for the young person. That is what the professional has spent years doing. The fact that on the basis of six days of training, volunteers have all this power is seen by some as quite insulting. On a practical level, the fact that the volunteers want to drag things on at the panel for usually an hour is seen as a waste of time when they [the YOT officer] could draw up a contract on their own in five minutes.

Youth Offender Panels: Process Issues

Youth offender panels are designed to be a more informal setting at which all participants can contribute to deliberations. This appeared to be borne out, with 62% of respondents agreeing with the statement that 'panels are more informal than expected'. One of the principal findings from evaluations of restorative justice developments, particularly in Australia and New Zealand, is that they have shown high levels of procedural satisfaction by the parties to the conflict (Morris and Maxwell 2000; Trimboli 2000). They are often seen to be fairer and accord more respect to the parties than do traditional courts (Strang *et al.* 1999). With this in mind, it is important that, as far as community panel members are concerned, they attach considerable import to issues of procedural fairness in the panel process. Eighty-eight per cent of respondents agreed to some extent (nearly half of whom strongly agreed) that 'panels are fair to all those who attend'.

Community involvement through the participation of panel members is a significant issue, not only because it enables young people to see the impact of their offending upon the community or because it brings 'ordinary people' and non-professionals into the process, but also because it enables the community to have an ownership of young people's problems and a responsibility to help in addressing them. In this vein, one community panel member commented that the most successful aspect of panels was the 'community taking responsibility for young offenders, rather than operating a culture where it is the fault of teachers/parents, etc.'. Another commented that the most successful aspect was 'communication and bringing this back into the community'.

Community panel members held generally positive views of the participation of young people, parents and others in the panel process. Over half (59%) agreed that 'young offenders contributed significantly to panel meetings', and an even larger majority (66%) agreed that 'parents/ carers contribute significantly to panel meetings'. Furthermore, 94% agreed to some extent (more than half of whom strongly agreed) that 'panels give everyone involved a chance to voice their feelings'. Together, this suggests that, as far as community panel members are concerned at least, youth offender panels do constitute a forum in which genuine deliberation about the young person, the offence and how to address future offending can, and often does, take place. Furthermore, this reinforces the views expressed by the young people and parents interviewed (see Chapter 10). In the light of the earlier discussion, it is interesting to note that only 14% of community panel members agreed (and 62% disagreed) with the statement that 'young offenders should be entitled to legal representation'.

As a process, many panel members were convinced by the way in which young people were challenged to take responsibility and acknowledge the harm that they had caused, and also contribute to how to try to repair the harm or make amends for their offending. Some community panel members suggested that the process helped empower young people to take control of their lives by giving them a chance to put their offending behind them. Approximately two thirds (66%) of respondents agreed with the statement that 'young offenders took responsibility for the harm they had caused', whilst only 8% disagreed. This would appear to be a strong endorsement by community panel members of one of the central aims of youth offender panels.

Community panel members who had experienced panels with a victim present suggested that their presence significantly altered the dynamics of panel meetings most often in a progressive manner. Of those who had experienced at least one panel at which a victim had been present, just over two thirds (70%) said that a victim's presence at a panel was either beneficial or very beneficial (see Figure 9.1). Almost nine tenths (88%) either strongly agreed or agreed with the statement 'having a victim present helps to make the young person recognise the effects of their behaviour' and just over three quarters (78%) either strongly agreed or agreed with the statement 'having a victim present places greater focus upon the offence'.

Those community panel members who had first-hand experience of sitting on panels at which a victim had been in attendance were asked to

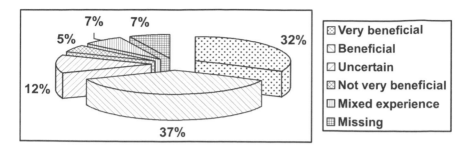

Figure 9.1 Community members' views regarding victims' presence at a panel

describe the effect on the panel meeting of having a victim present. Most respondents suggested the victim's presence helped focus the meeting upon the offence itself and its consequences. In addition, many highlighted the way in which the victim's presence often required the young person to acknowledge, and take responsibility for, his or her actions and their impact on others. The following comment from a community panel member is typical of the type of responses elicited by such an open-ended question:

> The whole dynamics change. The young person is usually unaware of the consequences on the victim and family. The victim being present emphasises that every action has a consequence. The victim gets a true impression of the offender, a physical, mental and emotional impression and realises that s/he is an ordinary youngster not a monster.

All community panel members were asked about the extent to which victims' experiences or views were represented at panel meetings at which victims were themselves not present. Here again, there was a mixed response. Thirteen per cent said that victims' views or experiences were very much represented; 44% said they were somewhat; 28% not very much; and 7% not at all represented. Generally, however, a majority of respondents (54%) agreed with the statement that 'the victim's perspective is given sufficient prominence in panels'.

It was the clear view of most community panel members that not enough was being done to encourage victim attendance at panel meetings. Eighty-five per cent of all community panel members who replied to the questionnaire agreed (40%) or strongly agreed (45%) with the statement that 'more should be done to encourage victims to attend'. This reinforces the views of others involved in the process and is discussed further in Chapters 10 and 11.

Contracts

As we noted in the last chapter the Youth Justice and Criminal Evidence Act 1999 states that a contract should always include some element of direct or indirect reparation and should also include activities to address the factors behind the offending behaviour. In this light, community panel members were asked to what extent reparation is a key element of the contracts that they had been involved with. Almost two thirds (64%) replied that reparation is always and 28% sometimes a key element of contracts.

Community panel members were asked to what extent the terms of the contract were decided before the panel began. Approximately one third of respondents (32%) indicated that contracts are often largely agreed before panels met. It was clear that community panel members saw the panel as having a fundamental contribution to make to the terms of the contract, albeit that the majority (61%) thought that the young person had made either a lot or quite a bit of a contribution to the decision-making process. Moreover, 68% of respondents later said that they agreed with the statement that 'young people are actively involved in determining their contracts'. Panel members had slightly differing understandings of the extent to which YOT panel members shape the content of the contract. Two fifths (39%) disagreed with the statement that 'YOT panel members determine the contents of the contract', whilst 33% agreed with the same statement.[3] Generally, community panel members considered that they have as significant an input (if not greater) into deliberations as YOT panel members – very much reinforcing the sense that the original intention of youth offender panels had in many ways been realised.

One of the issues raised by community panel members concerned their limited scope to construct tailored contracts in discussion with young persons and their parents (and victims where relevant) as a result of the lack of options available locally, particularly with regard to programmes of activity to address the young person's offending behaviour. This concern was also borne out by responses to the survey in which 61% disagreed with the statement that 'there are enough local programmes of activity for young people'. In the earlier interviews, concerns over the apparent lack of local programmes of activity for young people were related to questions of resources. A majority of community panel members (58%) believed there to have been fewer resources available locally than they expected.

Despite these limitations, community panel members tended to believe that 'contracts do actually address the young person's offending', 57% agreed and 19% strongly agreed with this statement. Moreover, they tended to believe that contracts were 'generally proportionate to the harm done'. Thirty-seven per cent believed this always to be the case, but the majority (56%) believed it sometimes to be true.

The Contribution of Community Panel Members to Referral Orders

Community panel members generally commented positively upon their own experiences of referral orders and youth offender panels. Community panel members also saw their role as crucial to the success of referral orders and youth offender panels. As one YOT manager said:

> It should not be under-estimated or taken for granted the amount of time commitment, and emotional energy volunteers are giving to this project. It will be this energy and faith in the success of panels, which will ensure 'offender panels' are seen as the way forward in constructively addressing youth offending in the community.

Despite some misgivings about working with community panel members and the perceived challenge to the professional expertise of YOT staff, it was universally recognised by referral order managers that as the community panel members had become more experienced over the course of the year, they were becoming increasingly professional, capable and competent. In several areas the YOT officers were playing a lesser role at the meetings, the overall approach was to 'let them get on with it'. The sheer commitment of the community panel members had been appreciated: 'it is the community panel members who have sustained us throughout with their commitment and their enthusiasm – they keep us going.'

Most referral order managers agreed that community panel members had brought a fresh outlook and approach to the work of the YOT and that they took their responsibilities very seriously. Although there was a concern that the panel members were not wholly representative of the community, they were felt to have brought a community perspective:

> They bring a fresh look at the situation. Kids that offend become the norm to us. The panel members are not ground down in the work of the YOT. They come with a different view. Some of the panel members live in areas where crime is the norm and they have to deal

with how that affects them on a daily basis. They will say to the young person 'this is socially unacceptable' and it seems to strike a chord with the young person. They do bring a fresh and different view to things.

One of the big problems identified was that sometimes panel members did not actually feel comfortable sitting on panels in their own community, so that aspect of the panels had been lost. However, their obvious enthusiasm and commitment to the work and the impact that they could have on situations was highly valued by all the managers:

> The panel members do see things from a broader perspective and they are a fairly strong and confident group of people. If they see things that are causing concern – like kids consistently coming from the same school – then they will write to the LEA and say something. One of our panel members is so concerned about one of the schools that he has been to speak to the governors and almost issued them with an ultimatum to start putting their house in order. They can do things like that and it seems to have more impact coming from them as members of the community.

Some criticism was levelled at the lack of resources that the panel members had brought to the process:

> I thought that one of the ideas behind this was that the volunteer from the community would come to the panels and say 'you have done harm to the community, this is what you can do to make amends'. But they have brought nothing in terms of ideas or resources. They have expected us to provide everything and it is all YOT based. I'm not sure that the idea of the community is coming through.

Overall, it was felt that the contribution of community panel members to panels was an extremely positive development. One of the referral order managers commented:

> I think restorative justice is about tackling the insularity of the criminal justice system and giving it back to the community, and I think that is where the panels are different. The panel is meant to be a representation of the community ... we have some way to go yet before we can say that they represent the community.

In all, the tension between lay panel members and professional YOT staff was seen to be a central dynamic in the operation of panels, one which needs to be carefully managed, such that each respects the contribution of, and constraints upon, the other. The involvement of lay panel members also adds an important challenge to the way YOTs work: how to integrate and use the skills of the panel members and respond to their different cultural assumptions. It affords a new interface between members of the public and the YOTs and offers vibrant opportunities for greater public participation in criminal justice (see Crawford 2001a). As such it can facilitate the 'opening up' of otherwise potentially introspective professional cultures, which militate against greater public participation. Accommodating such a challenge has been a vital aspect of implementing referral orders, as one of the referral order managers noted: 'The panels are a powerful organisation. They [community panel members] are a very confident group of people. They are a force to be reckoned with.'

It was clear that during the life of the pilots the community panel members grew into their roles over time and increasingly began to assert a greater independence from the YOT staff rather than being wholly reliant upon them. This placed YOT staff in a somewhat difficult position of giving up a certain amount of control, and presented a difficult balancing act, between allowing the lay panel members to take a greater lead and 'being directive and saving time at a panel because of their experience and professional knowledge' as one community panel member noted. Even those who felt that initially they had played an insufficiently determining role in the panel process believed that over time, they would take on a more independent role:

> It is taking a while for us to be independent and to make our own decisions ... At the moment we will bow to the professionals because we are trying to find our way. It will take a while for us to gain their [the YOT members'] respect but in the end we will want to be independent and set our own values on the panels ... it's a question of when – or if – they will relinquish some of their professional judgement over to us. There will come a point when they will have to trust us and allow us to exercise our judgement.

As this extract suggests, this meant YOT staff needed to learn to trust in the panel members. Building mutual trust and respect was important in developing constructive relations. A crucial element in establishing trust relations is making people aware of the limitations of their own and others' contribution, so that they neither try to 'do it all' nor have unrealistic expectations of what others can deliver. Most notably, YOTs need to accommodate the cultural shift required to embrace the role and implications of working with community panel members.

Conclusion

This chapter suggests community panel members enjoyed their work and generally felt valued members of what they considered to be an important initiative within youth justice. They were very supportive of the aims and intentions of youth offender panels and their restorative justice ideals. Community panel members' experiences suggest that they generally considered panels to be successfully meeting their objectives. Across the pilots, relations between community panel members and YOT staff were positive. Community panel members appear to have become confident and effective chairs of panel meetings and facilitators of inclusive deliberations. Their views were also generally positive about the con-tribution made by young people and their family members at panels meetings. Particular concerns were raised, once again, about the low level of victim involvement. However, those community panel members that had had experience of panels at which victims had attended suggested that their presence significantly altered the dynamics of the panel, most often in a progressive manner.

The experience of the pilots saw community panel members grow into their roles over time and embrace their responsibilities for facilitating panel meetings. In this they increasingly came to assert a greater autonomy from the YOT staff. This has seen relationships between YOT staff and community members mature into one premised upon a mutual recognition of what each side brings to the panel process. The contribution of community panel members has introduced an exciting and vibrant dynamic into the work of YOTs. This has also meant that YOTs have needed to accommodate the cultural shift required to embrace the role and implications of working with community panel members.

The timeliness of the provision of reports was important in influencing the extent to which community panel members felt able to contribute to panels. This suggests that they should be provided with a report on the offence, the young person and victim(s) (where appropriate) at least two days before the panel meeting. Other concerns cited included perceived insufficient programmes of reparation, and lack of resources/pro-grammes of activity for young people. This suggests that YOTs need to think creatively and identify a broad range of activities for potential inclusion into contracts, to facilitate panel meetings. Community panel members themselves may have a valuable contribution to make to this process. Nearly all concerns highlighted by community panel members related to problems of implementation rather than the general principles underlying referral orders.

Notes

1 This was changed during the passage of the legislation to a policy of 'lay community involvement' to include 'a broad cross-section of the community that has an interest in supporting young people and preventing offending' (Paul Boateng, Standing Committee E, House of Commons, 4th sitting, 15 June 1999 (afternoon), col. 76).
2 There is also a potential conflict of interests with regard to YOT panel members. As YOTs are required to have representatives from the police among their multi-agency staff, even if they are not 'otherwise involved in the case', nevertheless, a police officer may be privy to prejudicial information about a young person which may affect subsequent deliberations.
3 A quarter (26%) neither agreed nor disagreed and a further 3% was missing or not applicable.

Chapter 10

Young people and their families

A hallmark of youth offender panels is the active involvement of young offenders, their parents, victims and members of the wider community, as well as professional YOT staff, in a forum to discuss collectively the offence, the harm caused, how to deal with the aftermath of the offence and its implications for the future. In this chapter, we consider the primary subjects of the referral order process, namely young people and their parents or guardians. In so doing, we explore the role, involvement and experiences of young people and their parents and their views about youth offender panels and the referral order process.

The active participation of young people in decisions about how best to respond to their offending is premised upon a number of interlocking rationales. First, involving and giving young people a voice in participatory processes is a way of rendering them accountable for their actions. Second, involving young people in a dialogue with those most affected by their offending (both directly and indirectly) encourages them to recognise and acknowledge responsibility for the consequences of their offending behaviour. Third, engaging young people in a process over which they have some control and choice allows young people to take active responsibility for preventing further offending and changing their behaviour. Fourth, young people are more likely to adhere to agreements that they have contributed to or had a sense of choice in. Finally, Art. 12 of the United Nations Convention on the Rights of the Child provides a moral yardstick for giving young people the opportunity to express their views and have them taken into account in matters affecting them, most notably legal and administrative proceedings.

Similarly, there are a number of good reasons why involving parents or guardians may have beneficial effects. First, the involvement of parents can encourage them to take account and face the consequences of their child's behaviour. Second, parents and guardians are primary agents of care and socialisation and as such have a significant role in and influence over the lives of young people. Third, engaging parents in a process over which they have some control and choice encourages them to take active responsibility for preventing future offending by their child and changing their child's behaviour. Fourth, empowering parents in the decision-making process can help them deal with their child's offending through dialogue and through access to resources and support. Fifth, social control is likely to operate more effectively through informal relations of care and concern by family members and friends than through formal sanctions by socially distant professionals. The views of close acquaintances – notably family members – are likely to matter more to young people than the opinions and actions of those of remote criminal justice officials. Finally, parents and guardians can assist in the reintegration of offenders.

Referral orders and youth offender panels (as with other restorative justice interventions) demand an assessment of the way in which panels are experienced and perceived by key 'stakeholders': parents, carers, victims and community members (often marginalised within traditional processes of justice). The views of these key participants provide an important insight into the way in which the referral order process is experienced and perceived by those people who are intended to be most intimately affected by it. As documented in Chapter 7, we know that in over two thirds of cases (68%) the young person attended an initial panel with only one other person, usually the mother. In the following sections we examine the findings of in-depth interviews with a sample of young people and parents.

The Interview Sample

Between March and September 2001 a total of 90 young people and 75 parents or guardians were interviewed across the 11 pilot sites about their experiences of referral orders and panel meetings. The sample of young people interviewed was selected to represent the diversity of offenders of different ages, subject to referral orders of varying lengths and a range of offence types and seriousness. Similar criteria governed the selection of the parents/guardians for interview.[1]

The majority of the young people interviewed (64 out of the total of 90) came from the older age groups (15–17). No 10-year-old youths were interviewed. Although 18-year-olds are not eligible for referral orders, 7 young people were 17 years old when they received a referral order from the court, but had their eighteenth birthday before they were interviewed. Of those interviewed, 81 (91%) were male and 8 (9%) were female; 87% were white and 9% black Caribbean. The rest were Pakistani (2), Indian (1) and one 'other'. At the time of interview, 43 young people (48%) had successfully completed their order. Forty (44%) were still subject to an active referral order. Three young people had had their order revoked by the court due to reoffending, two did not know what the status of their order was, and in two other cases the information was missing. Over two thirds of young people (69%) had been given a referral order as a result of committing one offence, 14 had committed two offences and 10 had committed three offences. Three young people had each committed 4, 6 and 8 offences respectively (in one case the information was missing). A broad range of offences was represented, the most common being driving offences, theft, burglary and common assault (see Table 10.1). Those interviewed were broadly representative of the different lengths of orders available to the court. Approximately one third received 3-month orders and another third received 6-month orders.

Forty-nine of the parents/guardians interviewed (65%) were mothers, nineteen were fathers (25%), four were foster carers (5%) and three were other family members (4%). Ninety per cent of interviewees were white, with 7% black Caribbean and 3% Pakistani. In three cases the young person was no longer living with his or her parent/guardian at the time

Table 10.1 Offences committed by young people interviewed

Offence type	No. of young people	%
Acquisitive crime	28	31.0
Vehicle offences	22	24.5
Contact (including robbery)	20	22.0
Damage	8	8.5
Public order	5	5.5
Drugs	4	4.5
Fraud	2	2.5
Other	1	1.5
Total	90	100.0

the referral order was made. For the majority of those interviewed (59%), the age of the young person in their care was 16 and over at the time the order was made. The remainder (41%) were under 16, with some as young as 11, in which case a parent/guardian would have been ordered by the court to attend a panel. In addition, nearly half those parents/guardians of children who were 16 or over were ordered by the court to attend a panel. The children of nearly half the parent sample (43%) were given orders of 3 months and a slightly smaller number (38%) were given 6-month orders and only one was given a 9-month order. A further 11% were given 12-month orders, whilst the rest either had 4-month (5%) or 7-month (1%) orders. Again, this broadly reflects the picture across the pilots.

In sum, those young people and parents interviewed constitute a broadly representative sub-sample of those receiving and involved with referral orders during the pilot phase.

The Youth Court

In court, 27 of the young people interviewed (30%) had to pay compensation ranging from £10 to £600. A further fifth (20%) had to pay court costs and just over one tenth (12%) had to pay both costs and compensation. This left only just over a third who had neither costs nor compensation awarded against them. In most cases, the young person's parents made the financial payment to the court, but in many cases the young person had to reimburse his or her parents (at the request of his or her parents) either by working in the house or by making a direct payment to them. This repayment often became a term in the young person's subsequent contract (to which we return below).

Some young people felt that it was inappropriate that their parents had to pay costs or compensation as reflected by the following comment: 'I haven't got a job so it was wrong of the court to fine my mum. I was the one that did the thieving, not her.' Nevertheless, 80% of young people agreed that they had been treated fairly by the court.

Parents' and guardians' experiences of the Youth Court at which their child was given a referral order echo similar experiences of the young people themselves. Four fifths (81%) had attended the court when the referral order was made. Of those who had attended court, nearly one third (30%) said that the order had not been explained to them. Where the referral order had been explained to the parent/guardian in court this had been done in the majority of cases (57%) by a YOT member, in 27% of cases by a magistrate, 11% of cases by the court clerk and 5% of cases by a solicitor. Of those in court just over half (54%) said they understood what was expected of them. However, 15% did not understand what was expected of them. This appears to reinforce a picture of a court process in which key participants are neither clear about what is happening nor what the implications are for them. However, only 11% of those who attended court sought further information about what was expected of them, implying the experience was also disempowering. The most usual contact for further information was a solicitor or YOT member.

Those 13 parents/guardians who had not attended the court appearance at which the young person in their care had been given the referral order mainly found out about what was expected of them from the YOT, although some found out from another family member (who may have been at court) or their child.

Information about Referral Orders and Youth Offender Panels

Less than half the young people said they were given information by a solicitor about referral orders (48%), of which three quarters (78%) received this information at court. A further 54% received information about referral orders from somebody else, usually a YOT representative at court. Six per cent received information from a court official. By far the majority (93%) also received information about panels from a YOT officer after their court appearance and prior to their first panel meeting. A majority of young people was visited at least once by a YOT officer (56%). A quarter were visited twice and a small number (2%) had three visits before the initial panel meeting.

Most young people were given full and detailed information from YOT officers about appearing at their first panel meeting (see Table 10.2). They were told who would be there, what would happen if they did not fulfil the contract, that a report was being prepared about them (with the exception of one of the pilot areas) and that there would be community representatives present. The information which was most consistently given to young people concerned their appearance at the meetings (initial and review) and fulfilling their contracts. Most young people were not told that they could take a friend along as a supporter to the panel (67%) or that they did not have to agree to a contract at the first panel meeting if they wanted time to think about it (72%). Only 44% were told that the victim might be at the initial meeting. However, it should be noted that the YOT officer may not have known if the victim had agreed to attend at that stage.

Table 10.2 demonstrates a clear consistency between the experiences of young people and parents with regard to information given to them in

Table 10.2 Information given to young people and parents in preparation for the initial panel meeting (%)

Before the panel meeting were you told	Young people			Parents		
	Yes	No	Don't know/ Missing	Yes	No	Don't know/ Missing
A report was being prepared on you/your child for the panel members?	86	7	7	81	12	7
What might happen if you did not attend the panel?	90	6	4	77	16	7
Who else would be attending the meeting?	77	17	6	76	19	5
Who else could come to the panel meeting with you/your child?	82	11	7	48	44	8
At least two members of the community would be part of the panel?	76	17	7	73	21	5
The victim might be at the panel meeting?	44	38	18	41	36	23
A solicitor could not be present at the panel?	19	74	7	11	85	4
You/your child could take a friend along as a supporter to the panel?	27	67	6	25	63	12
Whether or not you had to agree a contract at the meeting?	86	9	5	85	7	8
What would happen after the meeting?	66	27	7	71	24	5
You/your child didn't have to agree a contract at the panel if you wanted to think about it?	18	72	10	29	61	10
You/your child would have to attend other panel meetings?	90	3	7	81	9	9
What would happen if you/your child did not stick to the contract?	93	2	5	88	5	7
You/your child will not have a criminal record if you/(s)he successfully completes the referral order?	76	14	10	69	19	12

preparation for the initial panel meeting. The only significant discrepancy was in response to the question about who else could accompany them to the panel. Whilst most young people (82%) felt that they were provided with this information, namely that their parent/guardian could accompany them, less than half of parents (48%) felt that they knew who, if anybody, could accompany them.

In the time between court and the first panel meeting most parents (81%) said that they had received further information or advice about youth offender panels. In nearly all instances (97%) this further information was provided by a YOT officer. Although more worryingly, 18% said that they had received no further information. Hence, most parents (80%) said that they had talked to a YOT officer prior to the initial panel meeting, although 16% said that they had not. Of those who did speak with a YOT member, three quarters only did so once. Only in two cases did the parent talk with a YOT officer on three occasions. Nearly all those who did talk with a YOT officer found this useful with half saying that this was very useful.

Interestingly, when asked if they would have liked more opportunity to prepare for the panel meeting three quarters of parents said that they would not (less than one tenth said that they would). As Table 10.2 suggests, most parents felt that they were provided with sufficient information about what to expect from the panel meeting, who would be there and what might happen. However, most young people (74%) and parents (85%) were not provided with information that a solicitor could not be present at the panel with them.

Restorative justice experiences from around the world have highlighted the importance of good preparation for all the parties, such that they understand the process, what is expected of them and have realistic expectations of what the outcomes might be. Table 10.2 shows that, by and large, those young people and parents interviewed felt prepared for the initial panel meeting. They had been provided with a range of information about the expected participants, process and outcome of panel meetings. In this the parents' experiences closely reflect those of the young people interviewed. Generally, however, most parents and young people seemed unaware of the fact that they could also bring along a friend or supporter. Nevertheless, it is somewhat concerning that of those parents and young people interviewed, over one third were unaware that the victim might be at the panel meeting and that nearly a quarter was uncertain about what would happen after the meeting. The fact that over one fifth of parents and just less than one fifth of young people said that they had not been given information that at least two members of the community would be part of the panel is of concern.

Given the emphasis in the *Guidance* on agreeing a contract on the basis of voluntary negotiation rather than imposing it upon the young person, we sought to understand the extent to which negotiation was balanced with the provision of information provided to the participants as to the limits of their required involvement. Most parents (61%) and young people (72%) seemed unaware of the fact that they did not have to agree a contract at the panel if the child and his or her parents wanted to think about it.[2]

The Initial Panel Meeting

According to the *Guidance* (Home Office 2001: para. 8.2) the primary purpose of the initial panel meeting is for the panel to agree a contract with the offender. In addition, it is also seen as crucial in providing for 'restorative justice in a community context'. When asked who had attended the initial panel meeting, many of the young people were very vague, not remembering exactly who was there. Some mentioned 'two women', or 'a couple of oldies' when clearly there had to be at least one member from the YOT also present. In some cases the young person identified the YOT officer by name, in others they were unsure exactly who the YOT officer was and often were unable to distinguish between YOT officers and community panel members. Some could not remember anybody who had been present at the panel meeting or were unsure who they were:

> Some bloke who we thought was a policeman or prison officer [community panel member], a woman who ran the panel [Chair] some woman who kept asking questions, I don't know who she was [panel member observing].

> Someone was there talking about the damage I had done, but I did not know who it was.

Young people were also sometimes vague about others that attended the panel meeting, making it difficult to say conclusively how many attended with their parent(s) or other supporters. However, of those who could remember, the majority attended with only their mother, a minority attending with their father or both parents and 13 young people interviewed attended an initial panel meeting with a victim present.

Young people were asked to put into their own words what they thought the purpose of the initial panel was. The majority mentioned some form of 'help' or 'sorting out'. The following comments are illustrative: 'To help me get through this situation and get through the contract and make sure I did get through this. To make sure that I was being good.' Another young person commented: 'Sorting things out and arranging all the stuff I have to do for community service.' A significant number said the purpose of the panel was to stop them reoffending. A few said it was specifically to stop them 'smoking' or 'drinking'. Only a small number of young people mentioned 'punishment' in any form.

Only three young people specifically mentioned the victim in describing the panel's purpose. One suggested that the panel's purpose was 'to say sorry to the man and for them [the panel] to try to help me'. Another commented: 'I thought I was going to meet the victim and I was going to be punished.' The third suggested that the purpose was: 'To sort me out, let me know what I'd done was wrong, to say sorry to the victim.'

Nearly a third of young people interviewed mentioned some form of reparation, by 'paying back' or making amends as reflected in the following extract: 'Because of what I had done I had to repay like community service.' Another commented that the purpose was 'to discuss and analyse what I had done and how I could make up for it'.

The young people were generally happy with their experience of attending an initial panel meeting. Despite their confusion over who the panel members were, they agreed (98%) that they had been introduced to all the other people attending the meeting. They also felt the purpose of the meeting was fully explained to them (72%) and understood what was going on at that meeting (91%).

Significantly, more than four fifths (84%) felt they were treated with respect. A similar number (86%) felt that the panel members treated them fairly and that they themselves got a chance to speak and explain their side of things during the meeting (87%). Three quarters responded that they did not feel pushed into anything they disagreed with.

The vast majority of parents interviewed (88%) attended all the youth offender panel hearings, though 7% attended some and 5% attended none. Hence, four of the parents interviewed had not attended the initial panel. Parents who attended the initial panel were asked how suitable they felt the venue was for holding the meeting. More than two thirds (68%) replied that it was very suitable and only 8% said that it was unsuitable. Similarly, 88% of respondents felt that the timing of the meeting was convenient. However, roughly one third (32%) had to make special arrangements to enable them to attend the meeting. In most cases, this involved either release from work commitments or childcare arrangements, but in a smaller number of cases it involved travel arrangements.

In two thirds (67%) of the meetings attended by the parent interviewed, the parent (usually the mother) was the only other person at the meeting apart from the young person and the panel members (this reflects the broader picture of panel attendance across the pilots during the fieldwork period noted earlier). In 13% of instances (from the interview sample) both parents attended with the young person. In all but one case parents/guardians were introduced to all the other people at the panel meeting. The vast majority of parents (91%) said that the purpose of the meeting was fully explained to them, as against 7% who said that the purpose was only partly explained and one parent who said that the purpose was hardly at all explained to them.

Parents interviewed were asked to explain in their own words what they thought the purpose of the panel meeting was. Generally, parents seemed clear about the panel's role. The following represent some of the responses given:

> The aim was to help my son mend his ways and apologise to the victim.

> For us all to understand the effect of what has happened. For my son to realise what he had done wrong and to make amends.

However, a small number of parents expressed views that suggest they were not entirely clear about the role of the meeting or they felt that they were being punished by the process:

> It was a shock when I went in there because no one had told me what to expect and I hadn't expected so many people to be there.

> One of the problems was that when they explained things they made us feel like we [the parents] were being punished.

These comments reinforce the importance of preparing all the parties, not merely the young person, as to the purpose and nature of the meetings and managing their expectations.

Comparing the Experience of the Initial Panel Meeting with Court

When asked how nervous they were 'about attending the initial panel meeting' 59% of the young people interviewed said that they were nervous (17% of whom said they were very nervous) and 36% said they were not nervous at all. This compares with over three quarters (77%) of young people who said they were nervous about attending court (37% of which said they were very nervous) and 18% said they were not nervous at all.

Table 10.3 highlights the comparative experiences of young people attending an initial panel meeting as compared to the Youth Court at which they were given the referral order. Whilst three quarters (74%) of young people agreed that they understood what was going on at court and 6% strongly agreed, this figure rose to 79% who agreed and 12% who strongly agreed that they understood what was going on at the initial panel meeting.

Panels were introduced as part of a 'step change in the culture of the Youth Court' (Home Office 1997d: 31–2) away from a 'court-based judicial model' towards a 'party-centred deliberative model' of justice. As such, respondents were asked a series of questions about their experience of the initial panel meeting. Moreover, those respondents who had also attended the Youth Court hearing at which their child was given the referral order were asked a number of the same questions with regard to both the court and panel experience in order to gauge a sense of comparison.

Table 10.4 suggests that, on the basis of their experience, parents accord a significantly higher level of understanding of the process and how the parties had been affected by the offence, as well as opportunities to participate and a sense of procedural fairness with regard to initial panel meetings as against Youth Court appearance. Whereas approximately three quarters (78%) of parents agreed that the court had treated them with respect, parents were almost unanimous (97%) in agreeing that the initial panel had treated them with respect. Similarly, 79% of parents agreed that they had understood what was going on in the court, whilst parents were virtually unanimous (99%) in agreeing that they had understood what was going on at the initial panel meeting.

Three quarters (77%) of parents agreed (or strongly agreed) that the main purpose of the court was to punish their child. By contrast, only 38% agreed that this was the main purpose of the panel. Whilst 68% of respondents agreed that the main purpose of the court was to help their child get on with his or her life, a significantly larger number (89%) said this was the main purpose of the initial panel.

Principles of Justice

As well as highlighting comparative differences between court and initial panel meetings, Tables 10.3 and 10.4 also reveal interesting information

Table 10.3 Experiences of young people of initial panel meeting (IPM) as compared to the Youth Court (YC) (%)

To what extent do you agree with the following statements?	Strongly agree (YC)	Strongly agree IPM	Agree (YC)	Agree IPM	Neither agree nor disagree (YC)	Neither agree nor disagree IPM	Disagree (YC)	Disagree IPM	Strongly disagree (YC)	Strongly disagree IPM
You understood what was going on	(6)	12	(74)	79	(9)	2	(10)	3	(2)	0
You felt that you were treated with respect	(3)	14	(67)	70	(18)	4	(8)	7	(1)	0
You had an opportunity to explain your side of things	(2)	19	(52)	68	(21)	1	(21)	8	(1)	0
If the court/panel got the facts wrong you felt able to get things corrected	(2)	10	(40)	42	(37)	32	(11)	10	(0)	0
You felt that the court treated you fairly/the panel members were fair	(4)	22	(76)	64	(7)	3	(8)	6	(3)	1
The main purpose of the court/panel was to punish you	(10)	3	(61)	40	(11)	14	(14)	38	(1)	1
The main purpose of the court/panel was to help you get on with your life	(2)	19	(43)	60	(26)	10	(22)	8	(2)	0
You had a clearer idea of how people had been affected by the offence after court/panel	(0)	12	(46)	57	(36)	18	(12)	7	(0)	0

Table 10.4 Experiences of parents/guardians of initial panel meeting (IPM) as compared to the Youth Court (YC) (%)

To what extent do you agree with the following statements?	Strongly agree (YC)	Strongly agree IPM	Agree (YC)	Agree IPM	Neither agree nor disagree (YC)	Neither agree nor disagree IPM	Disagree (YC)	Disagree IPM	Strongly disagree (YC)	Strongly disagree IPM
You understood what was going on	(19)	27	(60)	72	(8)	0	(11)	1	(2)	0
You felt that you were treated with respect	(15)	35	(63)	62	(11)	1	(8)	1	(3)	0
You had an opportunity to explain your side of things	(7)	30	(31)	62	(32)	7	(29)	1	(2)	0
If the court/panel got the facts wrong you felt able to get things corrected	(8)	23	(37)	42	(38)	32	(13)	3	(3)	0
You felt that the court treated your child fairly / the panel members were fair	(18)	49	(53)	48	(2)	0	(17)	1	(10)	1
The main purpose of the court/panel was to punish your child	(21)	6	(56)	33	(12)	14	(12)	38	(0)	10
The main purpose of the court/panel was to help your child get on with his or her life	(12)	30	(56)	59	(20)	6	(12)	6	(0)	0
You had a clearer idea of how people had been affected by the offence after court/panel	(7)	19	(53)	49	(34)	22	(7)	8	(0)	1

about how young people and parents experienced youth offender panels as forums of justice. The interviews were deliberately designed to evaluate the extent to which panels meet different notions of justice from the perspectives of young people and parents.

Procedural justice

We sought to test young people's sense of procedural justice, defined as being treated fairly and with respect and having a voice in the panel process. The findings in Table 10.4 show that offenders reported considerable levels of procedural justice. Some 84% of young people agreed that they were treated with respect; 86% agreed that the panel members were fair (including a fifth who strongly agreed); 91% agreed that they understood what was going on at the panel; 75% agreed that they did not feel pushed into anything they disagreed with; and 87% agreed that they had an opportunity to explain their side of things. They also suggest that panels were experienced by young people and parents as fairer and accord more respect to the parties than do courts. The greatest discrepancy between court and the panel for the young people was having the opportunity to explain their side of things at the initial panel meeting. For many, they welcomed the opportunity to speak for themselves and to be listened to by the panel members. One young person commented: 'I had people talking to me that showed me respect and told me what I am capable of.' This high level of procedural satisfaction is in line with findings from other restorative justice initiatives around the world (Strang et al. 1999; Daly 2001).

This is significant in that, as Tyler (1990) suggests, people are more likely to comply with a regulatory order that they perceive to be procedurally just. There is some evidence emerging from the RISE research into the community conferencing initiative in Canberra that citizens' personal judgement that the law is moral may depend upon their judgement that the human agents of the legal system have treated them with respect (Sherman et al. 2000b). The more legitimacy that such agents (namely conference facilitators and panel members) can create, the more likely they are to impact positively upon higher levels of future compliance with the law and reduce reoffending.

This sense of procedural justice is also reflected in the responses by parents interviewed about their experience of the initial panel meeting (see Tables 10.4 and 10.5). In particular, three quarters of parents agreed that they felt the panel took account of what they had said in deciding what should be done.

Table 10.5 Experiences of parents/guardians of initial panel meeting (%)

To what extent do you agree with the following statements?	Strongly agree	Agree	Neither agree nor disagree	Disagree	Strongly disagree
All sides got a chance to bring out the facts	29	61	10	0	0
You were able to discuss issues that you felt may have contributed to your child committing the offence	30	61	7	3	0
You felt pushed into things you did not agree with	1	3	16	53	27
The panel took account of what you said in deciding what should be done	24	51	17	7	1
The contract was too harsh	1	7	9	49	34
You felt that your child got off lightly	12	27	12	44	6
You found it was easy to decide what should be put in the contract	0	53	36	10	1
You just went along with whatever the panel suggested	7	37	19	33	4
You would have liked to have had some other people present with you to provide further information or support	0	7	34	53	7
You would have liked some time alone with the people that came with you to think about what should be in the contract	0	8	39	49	3

Restorative justice

Restorative justice was defined in terms of the parties' perceptions about the repair of harm, the degree to which the offender and the victim recognised (or empathised with) each other and were affected by the other and the potential for the reintegration of the offender. Over two thirds of young people (69%) said they had a clearer idea of how people had been affected by their offence after attending the panel meeting. This compares to 45% who said the same after attending court. Only 13 young people interviewed had a victim present at their panel meeting, so the other young people may have developed this understanding from the input of others (particularly panel members) attending the meeting. With regard to the possible reintegration of offenders beyond the referral order process, over two thirds (69%) of young people interviewed felt that attending a panel meeting made them feel they could put the whole thing behind them, whilst 16% disagreed with this suggestion. As one young person commented: 'It gives you a chance to start again and you have no criminal record.' Furthermore, four fifths (79%) of young people agreed that for them, the main purpose of the panel was to help them get on with their life. However, young people had mixed views about the role of punishment within panels. Whilst 43% agreed that punishment was a main purpose of panels a similar number (39%) disagreed. This suggests that youth offender panel deliberations allow the expression of several different justice principles, including punitive sentiments. From our sample there appears to have been relatively less evidence of 'restorativeness' than procedural justice.[3] In large part, this may be due to the relative absence of direct victim input (see Chapter 11).

Substantive justice

Substantive justice was defined in terms of the parties' perceptions of the sanction received by the young person. By and large, parents and young people felt that contracts were appropriate, albeit that a significant minority of parents had misgivings about some contractual elements (we return later in this chapter to a fuller discussion of contracts). When asked, four fifths (81%) of young people disagreed with the suggestion that their contracts were too harsh, although 10% agreed. When asked if they felt they had got off lightly, only just over a third (37%) agreed, whilst over two fifths (43%) disagreed. Parents also tended to disagree (83%) that their child's contract was too harsh; a third of these strongly disagreed. Whilst over a third of parents (39%) felt their child had got off lightly, half disagreed.

The Presence of Victims

The restorative nature of a panel is clearly enhanced by the participation of the young person's victim(s). However, only 13 young people interviewed attended a panel at which a victim was present.[4] Approximately three quarters (10) felt it was right that the victim attended. Most did not find the victim's presence unduly difficult (although four did find it difficult). Most (9) said they were glad to have had the chance to explain their side of things to the victim and eight felt that this gave them the chance to make up for the harm they had caused. Three quarters were affected by what the victim said about his or her experience, whilst three were not affected. In addition, three quarters said that it would make them think differently in the future (only one disagreed with this proposition). These findings suggest that for the small sub-sample of young offenders who attended an initial panel with a victim there was a degree of movement on behalf of the offender as an indicator of restoration. As a result of the panel process, most of these offenders appear to have recognised the victim's perspective and been affected by his or her participation. The following comments by young offenders illustrate this recognition: 'It made me realise that small things you do, for small reasons, affect people for a long time'; 'It made me think what I did was wrong, made me understand better'; and 'the victim was a carer for old people and we stole her moped which she used to get to their houses – it felt really wrong.'

The restorative nature of panels also allows a similar movement on behalf of the victim as the following young person's account suggests:

> They [the victim's parents] were looking at me like I was a nasty piece of work, they only know one side of the story from their son and that really annoyed me. Their attitude changed a bit during the meeting – they listened to me towards the end. At the beginning they didn't want to listen to me at all. I had wanted them to leave after their bit but they refused so they stayed but then they started listening to me.

Of the other 77 that did not have a victim at the meeting, most (63%) said they would not have wanted them to have been present for various reasons, some of which suggested that it would have been easier for the young person without the victim's presence:

> I would have been a bit worried if they had been there – they could lay down harsher terms in the contract.

No, he would tell people who knew me all about it and I would get 'jipped' about it from my mates. I didn't want anyone to know what went on.

However, a fifth (22%) said that they would have wanted their victim to be present, either so that they could apologise or address any unanswered questions: 'Yes, it would help me get things off my chest and explain things to them'; 'Yes to let them know I'm getting dealt with so they can't do anything else about it' [i.e. take the law into their own hands]; and 'so I could apologise and say I didn't mean to frighten him.' When presented with the statement 'victims should always be invited to attend panel meetings', the young people were equally split in their views (Figure 10.1).

Figure 10.1 Young people's response to the suggestion that victims should always be invited to panels

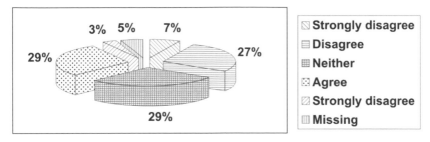

Similarly, many parents offered generally positive views of the presence of the victim at a panel meeting. Only nine of the parents interviewed had attended a panel at which a victim had also been present. Of these, most disagreed that it was 'a difficult experience having the victim at the panel'. All agreed that 'it was right' that the victim was present. But they were evenly split as to whether hearing from the victim had made them think about things differently. When prompted, one parent who had agreed that he had been affected by the victim's presence went on to elaborate: 'I'm sympathetic towards the victim – I've known him for years and we don't get on but I did feel sorry for him.' Another parent who was uncertain as to whether hearing from the victim had made her think differently about things, commented:

I think I was more embarrassed than him [the young person]. My son just hung his head but I felt really embarrassed. It was worse for me having the victim there.

Nevertheless, three quarters of the parents who had attended a panel with a victim agreed that they were glad that they 'had a chance to talk to the victim'. Importantly, all but one parent agreed (and two strongly agreed) that meeting the victim helped their child 'to try and make up for the harm caused'. Finally, all but one parent disagreed (three of whom strongly disagreed) with the proposition that 'it would be better to meet the victim without the rest of the people at the panel'.

As with the young people, all the parents/guardians interviewed were asked whether victims should always be invited to attend panel meetings (see Figure 10.2). A majority (55%) either replied in the affirmative or that it depended upon the circumstances, while nearly a third said no.

Figure 10.2   Parents' views on whether victims should always be invited to attend panel meetings

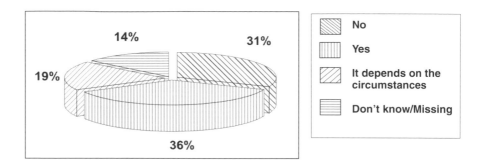

The Contract

All but one of the young people interviewed signed a contract at the end of the initial panel meeting. The one that did not sign explained: 'I wanted more time to think about it.' Most were happy to sign their contract, but 11 young people (12%) said that they felt pressured to sign. We noted above that not many knew that they did not have to sign their contracts at the initial meeting (18%) and 15% said they would have liked to have had more time to think about it. One fifth of the young people interviewed could not remember some or all of the elements in their contracts (most had completed their referral orders at the time of interview, suggesting that it had been put behind them).

When asked if they could elaborate on any reparative element in their contracts, most young people could not. Of those who could, the majority commented positively feeling that they had learned from their experience and enjoyed it:

> I knew I had done wrong so writing the letter was OK, I was glad to say I was sorry. Doing the football at the community centre was great 'cos I love football and enjoyed it.

Most young people found it easy to decide what should be in their contracts. However, when asked if they just went along with what the panel suggested, 44% agreed that they had done so. Five young people objected to something in their contracts and one young person would have liked something in the contract which was left out.

Most young people felt that the contracts had been useful and helped keep them out of trouble. Three quarters (76%) of young people agreed that their contract was useful (including 12% who strongly agreed) and an even larger proportion (78%) agreed that it had helped keep them out of trouble (including 28% who strongly agreed). Interestingly, 8% who felt that their contract was not useful, nevertheless agreed that it had helped them stay out of trouble. This suggests that being involved with the referral order process itself – having to attend meetings and taking responsibility for their behaviour – not just being party to a contract, is significant in how young people perceive they have been treated.

Young people were evenly split as to whether they enjoyed elements of the contract (45% agreed and 36% disagreed). Of the 42 young people who had completed their contracts at time of interview, 72% said they did so to get rid of their criminal record, 75% also said they did so because they did not want to go back to court.

The contracts of the children of parents interviewed were broadly in line with the experience across the pilots. Most had two or three elements. According to the parents, three quarters of the young people had completed all of the elements of the contract. However, some contracts were still ongoing at the time of interview. A number of parents commented that the one-to-one meetings with YOT staff had proved particularly useful:

> It's good that he can have a good one-to-one with someone and a chance to look at himself.

> They try to help the young person. He seems happy to talk to the YOT – they stick to one person and they get to know them and can help them.

When asked about the reparative elements of contracts, parents made some interesting observations about their implications and impact. Writing a letter of apology, where part of the contract, was a particular subject which parents commented upon:

> It was hard for my son to write the letters, but it did him good, helped him understand.

> Writing the letter was the hardest thing. It was only basic but it was from him and it was genuine.

Although one parent stated: 'It would have been better to apologise face to face rather than write a letter of apology.'

A small number of parents (10) said that they felt that there were things which they would have liked to have seen in the contract but which were left out. By and large, these parents were of the view that the content of the contracts had not been harsh or exacting enough. The following were the types of comments typically made by these parents: 'He could have done more to make up to the public and the community'; 'the contract wasn't harsh enough'; 'I would have liked the contract to be a lot harder for him'; and 'He should have got more. I was disappointed that he didn't get more. It was too light.'

When asked about the value and impact of the contract for the young people and the family, parents were generally very positive (see Table 10.6). Nearly three quarters (72%) agreed that the contract elements were useful. However, somewhat ambiguously, just under a half (45%) believed that the contract had not made any difference to the young person's behaviour, albeit that nearly three quarters (74%) agreed that the contract had helped the 'young person stay out of trouble'. This may suggest a belief on the part of the parents that whilst the contracts had helped the young person, changing his or her behaviour may be more difficult and the subject of wider factors not necessarily addressed by contract elements. It may also reflect the fact that some parents and young people perceived the contract alone to be less important than the whole referral order process including the experience of the panel.

Subsequent Panel Meetings

Sixty-seven young people interviewed (74%) said they had attended more than one panel meeting. However, when asked this question some young people confused the panel meeting with a meeting with their YOT officer

Table 10.6 Views of parents/guardians about the contracts (%)

To what extent do you agree with the following statements?	Strongly agree	Agree	Neither agree nor disagree	Disagree	Strongly disagree
The things in the contract were useful	17	65	8	6	4
The whole thing has been a waste of time	5	5	7	59	23
The contract has helped provide support services to the family	7	48	28	15	1
The contract hasn't made any difference to his or her behaviour	10	35	14	29	12
You have been able to approach people for help more easily because of the contract	4	44	36	14	1
The contract has helped your child stay out of trouble	32	42	10	12	4

as part of their contract. It is interesting to note that some young people were not distinguishing between these two activities, but considered them all to be part of their referral order.

Of the 62 young people who had attended more than one panel meeting, 32 (36%) had the same panel members at subsequent meetings. In one fifth of cases some were the same and in one tenth of cases none were the same. However, when asked, half said they would have preferred the same panel members: 'They could then talk about how I felt now compared to the first panel meeting' and 'It makes it more personal, like they knew me and what I'd done.' The other half said they really did not mind. However, 62% said they felt more at ease at later meetings – some of whom will have had at least some new panel members present, six of whom had no familiar panel members at their review meetings.

The majority of parents (59%) had attended two or three panel meetings, although a significant number (29%) had only attended one meeting and a few had attended four or more meetings. The vast majority of those parents that attended later panel meetings (87%) said that they 'felt more at ease'. Of those who had attended more than one meeting, most (58%) had all the same panel members at subsequent meetings. But where only some or none of the panel members were present at subsequent meetings, a significant number of parents said that they would have preferred the same people to have been present. One parent commented: 'the same faces would have been nice so they could see how everything was OK.' However, a slightly larger number of parents indicated that, for them, this 'did not matter'.

General Views

Most young people interviewed were positive about their experience of referral orders. They were pleased to have had the opportunity to tell their story and be listened to by ordinary, caring people:

> It makes you think about what you are doing. Talking to people was good because it made me realise that I had a problem. I've been arrested a few times for this so now I realised that I had to do something. I had a problem and they helped.

When asked what the worst thing about the referral order was, just under half of the young people (47%) could think of nothing negative to say at all. Of the rest, the most negative comments were about the inconvenience of having to attend the panel meetings, rather than any criticism of the interaction with panel members or implementation of their contract. One young person commented that he did not like: 'Attending meetings at awkward times – I might be doing something else.' Another young person summed up her experience as 'not the best thing in the world, but it helps a lot'. A common refrain by parents when asked what they thought was the best thing about the referral order or panel was that this had provided their child with 'a chance': a chance to make amends for what he or she had done wrong; a chance to reflect upon what he or she had done and where he or she was heading; a chance to speak for him or herself; and a chance not to get a criminal record. Many parents spoke in a similar vein of the fact that the referral order had made their child 'realise' certain things and made him or her 'think' about and account for his or her actions, namely the wrongfulness of his or her actions and the impact of his or her offending on others: 'It helps them to realise their mistakes and the consequences of their actions.' The following extracts are illustrative of this:

He realises that there are two roads that he can go down and he's seen what the wrong path can be like. One of the best things was that when it was over they really praised him and that lifted him and made him feel good about himself again.

It impacts on a child that this is serious and the consequences of offending behaviour, it makes them think and gives them a chance.

The last quotation neatly combines both the idea of a referral order as providing a space to think about things and offering the young person a chance. In addition, some parents were particularly positive about the support provided. One commented: 'I felt as if there was a lot of support for me as well as my son.' Another observed that:

She [the young person] needed some help and she got it. I think the whole thing has been really marvellous and has taught her a lesson and helped her.

Some parents alluded to the beneficial impact of the involvement of community panel members:

The fact that the panel members were in charge and he [the young person] had to listen to them helped. It helped us give him the discipline. It helped that they were strangers.

It is good that community panel members are not in an authority position as well.

Others commented upon the important human and interpersonal dynamics of panel meetings, particularly those engendered by the central involvement of lay people:

The panel took note of her [the young person] as an individual, not just part of the system. They treated her very well in the end, and the community people were really excellent and treated her as an individual. They recognised that she had had family difficulties and her behaviour wasn't bad.

Parents also emphasised the important deliberative qualities of panels as places to discuss important issues about a young person with his or her parents, which might not otherwise be discussed:

If the referral order hadn't happened then he would have kept on reoffending, I am sure. But we discussed things openly and now things are a lot better and he has changed quite a lot.

Some of the parents who had voiced critical concerns throughout the interviews had done so, in part, because they had felt that their child had been given a referral order for a minor offence, which to their mind did not deserve such intensive intervention. Nevertheless, even some of these parents saw the benefit of referral orders for other, more serious young offenders. The following is an example of such views:

I'm not against it but I don't think my son should have gone to court – but I like this idea and I think it can be good, it can give the youth a chance to express themselves where they can't in the court room.

These critical comments expressed by a small number of parents were echoed when asked what, on the basis of their experience, they thought was the worst thing about referral orders or youth offender panel. As the following suggested: 'The offence did not justify what he had to do' and 'It is not appropriate for trivial cases.' By contrast, some parents (notably those whose child had received a short order) would have liked the intervention, and thus the support, to have gone on for longer. One commented that: 'The time-span of the order could have been a bit longer to give him more time to get into things.' Another remarked: 'I wish they went on longer, three months isn't long enough.'

A small but significant minority of parents suggested that the process and contracts were not sufficiently harsh or punitive, some suggesting that their child 'got off a bit lightly', as indicated by the following comments:

If I had any criticisms, it is that it was far too lenient. My son thought his boat had come in when he got out of the first panel, so I think it could be harder.

If I have any criticisms about it, it is that the whole thing could have been a lot harder. If anything, I do think that it was a bit too light and he should have had harsher things.

Interestingly, some parents emphasised that they felt that the reparative element had been underemphasised. When asked to highlight the worst thing about referral orders the following parent noted it to be: 'Limitations on community service that they can offer. He should be made to put more back into the community.'

Finally, all respondents were invited to comment what they would tell a friend who had a child in trouble with the law who asked them what a referral order was like. The responses were nearly all positive. A recurring theme in many of the responses was that the panels are 'there to help' and that it is a 'useful experience':

> They are going to help, they will be there. They listen and sort out problems and get the young person on the straight and narrow. They are there to help you, the victim and the whole thing.

> It is a helping hand if someone is willing to reach out and grab it.

> It is a practical strategy, the strength of it is that it gave [the young person] a voice in what happened to him.

Some Critical Concerns

By and large the parents interviewed were very supportive of the idea and practice of referral orders and youth offender panels. The few parents who voiced critical comments mainly fell into one of three categories. The first group was those parents who felt that their child had done sometime too trivial to warrant the intervention of a referral order. Consequently, they were critical of many aspects of the subsequent process on the basis that their child should not have been put through it in the first place. In contrast, the second group included those parents who felt that referral orders were not sufficiently punitive. The third group of critical concerns was voiced by those parents who felt that they were made to feel inappropriately 'on trial' for their child's behaviour.

The fact that parents/guardians can be quite harsh on their children reinforces the argument that young people should also be encouraged to have a 'supporter' with them at panel meetings, to ensure that someone who knows them and cares about them can speak up for them. It is also important that panel members offer some kind of balance in these situations, but they may be disadvantaged by the lack of intimate knowledge of the young person and his or her relations with his or her parents/guardians.

Panels can place parents in ambiguous positions. First, they may be simultaneously the victim *of* and carer *for* the young person, and in some cases, this can put parents in a conflicting position. This sense of victimisation may be direct, where the young person has received a referral order because of the victimisation suffered by a parent/guardian, or it may be more indirect, for example where the parent has had to pay the compensation or costs awarded by the Youth Court in the case of his or her child. As a consequence, the panel may focus upon how the parent/ guardian is to be compensated for his or her loss.

Second, the parents may be both compelled to attend a panel (by order of the court) and may be a voluntary contributor to deliberations about the contract for their child. As we have seen, some parents felt that they were perceived to be 'at fault' or 'on trial'. And yet, they may also be enlisted in ensuring the fulfilment of contractual terms (such as school attendance, etc.). These competing tensions can place parents in demanding positions throughout the referral order process. Nevertheless, most parents accepted and welcomed the active responsibility that panels encouraged them to embrace with regard to their child's future behaviour.

Conclusion

Despite these critical concerns the young people and parents interviewed were largely very supportive of the idea and intentions of referral orders and youth offender panels. What is more, their own comments and views suggest a positive experience. From the perspectives of young people and parents the panel process and outcomes are viewed as satisfying significant levels of procedural, restorative and substantive justice. Both young people and parents accord to panels high levels of procedural satisfaction. They were generally experienced as having been treated fairly and with respect. Parents and young people also felt that they were accorded a significant degree of agency and voice in the process. In addition, for some of the young people, notably those who attended a panel at which a victim participated, panels allowed a degree of restoration as a result of which offenders appear to have recognised the victim's perspective and the harmfulness of their actions. With regard to the substantive justice of panel outcomes, despite some parents' concerns that the contracts were not harsh enough or in some instances too intensive given the trivial nature of the offending, many of the respondents felt that the elements of the contracts agreed at the panel were worth while and appropriate. The involvement of the parties in deciding the contract, as well as the incentive not to have a criminal record, appear to have been important in encouraging young people to fulfil their contracts.

Notes

1 Those selected were not necessarily the parents/guardians of the young people interviewed, although in a small sub-sample this was the case.
2 Whilst conducting the interviews, it was noted by several of the interviewers that a number of respondents felt strongly that they should have been informed of their rights fully and were disappointed that they had not been told that they did not have to agree a contract at the initial panel meeting.
3 This reflects the findings of Daly (2001: 76) with regard to conferencing in South Australia.
4 This figure is not strictly representative of young offenders' experiences broadly as we deliberately boosted the sample of young offenders who had attended a panel at which a victim had been present, in order to ensure a decent sub-sample size.

Chapter 11

Victims and referral orders

Traditionally victims have constituted the 'forgotten party' within criminal justice. In this, youth justice has been no different. Despite the more recent political fervour for championing victims, their role within criminal justice processes of deliberation remains marginal. By contrast, the active and voluntary involvement of victims in youth offender panel meetings lies at the heart of the restorative justice potential of referral orders. Ideally it enhances the impact of the referral order process on offenders and can be beneficial to the victims themselves. It allows a space in which to respond to the harm and hurt experienced by a victim, address his or her fears and anxieties and render the young person accountable for the consequences of his or her actions. Rationales for victim involvement in panels are, first, that it offers an appropriate forum in which to consider the views of the victim(s) and allows victims an opportunity to express the harm experienced and for this to be recognised. Second, it forces young offenders to confront the consequences of their offending behaviour and the harm caused and acknowledge their responsibility for it. Third, it enables victims to address concerns or questions they may have by meeting the offender and the offender's family face-to-face so that they can better understand their attitudes and why the offence occurred, as well as assess the likelihood of it reoccurring. Finally, it allows for victims to receive some kind of emotional and/or material reparation.

The involvement of victims, and in particular their attendance at panel meetings, across the pilot areas was both lower than was originally anticipated and significantly lower than comparative experiences from restorative justice initiatives around the world (see below). Of the cases closed before 31 July 2001, where information on the victim was available (from YOT records), it was possible to identify a victim in 457 (77.5%) of the cases. There was contact information for 411 of these cases and in 319 the victim was contacted (i.e. 70% of the cases where there was an identifiable victim). Only 22% (71) of the victims who were contacted attended any of the panel meetings. Put another way, a victim attended a panel meeting in only 13% of cases where at least an initial panel was held and for which we have firm data that there was an identifiable victim (see Table 11.1).[1]

In 120 cases victims made some other form of input into the panels, such as a statement or consent to personal reparation. Of these victims 84 did not attend any of the panels. Consequently, defining the term 'victim' in its broadest sense, we can identify only 155 cases[2] in which there was some victim involvement in the referral order process. This constitutes 28% of the cases where the data identify the potential for such involvement. It is probable that some of the victims were also parents/ guardians who would have had additional reasons to attend (potentially even under a court order). Where a victim did attend a panel, this was invariably an initial panel meeting.

In addition to data from YOT records on cases closed by 31 July 2001, data were collected on victim attendance at the panel meetings where panel assessment forms were completed until the end of September 2001. This does not represent all the panels held, but it does reflect the low level of victim attendance in the 1,066 monitored. This is set out in Table 11.1. On the basis of these data it would be wrong to assume that victims simply did not want to attend panels or that the referral order process is not suitable for victim attendance. The comparative experiences from similar

Table 11.1 Victim representation at panel meetings (by type)

Victim representation	Initial	%	Review	%	Final	%	Breach	%	All	%
Some victim representation	88	8	2	1	2	1	1	2	93	5
No victim representation	978	92	370	99	277	99	42	98	1,667	95
Total	1,066	100	372	100	279	100	43	100	1,760	100
Actual victims present	67	6	2	1	1	0	1	2	71	4
Victim also family member	14	1	0	0	1	0	0	0	15	1
Victim representative present	21	2	0	0	1	0	0	0	22	1

restorative initiatives across the world and the fact some pilot areas were more successful than others at encouraging victim attendance and input suggest that the low level of victim attendance is largely a result of poor implementation, rather than problems with the general principles underlying referral orders.

Table 11.2 breaks down victim attendance in cases closed by 31 July 2001 across the different pilot sites. It shows that the level of victim representation was variable across the pilot areas. Only Nottingham City and Oxfordshire show significant numbers of victims attending panel meetings. Given the low number of referral orders in West London, Hammersmith & Fulham and Westminster have relatively high proportions of victims attending panels. The higher levels of victim attendance in Nottingham City and Oxfordshire, as well as Westminster and Hammersmith & Fulham, are in large part due to the higher priority accorded to victim contact (notably in the first year of implementation) by the YOT in those areas. In the West London sites, this was also assisted no doubt by the low level of cases that allowed greater time to be given to victim work. Despite the small numbers there is some indication that victim attendance may have a positive impact upon young people. In analysis of the Nottingham City cases completed by 31 July 2001, their success rate (in terms of young offenders successfully completing their contract) is significantly higher where the victim attends, namely 80%, as against the overall success rate of 63%.

Table 11.2   Victim representation at at least one panel meeting by pilot area

Pilot area	Cases	No victim	Identifiable victim	Don't know	Victim attendance	%
Blackburn with Darwen	49	15	34	0	5	15.0
Cardiff	86	24	59	3	2	3.0
Nottingham City	137	12	112	13	31	28.0
Nottinghamshire County	80	7	66	6	1	1.0
Oxfordshire	105	19	85	1	15	18.0
Suffolk	102	13	88	1	0	0.0
Swindon	46	14	32	0	2	6.0
Wiltshire	56	16	40	0	5	12.5
Hammersmith & Fulham	21	4	17	0	7	41.0
Kensington & Chelsea	3	1	2	0	0	0.0
Westminster	11	3	8	0	3	37.5
Total	696	128	544	24	71	13.0

Comparative Experiences

Victim input in the referral order pilot areas was considerably lower than that in comparative restorative justice experiences around the world. For example, Maxwell and Morris (1993) found that in the early years of the introduction of family group conferences in New Zealand, despite implementation difficulties, victims attended in 51% of cases in which there was an identifiable victim. Furthermore, follow-up research into those victims that did not attend revealed that only 6% did not wish to meet their offender. This indicates that, in New Zealand at least, most victims are willing, and may actively desire, to meet their offender in a forum such as a family group conference. The evidence from Australia with regard to victim attendance is even more impressive. In Queensland evaluators found that 77% of conferences took place with victims in attendance (Hayes *et al.* 1998) and the RISE initiative in Canberra saw victims attend in 73% of conferences held for offences against personal property and 90% for violent incidences (Strang *et al.* 1999). However, our findings would seem to confirm the low level of victim involvement highlighted in the earlier research into the work of YOTs in the Crime and Disorder Act pilots in England and Wales (Holdaway *et al.* 2001).

The fact that levels of victim involvement vary considerably among the pilots, together with evidence of restorative practices elsewhere, suggests that there are techniques that can be used to improve on the current situation. This wider research literature suggests that victims are keen to and will attend restorative justice interventions (such as conferences and panels) if they are invited to attend at a time and place suitable and convenient for them.

Managing Victim Contact

In part, the low level of victim attendance stems from a degree of unfamiliarity in some of the pilot areas with the best ways of involving victims in restorative processes. There was also some reticence among some staff within YOTs about the value and purpose of doing so, as well as concerns about the resource implications of fully involving victims. The experience of the pilots reinforces the message from earlier research that victim contact work is labour intensive and, as such, requires significant resources. Moreover, it requires not only time, but also considerable commitment and training. Pilot areas that were more successful in involving victims tend to be those that dedicated the resources and personnel to invest significant time and effort in victim contact and pre-meeting preparation of the parties.

Many of the pilot sites experienced difficulties implementing victim contact procedures with the result that the subsequent participation in the process and particularly attendance at panels by victims was significantly lower than originally anticipated. The cornerstone of restorative justice is that victim involvement should be entirely voluntary. For understandable reasons, victims may choose not to attend a panel meeting or not to contribute in any way to the panel process. Such views must be respected. Nevertheless, there are diverse ways – notably through the provision of documentation and discussion – in which victims can be provided with information, facilitated and encouraged to consider attending a panel meeting or making some other form of input or contribution to the process. There are, arguably, eight crucial steps in the victim contact and consultation process:

- Identifying victims.
- Contacting victims.
- Providing victims with choices.
- Securing victims' consent.
- Assessing victims' suitability to attend a panel.
- Facilitating victim attendance through practical measures.
- Victim input at initial panel meetings.
- Follow-up – keeping the victim informed of progress.

With regard to each stage there are ways in which victim attendance could be encouraged. The practice implications of these were covered in some detail in the second interim report published by the Home Office (see Newburn et al. 2001b). There, we noted the lack of coherent consultation procedures in existence in many of the pilots and the significant problems around data protection. We also highlighted a number of other specific obstacles to victim participation experienced in various pilot areas, including: pressures of time; lack of commitment by YOT staff; lack of training of YOT staff; lack of public awareness about youth offender panels and referral orders; and difficulties presented by travel and the timing of panel meetings (particularly in rural areas). The following specific lessons arose out of the pilots:

- The experience of the pilots to date illustrates some of the difficulties of identifying victims and, more particularly, in encouraging 'corporate victims' to attend panel meetings.

- Contact by telephone, rather than by letter, appears more personal and effective. 'Opt in' letters appear the least effective.

- The evidence from the study suggests clear thought needs to be given to providing victims with alternative means of input to youth offender panels.

- At the current time there appears to be a tension between the requirements of informed consent and the aim of involving as many victims as possible in the referral order process.

- Most pilot sites did not have a clear or formal set of criteria to guide the assessment of victims' suitability to attend a panel.

- In the absence of significant victim attendance there are obvious concerns that victims issues are insufficiently represented.

- In most areas victims only appear to be kept informed of progress when, and if, they specifically request this.

- The experience of the pilots reinforces the understanding that victim contact work is labour intensive, requires significant resources, time, commitment and training.

The victim contact arrangements did not work well across all the pilots. As a consequence, the victim perspective was not adequately represented at panels and direct attendance at panels was lower than anticipated. The wide range of options for encouraging victim involvement in the process was not effectively explored and developed. The low level of victim participation was recognised by many involved in the implementation of referral orders as a legitimate cause of concern. Without exception, all the referral order managers interviewed during the implementation recognised that victim work had not been given sufficient attention.

Across the pilot sites, managers attributed the low victim attendance at panels to a number of causes. First, it was acknowledged that a lack of awareness of the principles and practice of restorative justice meant that victims were not able to make properly informed decisions about attending panels. This could be linked to the limited nature and extent of training provided for YOT officers about what could be done for victims. In some respects, this general lack of awareness and understanding fuelled a general lack of motivation for pursuing the victim work. Second, victim contact work was often not given priority by YOT workers with large caseloads and tight targets to achieve in line with national standards. Third, many managers felt that the recent emphasis upon speeding up the court and sentencing processes had created tensions with regard to engaging victims in referral orders. Fourth, data protection problems were highlighted as militating against victim contact. The combination of these factors, plus the experience that where contacted some victims preferred not to be involved, meant that victim work was accorded a reduced priority.

With regard to data protection issues, it is clear that the police play a highly influential role when it comes to victim contact. Many of the pilot sites acknowledged that the police officers were integral to the whole team and were highly committed to developing the work with victims. However, several areas noted difficulties with police procedures which effectively blocked victim contact. Data protection constraints can significantly impair the process. In most of the pilot sites, local victim contact protocols between the YOT and the police force had not been established. Many suggested that there was an urgent need for existing data protection protocol to be varied to facilitate victim engagement – perhaps establishing local data protocol among steering group agencies under the Crime and Disorder Act 1998. The excessive workload and time constraints faced by YOT police officers was also considered to impede the process.[3] This could particularly affect the quality of the initial contact and subsequent engagement with the victim.

The experiences of referral order pilots highlight important organisational and cultural issues. The referral order experience reinforces the conclusion of the researchers into the earlier YOT reforms who highlighted cultural resistance from long-serving staff, poor consultation procedures and, in particular, data protection problems as having influenced the low level of victim consultation and input (Dignan and Marsh 2001: 94).

In response to, and on the basis of, our findings and recommendations (Newburn et al. 2001b) many of the pilots introduced new victim contact procedures and encouraged greater staff commitment towards the end of our fieldwork in mid-2001. Preliminary evidence suggested that these new developments were producing greater success in encouraging victim attendance and input at panels. In a number of pilot areas, specialist victim liaison officers were appointed to develop and encourage victim contact and participation in the process. It was thought that they were beginning to make a significant contribution to increasing victim involvement. In some areas, outside agencies were contracted to do the victim work. Whilst this relieved the burden on YOT staff, it did run the potential risk of complicating the process by creating yet another set of referral arrangements and was totally dependent on good communication and exchange of information. Across all the pilot sites, a range of creative and innovative approaches to victim work were being developed including letters and statements from victims being read at the panel (sometimes by the police officer or a proxy representative) and the use of video and audio presentations were being considered in a number of areas. However, these developments arrived too late to impact upon the data presented here.

Views and Experiences of Victims

Between July and September 2001, interviews were conducted with 76 victims of young offenders who had received a referral order. This comprised a broadly representative sample of victims, including both those victims who had attended a panel meeting and those who had not, whether by choice or for some other reason.

Of the 76 victims interviewed more than half (44) were personal or individual victims and the remaining 32 were corporate representatives.[4] Of the total interviewed, 46 victims (61%) had attended a panel meeting and 30 victims (39%) had not (see Table 11.3).

Table 11.3   Interview sample analysis

Victim classification	Attended panel meeting	Did not attend panel meeting
Personal	29	15
Corporate	17	15

Of the 44 personal victims interviewed, the majority (55%) was male. In terms of ethnic origin, most personal victims interviewed (89%) were white, only five (11%) were black or Asian. Five victims (11%) under the age of 18 were interviewed, the youngest being 9 years old. Five victims (11%) were aged between 19 and 29, eight (18%) were aged between 30 and 39, fifteen (34%) were aged between 40 and 49 and seven (16%) were aged between 50 and 59. Two victims were aged over 60. Of the 32 corporate victims interviewed, a number of organisations were represented. These can be classified into those from the retail sector, the educational sector, health service, local authority housing sector, city or borough councils and the church. Representatives from the retail sector interviewed, who were largely the victims of acquisitive crimes (theft, shoplifting, etc.), did not generally attend the subsequent panel meeting.

The initial stages

Thirty of those interviewed (40%) had been told of the making of a referral order via a telephone call from someone in the YOT, and a further 14 people (18%) were informed by a police officer. One fifth of the victims (20%) had received a letter or leaflet with information about the referral order. Six people (8%) had actually been in court at the time and had heard about the referral order in person. In the initial stages, only seven victims (9%) actually received a visit from someone in the YOT. Following this initial contact, victims who had expressed an interest in the process or wanted to receive more information about what would happen to the young offender, indicated that they had received further information in the form of at least one and sometimes two telephone calls from someone in the YOT (47%) or they had received at least one and sometimes two visits from a YOT officer (49%).

Information about the youth offender panel meeting

In terms of the specific information that victims were given about the referral order, over four fifths of those interviewed (82%) were told that the offender(s) would have to attend a panel meeting to decide exactly what would happen, and that they could attend the meeting and contribute to it if they wanted to. Almost two thirds of victims (63%) were told that the offender(s) would be expected to try to make up for what they had done in some way and similarly (60%) were told that they could make suggestions about what the offender might do. Over half (59%) were told that if they did not want to attend the panel, their views could still be included in the meeting.

Overall, just over half (59%) of the victims interviewed felt they were given sufficient information about the referral order and what would happen at the meeting. However, just over one quarter (28%) felt that they were not given sufficient information. Several victims indicated that the documentation they received had not been particularly useful and that more information about how the panel would be run and what to expect at the meeting would have been helpful. Although just over half of those interviewed (55%) were told that there would be two members of the local community present at the meeting, less than half (45%) were told how the meeting was likely to be run. Whilst over two thirds (70%) knew that the young person would be at the panel meeting with members of his or her family, less than half (43%) were aware that the community panel members would be talking to the young person about his or her family, home life, school life and hobbies. Only one quarter of those interviewed were told that there would be further panel meetings that they could attend if they wished. Less than one third (29%) were told that they could have a friend or other supporter with them at the meeting if they wanted. Two thirds of the victims (65%) attended the panel meeting alone. Others (30%) attended with someone else, most notably a partner, son or daughter or other family member.

A number of personal victims commented that they had not found the panel process particularly easy and would have welcomed some personal support:

> If I could have had a friend with me at the panel it would have been better, I was not told that I could take anybody with me … if I was victimised again I might attend a panel if I could take somebody with me.

Overall, it appears that there were some aspects of the structure and organisation of the panel meeting about which the victims could have been provided with more detail. Several victims had some general awareness and knowledge of the restorative justice process through their work but still felt that they would have benefited from more information: 'I had an advantage having knowledge of the restorative justice process, but if I had been an ordinary member of the public then I don't think I would have got sufficient information.' Of those 30 victims who did not attend the panel meeting, half were never offered the opportunity to do so. They were either contacted too late or had not been told about the panel meeting. Some of these victims indicated that had they been given the information and choice, they would have attended the meeting.

Victims who Did not Attend the Initial Panel Meeting

Victims who did not attend a panel meeting can be categorised broadly into three main groups:

- Those who would have attended if they had been given the opportunity (53%).
- Those who either planned to attend the meeting but eventually were unable to do so or attended a panel meeting that was cancelled due to the non-attendance of the young person and were unable or not invited to attend the subsequent rearranged meeting (23%).
- Those who did not wish to participate in the process (23%).[5]

Thirty victims who had not attended a panel meeting were interviewed. This comprised 15 personal or individual victims and 15 corporate representatives. Although this is a relatively small sample, some interesting issues emerged. Table 11.4 illustrates the principal factors that the victims gave as reasons for not attending the panel meeting, and indicates whether they would have attended if they had been able to.

Table 11.4   Reasons for not attending the panel meeting

Factors involved in not attending the panel meeting	Did not attend the panel meeting	Would have like to attend
Was not offered the opportunity or was contacted too late	13	6
The timing of the panel meeting was inconvenient or too short notice	3	2
Wanted to attend the meeting but domestic issues prevented subsequent attendance	5	4
Attended a panel meeting where the young person failed to attend	2	2
Did not feel could add to the process/did not want to attend	5	0
Too angry	1	0
Did not have the time to get involved	1	0
Totals	30	14

Half the victims interviewed (53%) had not been offered the opportunity to attend the panel meeting. Almost half of these indicated that they would have attended if they had known about it or had been offered the chance. The majority thought that the referral order process sounded like a positive initiative and would have welcomed the opportunity to make a constructive contribution. One of the corporate representatives was disappointed that they had not been made aware of the new initiative:

> I would have liked to attend the panel because it would have helped me understand about the process and come up with a way of dealing with it, or helping what the YOT are trying to do. My personal philosophy is that it is only right that people should face up to what

they have done. When they are young, you can't write them off, there must be a reason why they are committing crime ... I think if everyone tried to understand the motivations a more workable solution could be found.

Three victims could not attend because the panel meeting had been arranged at a time that was inconvenient to them or had been arranged at too short notice for their participation.

Nearly a quarter of these victims (23%) had wanted to attend the panel meeting. Five people had wanted to attend but had been unable to at the last moment due to a number of unforeseen domestic circumstances. However, these panels were not rearranged. Two victims had actually attended the panel meeting but the young person had failed to attend. Rather worryingly, it appears that they were not invited to attend the rearranged meeting.

Nearly a quarter of the people interviewed (23%) did not want to become involved in the process and actively rejected the invitation to do so. Five victims felt that they did not want to meet the young person, either because they did not wish to 'personalise it', or because they felt unable to make a contribution to the process. When offered the opportunity to attend, one victim said that she felt 'strange' about it:

It was a minor offence and to come face to face with him [the offender] would have been quite harrowing for him. I already knew the circumstances of the offence and the offender. There wasn't much more that I needed to know. I couldn't see any benefit in attending for ourselves.

Only one victim stated directly that he was too angry to attend the panel meeting.

Support services and information

Half the victims that had not attended a panel had not received any support or services after the offence had been committed against them. Nearly one fifth (17%) had received some support from the police. Nine victims said that someone from the YOT had spent some time with them asking them to think about what they would like the offender to do to make up for the offence. The majority of these said that this had been very useful.

Over half (53%) had not received any information about the terms of the contract agreed at the panel meeting. Two thirds of these would have liked to have been informed. Similarly, the majority of victims indicated that they had not received any information about the progress of the young person in completing the terms of the referral order. Two thirds (67%) did not receive an invitation to attend subsequent review panel meetings. However, the majority indicated that they would have chosen not to attend review meetings as it was too long after the offence.

Reparation and letters of apology

Nine of the victims had received a verbal or letter of apology from the young person. Of these, the majority felt that the young person was genuinely sorry. Several victims were not convinced that the apology was genuine; one described the apology he received as 'totally hollow', one had been told that the letter he had received had been written by the offender's mother and one corporate representative thought that one of the offenders who had visited his office for a direct face-to-face apology acted like it was a 'huge joke'. One victim who had not been given the option to attend the panel meeting felt strongly that letters of apology were not meaningful if the young person was told to write them: 'If they do it off their own back it's okay, but if they are just doing what they are told it's no good at all – it's got to come from them – it's got to come from the heart.' Four victims had received some direct or indirect reparation. Responses to this were rather mixed. Several expressed concern about the supervision of the young person when he or she had come to do the reparation activity, and one felt strongly that the reparation had been organised at the convenience of the young person:

> We wanted them to come on a Saturday but he [the offender] said he couldn't because he was playing football. It had to be arranged after 6 p.m. but then that inconvenienced me. We should have put them out and inconvenienced them … the whole thing shouldn't have been organised to suit them.

Victims who Attended the Initial Panel Meeting

The invitation to attend

Victims were asked how they had felt when they were first offered the opportunity to attend a panel meeting and meet the offender.[6] Initial reactions appeared to be rather mixed. About one third admitted to being extremely apprehensive and nervous about attending the meeting and were unsure whether they wanted to. Almost one third (30%) of victims said they were very, somewhat or a little nervous about attending the meeting. Two thirds (65%) said that they were not at all nervous. Overwhelmingly, corporate representatives indicated that in their professional capacity they were not at all nervous about the meeting. Several victims indicated that despite feeling that they wanted to go to the panel, they recognised the experience would be difficult and potentially very challenging for them. A number expressed concern about the prospect of coming face to face with the offender: 'I was very apprehensive about meeting him, I didn't know what to expect in terms of what he would say.'

The importance of the victim receiving adequate information about how the panel would be run, and given appropriate support was emphasised by a number of interviewees:

> I was very apprehensive. I asked so many questions [before deciding to attend] because I needed to make sure exactly what it would be like. I needed to clarify a lot of things.

About a third of the victims felt that the panel process 'sounded like a good idea' and felt very positive about attending, particularly if they felt that some good would come out of it:

> I thought it sounded interesting. Initially I had slightly mixed feelings but I thought it was incumbent upon me to do something about it. I have an overall feeling that when crime happens we never do anything about it, but this sounds like a good initiative and it may reduce crime in general.

Corporate representatives were particularly keen to contribute to the process and take the opportunity to discuss the impact of crime on individuals, organisations and the community in general. The representative of a company where vandalism costs them an estimated £3,000 per week was keen to support the initiative: 'I wanted to let them know about the costs of the offence to us, and say that there is no way we will tolerate them showing disrespect for individuals or property.' Similar views were expressed by a different corporate representative:

> I wanted the victim and the hospital generally to be represented. Assaults on medical staff are common. The hospital now operates a zero tolerance policy and we are anxious to demonstrate that assaults will be taken seriously. Recruitment and retention of hospital staff is a huge problem. If people are afraid to come to work for fear of being attacked it is difficult. I wanted to get across that it is

unacceptable behaviour, and it was also to show staff that we support them.

A number of victims indicated that they wanted to meet the offender so that he or she could understand how he or she had made them feel. A victim who was just 9 years old said:

> I wanted to tell him that I was angry that he had taken my bike because it was my birthday present. I wanted to see him and try and find out why he took my bike.

Other victims thought the panel might be a good opportunity to express their hurt and put their point of view over to the offender or to get answers to specific questions such as 'why me?' Nevertheless, several victims expressed surprise at being invited to be involved in the process, and were pleased that there was involvement for the victim.

Expectations of the panel meeting

The majority of victims appeared to have approached the meeting with a fairly open mind and either did not have any preconceived expectations, or did not expect too much from the meeting. The extent to which victims had had the process fully explained to them beforehand appeared to influence their subsequent expectations. Although one victim thought it would be 'boring, rather like a committee meeting', the restorative ideals behind the process were understood by a number of victims, one of whom hoped that 'the offender would in some way understand the problems and difficulties caused and through joint negotiation there would be a satisfying result'. However, remarkably few victims said that they expected a 'result' from the meeting. Most simply expressed the hope that the offender would acknowledge responsibility for the offence and show some remorse or offer an apology: 'If he [the offender] understands what he has done and realises that he must not do the same things again then I would be happy.'

The purpose of the panel meeting

In interviews, victims described their understanding of the purpose of the panel to be both educational and restorative. First, as an educational process, it was felt that the young person would be made to think about what he or she had done, appreciate the consequences of his or her actions and understand the link between his or her offending behaviour and the community. Second, as a restorative process, it was felt that the panel was a forum to establish whether the young person was willing to make amends to prevent further offending. A number of victims described this in broader terms of 'helping the offender', or getting him or her to 'see the error of their ways'. However, others suggested that this involved arranging what 'punishment' the offender would undertake. As a response to youth crime, it was felt to be extremely positive, as the following comment suggests: 'For me, it was not about revenge but the idea of trying to help the offender, or get help for him so that he would stop offending.'

The decision to attend: motivating factors

Victims were asked what had influenced or motivated their decision to attend the panel meeting. Over three quarters (78%) said that the opportunity to express their feelings and speak directly to the offender had been very important. A victim of dangerous driving said that attendance at the panel and speaking directly to the offender was about 'getting some control back into her life'. She elaborated upon this:

> I was conscious that the young person could have been killed and he could have killed me and my children. I wanted him to know me. I needed to know who he was, what he was like. I wanted him to know that when they were arresting him, I was trying to calm down two very frightened little children. And the next day, when he was probably lying in bed nursing his hangover, I was still clearing up the mess. I wanted him to know that it might have been a big joke to him and his mates, but my family were nearly wiped out by him.

Half the victims interviewed felt that it was very or somewhat important that they attended to ensure that they would be repaid for their harm or loss. Many acknowledged that the offender would never be able to repair the harm. Whilst no victims were put under any pressure to attend the panel meeting, one third (35%) felt that they should attend. One victim felt that he should attend 'out of duty – I needed to be seen going'. Nearly half the victims (43%) felt that it was very important that they should have a say in how the problem was resolved. Ensuring that the penalty for the offence was appropriate was not a motivating factor for over half (52%) although some clearly felt that their attendance at the meeting could reinforce the impact of the offence:

> We spend £1 million a year on vandalism. I wanted to say to him [the offender] that the money could be better spent improving services

for him and other local authority tenants. What he did affected the whole community. I wanted to get that message across to him and his mum.

A sizeable majority (60%) attended largely out of curiosity because they wanted to see how a youth offender panel worked. As indicated in Table 11.5 over half the victims (54%) who attended the panel meeting did so because they felt that it was somewhat important or very important to try to help the offender.

Table 11.5 Motivating factors for attending the initial panel meeting

Motivating factors (%)	Not at all	Not very	Somewhat	Very
To express feelings and speak directly to the offender	4	9	7	78
Because they felt pressured to attend	100	0	0	0
To ensure that the penalty was appropriate for the offence	52	11	20	15
Because they felt they should attend	57	4	24	11
To have a say in how the problem was resolved	22	4	28	43
To ensure that they would be repaid for the harm/loss that they had experienced	33	13	15	35
Because they were curious and wanted to see how a youth offender panel worked	24	15	17	43
To help the offender	28	13	26	28

Many victims said that it was important that the young offender understood and appreciated the seriousness of his or her actions on the victim and the wider community, but also received help and support to prevent further offending. One victim felt that the panel process offered a golden opportunity to the young offender:

This lad [offender] is at a crossroads and it is up to him if he chooses the right or wrong way ... we need to give young people a chance. It is up to them whether they take it or not.

Preparation for the panel meeting

Prior to the initial panel meeting, just over a third of the victims (35%) indicated that they had spent a lot of time thinking about, or preparing, what they would do or say at the meeting. A similar number (41%) had spent a little time, but a quarter (24%) indicated that they had spent no time at all preparing for the meeting. In the majority of cases (59%) a YOT officer (or specialist victim liaison worker within the YOT) had spent some time with the victim asking him or her to think about what he or she wanted to say at the meeting. However, in a significant number of cases (37%) no one had spent any time with the victim. Similarly, in two thirds of cases (65%) the YOT officer had spent time with the victim asking him or her to think about what he or she would like the offender(s) to do to make up for the offence. In some of the pilot areas, the YOT officer and the community panel members held these discussions with the victim immediately prior to the panel meeting. More worryingly, in just over a quarter of cases (28%), the victim had received no support or advice. Of those victims who had spent some time talking with someone in an official capacity before the panel, the majority indicated that they had found this very useful.

'Having their say' at the panel meeting

As indicated earlier, the opportunity to express their feelings and speak directly to the offender was a significant factor for the majority of victims. Before the panel meeting, three quarters (74%) felt it was very important that they told the young person how much they had been affected. As well as wanting to explain the effects and consequences of the offence directly to the young person, many victims wanted to understand the motives behind the offence ('why did you do it?') and sought reassurance ('was it personal?'). For some victims, expressing the anger, fear and hurt that they, and other members of their family had suffered, was the sole purpose for attending the panel. To reinforce their point, a number of victims provided descriptions of injuries suffered; one victim took photographs, documents, statements and other pieces of evidence to demonstrate to the young person and the community panel members how traumatic the incident had been. One victim said that he had found it difficult to remain 'controlled and articulate in the circumstances'.

Through their personal accounts, some victims tried to impress upon the offender that the consequences could have been much worse:

> I wanted him [the offender] to know that the stone hit the back of my
> head and made me ill and was painful and distressing but it could

have been much worse. If he had hit my face I could have lost an eye. If it had hit a child it could have been really serious. This caused a lot of upset and anger, not just at the school amongst other staff and pupils but also my family. My family lost quality time with me whilst I was sick and recuperating. It was traumatic and I wanted him to know that.

Younger victims, or those who worked with young people, felt that they could bring a particular perspective: 'Because he [the offender] was the same age as me, I wanted him to see that I wasn't so different from himself.' A teacher representing a school commented: 'I wanted to tell him that his offences were not victimless, that the children at the school were badly affected and upset by his actions and that it might just have been some school equipment to him, but to the children it was part of their school life.' Over half those interviewed (52%) thought that it was very important that the offender made amends for what they had done.

Panel location and timing

Two thirds of the victims indicated that the panel meeting had been held at a time and place that was convenient for them. Some (22%) indicated that the meeting had been held at a reasonably convenient time but they had had to rearrange personal or work schedules in order to attend. We asked what would have made the panel more convenient and a number of responses indicated that some victims had not been offered a choice, they had merely been told when and where to go, and this had almost excluded their participation. A number of victims questioned the suitability of certain venues for the panel meeting. One victim attended a panel meeting in the YOT building and had felt intimidated:

> In the reception area I was surrounded by all these young offenders who were asking for money from me and some other adults who were there. It was a totally inappropriate place to hold a panel meeting.

Similar views were expressed by at least one referral order manager (where YOT offices were used in the pilots) who thought that the YOT building was not a victim-friendly environment. Several other victims said they had not been given adequate directions on how to find the venues and felt vulnerable and uncomfortable trying to find 'obscure buildings' in areas in which they were not familiar. This research suggests that more consideration should be given to the needs of victims when selecting locations and venues of panel meetings.

The initial panel meeting

The victims' experiences of the initial panel meeting were overwhelmingly positive (see Table 11.6). Nearly all victims agreed or strongly agreed that they had understood what was going on at the panel meeting (94%); that they had been given the opportunity to express their views (92%) and explain the loss and harm that had resulted from the offence (91%). The vast majority of victims accorded to the initial panel meetings high levels of satisfaction in relation to measures of procedural justice: 91% agreed that they had been treated with respect, including more than half who strongly agreed; 85% felt that the community panel members had been fair (the majority of whom strongly agreed); and 84% agreed that the panel had been sympathetic towards them, roughly half of whom strongly agreed.[7] Furthermore, victims generally felt that they were given sufficient opportunity to voice their views and feelings and contribute to the panel process. For instance, 92% agreed that they had the opportunity to express their views in the panel, including 57% who strongly agreed. Over three quarters felt that all sides had been given a fair chance to bring out all the facts (78%) and two thirds that the panel had taken account of what they had said when deciding what should be done (70%). Victims felt a considerable degree of control over their contribution to the panel proceedings with 79% disagreeing with the proposition that they felt pushed into things they did not agree with. Moreover, 87% disagreed that they felt intimidated by the offender or his or her family (including 63% who strongly disagreed) suggesting that victims felt safe at panel meetings.

With regard to measures of restorative justice, by the end of the panel meeting the majority of victims (69%) felt that the offender had a proper understanding of the harm that had been caused (Table 11.6). However, less than half the victims (48%) felt that the young person had expressed remorse for what he or she had done or felt that the panel had allowed the harm done to them to be repaired. Similarly, less than one third (30%) agreed or strongly agreed that the panel had made them feel that they could put the whole thing behind them. Compared to the high levels of agreement on measures of procedural justice, this reflects relatively less evidence of restorativeness from the victim's perspective. This reinforces the findings from the perspectives of young people and parents outlined in the previous chapter, and suggests that there may be limits to the restorativeness of panels as currently organised. Nevertheless, these findings also suggest that restorative justice interventions can offer opportunities for emotional harm to be repaired.[8]

Table 11.6 Victims' experiences of the initial panel meeting (%)

To what extent do you agree or disagree with the following?	Strongly disagree	Disagree	Neither	Agree	Strongly agree
You understood what was going on	0	4	0	57	37
You feel you were treated with respect	0	2	4	37	54
The panel members were fair	0	7	7	39	46
If the panel got things wrong, you felt able to get things corrected	2	13	30	35	15
You had an opportunity to explain the loss and harm that resulted from the offence	0	7	0	30	61
All sides got a fair chance to bring out the facts	0	9	9	48	30
You felt you had the opportunity to express your views in the panel	0	7	0	35	57
You felt you had enough control over the way things were run in the panel	2	22	15	41	13
You felt pushed into things you did not agree with	22	57	15	0	2
The panel took account of what you said in deciding what should be done	4	13	9	35	35
By the end of the panel, you felt the offender had a proper understanding of the harm caused to you	9	15	4	39	30
After the panel you felt it allowed the harm done to you by the offender to be repaired	4	24	11	37	11
The panel was concerned primarily with the offender's interests	0	33	13	30	22
The panel was sympathetic to you	0	7	4	43	41
The young person expressed remorse for what he or she had done	11	24	15	28	20
It was very difficult for the young person to explain him or herself to you	11	26	15	26	17
You felt intimidated by the offender or his or her family	63	24	4	4	0
The panel made you feel you could put the whole thing behind you	7	17	30	26	4
It would be better to meet the offender without the rest of the people at the panel	24	24	37	4	0

Involvement in the panel meeting

One area of dissatisfaction about the panel process expressed by a significant number of victims concerned the limits to their involvement and participation in the whole panel meeting. Over half the victims (57%) did not stay for the whole panel meeting. The majority of these (80%) did not choose to leave the meeting but were, in the majority of cases (88%), asked to leave either by the YOT officer or by the community panel members. Although some victims acknowledged that certain issues being addressed in the panel meeting were personal and confidential to the offender and his or her family, being asked to leave the panel meeting after 'having their say' did not find favour with many. Several victims said they were 'annoyed' or found it 'totally unacceptable' that they were asked to leave. One victim felt that being asked to leave the panel meeting rendered the whole process futile:

> I was outraged. I was allowed to have my say and then asked to leave. I could see that she [the offender] didn't want to face me but I felt that the whole panel was for her benefit. It was a waste of time for me.

Several victims indicated that they had felt excluded and had been made to 'feel like an outsider'. One said that she had not felt fully involved in the meeting and although she wanted to know what happened to the young offender 'the panel seemed very keen that I leave quickly'. Of more concern perhaps, is that a significant number (70%) of those victims who did not stay for the entire panel meeting, did not receive any information about the content of the contract that was eventually agreed at the meeting. These victims indicated overwhelmingly that they would have liked to have been informed. As one victim pointed out: 'Having made my contribution and suggestions for changing his criminal directions, I wanted to know the outcome.' This was a recurring theme throughout many interviews with victims.

The contents of the contract: substantive justice, reparation and apology

Victims' perceptions of substantive justice, on the basis of the appropriateness of the sanction received by the young person, entirely depended upon being informed of the eventual outcome. Those victims that stayed for the entire panel meeting or who were subsequently informed about the contents of the contract largely agreed or strongly agreed (78%) that the contract was fair. This suggests that where victims are included within all

deliberations over contractual outcomes and informed about their
contents they are more likely to be satisfied. Those victims who had been
included in the discussion about the contract felt that their input had been
useful and appreciated by the YOT. Whilst over a half (54%) disagreed,
over a quarter (28%) agreed that the contract was too lenient on the
offender. This suggests that some victims are not always likely to be
satisfied. However, only six victims (13%) indicated that things were left
out of the contract that they wanted to see included.

As indicated earlier, a significant number of victims felt that the young
person had not expressed remorse or offered an apology at the panel
meeting for his or her behaviour. Some victims were concerned that after
the panel meeting they had not received a letter of apology even though
they had been promised one. They had believed that this had been
included in the contract.

In terms of reparation, the victims interviewed felt that the sanction
should somehow be related to the nature of the crime itself. A significant
number expressed disappointment at the limited amount of reparation
hours young people were being asked to fulfil or felt uncomfortable with
the kind of activity that was eventually undertaken:[9]

> There was a strict limit on what he could do which has left us with a
> niggling feeling. I feel that the number of hours it has taken me to
> repair the damage done by the offender is actually more than what
> the offender has had to do to make up for the offence.

Corporate representatives, notably those who were representing organisations or businesses where the young persons' offending behaviour had
cost them many thousands of pounds, appeared more likely to be dissatisfied with panel outcomes. Although there was a universal desire to
attend the panel meeting to 'get the message across' about the wider
implications of offending, such as damage to property and loss of jobs and
the potential wider effects to the community, there was considerable
disquiet about whether their message was being reinforced by the
contract. One company representative thought it was 'disgraceful' that
someone who had caused damage to public property worth £114,000
received only 20 hours' community reparation, specifically cleaning out
bus shelters.

Concerns were also expressed that some of the decisions of the panel
were not particularly balanced. It appeared to some victims that panels
were 'trying to please the young offender ... bending over backwards to
help him' or were 'pandering to the young person trying to get him to
behave'. It was recognised that finding suitable reparative activity for

young people to undertake was not always a straightforward issue with concerns about security, health and safety, as well as supervision and monitoring sometimes militating against direct reparation.[10]

Three quarters (78%) of the victims were not invited to subsequent review panels. However, when asked if they would have liked to attend further panels, only a quarter (26%) indicated that they would. This was primarily to see if the young person was 'progressing positively' or to learn whether 'anything constructive' had come out of the process. Nevertheless, the vast majority of victims indicated that they would appreciate feedback about the young person.[11] Over two thirds (70%) had not received any information about the progress of the young person in terms of completing the contract. Indeed, victims only appeared to be kept informed of progress when and if they themselves specifically requested this. They indicated that they would appreciate information on three basic issues:

- The contents on the contract (what was actually agreed) and some idea of what the young person was actually doing, particularly in terms of reparation.

- The progress of the young person and whether the contract was successfully completed.

- If the young person had managed to stay out of trouble. One of the most important factors for many of the victims was 'has it worked?'

This suggests that where victims attend an initial panel meeting they may prefer not to attend subsequent review meetings, but would nevertheless want to be kept informed of the young person's progress.

After the initial panel meeting

In order to provide an overall assessment of the impact of the panel meeting on the victim, namely whether attending the panel meeting had reduced any physical and/or emotional affects or offered any re-assurances, victims were asked to think back to when the offence was committed (before the panel meeting) and indicate the level of their emotional feelings in a range of categories. We then asked them to reflect on these responses immediately after the panel meeting. Table 11.7 illustrates the shifts in the before and after responses. For those victims who indicated that before the panel they had felt very angry, hurt and frightened towards the offender, or were concerned that they would be re-victimised by him or her, there was a significant reduction in these heightened feelings after the panel meeting. This suggests panel meetings

Table 11.7 Victims' attitudes and feelings before and after the initial panel meeting (%)

Thinking back to before the panel *Reflecting on your feelings after the panel*	*Not* *at all*	*A little*	*Somewhat*	*Very*	
How hurt did you feel by the offence?	26	11	7	50	Before
	46	*20*	*7*	*15*	*After*
How angry did you feel towards	24	9	17	46	Before
the offender?	*48*	*17*	*9*	*20*	*After*
How frightened did you feel of	74	9	2	11	Before
the offender?	*78*	*13*	*0*	*4*	*After*
How sorry did you feel for the	70	13	9	4	Before
offender?	*48*	*28*	*9*	*11*	*After*
How concerned were you that	52	11	13	13	Before
they might commit another	*63*	*15*	*4*	*7*	*After*
offence against you?					

Figure 11.1 How sorry did you feel for the offender?

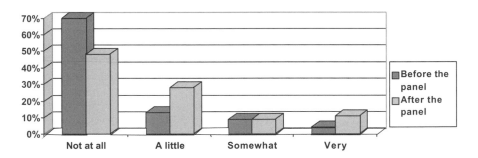

were beneficial in helping victims overcome sentiments of fear, feelings of anger and concerns over future safety (all important indicators of 'victim restoration').

One slight change in attitude related to how sorry the victim had felt for the offender before and after the panel. Before the panel, perhaps not surprisingly, over two thirds of victims (70%) did not feel at all sorry for the young person. Figure 11.1 indicates that after the panel meeting, these hardened attitudes changed slightly. This may suggest that the process of meeting the offender and gaining some insight into his or her circumstances or background, may have helped victims put the offender into a different perspective. Figure 11.1 shows a limited but significant movement on the part of some victims as an indicator of restoration, which reinforces some of the indications or parallel shifts on behalf of the sub-sample of young offenders who met their victims (discussed in Chapter 10).

Victims were also asked how sympathetic they had felt after the panel meeting towards the offender's family. Attitudes were divided with nearly half (48%) saying they were not at all or only a little sympathetic to the offender's family. A number of victims indicated that they thought 'the family was as bad as the kid' or expressed disappointment that the young person's family had not displayed any sympathy or understanding towards them. Nearly half (45%) the victims indicated that they were somewhat or very sympathetic to the offender's family. A number of victims recognised that the panel meeting had been a difficult process for the parents of the young person and expressed some empathy: 'I felt sorry for his mum and dad because I know what kids can be like so I know how they feel.'

Would you recommend this to a friend?

Asked what advice they would give to someone they knew if he or she had an offence committed against him or her and were invited to attend a panel meeting, victims said emphatically that they would encourage other people to attend. As a forum where victims could have their say, interviewees felt that it had been a useful and helpful experience to meet the young offender. However, it was recognised that the nature of the offence – whether it was a personal, violent or property crime – was a crucial factor. Some felt that the seriousness of the offence and the level of trauma experienced by the victim could act as a deterrent to attendance. There were a number of inter-related issues which victims felt needed to be recognised by anyone considering attending the meeting:

- Attending the panel is not an easy process; many had found it a hard experience.

- Preparation and support were seen as vital, particularly when faced with the perpetrator.

- Being prepared, thinking about the questions they wanted to ask and being clear about what they wanted to say were regarded as extremely important.

- Taking a supporter with them to the panel was strongly recommended, particularly as it was impossible to predict how people would react when face to face with the offender.

Overall Views of the Referral Order Process

On the whole, the victims that we interviewed appeared extremely positive about their experience of the referral order process. When expressing their general views about the process, a number of themes emerged.

First, whilst all the victims we interviewed had very different reasons for wanting to participate in the process, almost all described youth offender panels as a 'good idea' and a positive initiative. Several people indicated that they were surprised to hear that the YOT even existed, or had not appreciated the multi-agency interests involved in tackling youth offending. This suggests a role for greater public awareness about the work of YOT and the operation of referral orders.

Second, meeting the offender and gaining an understanding of the young person and their circumstances were regarded as beneficial, enabling victims to come to terms with the offence that had been committed against them. Victims recognised that the offenders needed to have their story heard. However, concern was expressed by some victims that there had been a lack of balance in the process, and that too much emphasis had been paid to the offenders' needs to the detriment of the victims' perspective. One victim commented:

> I felt it was a waste of time. It was too informal, too lightweight and goody-goody, all sitting around in a circle and trying to understand the offender. I have heard of this thing called restorative justice. Well, it wasn't justice and it hasn't restored anything.

Third, the involvement of parents in the process, and particularly the presence of parents at the panel, was felt to have strengthened the whole process. One victim felt that the panel could potentially impress upon young people the threat they caused to both the individual victim and the wider community:

> The youth offender panel has enormous potential to make young people face up to their actions and will give them [the offenders] a sense of isolation. I think engaging parents in the process is a good idea.

Fourth, the victims were generally impressed with the genuine commitment and 'professionalism' of the community panel members. Their skills at working with sometimes uncommunicative young people in the occasionally difficult and charged atmosphere of the panel meeting were widely applauded. A number of victims felt that criminal justice policy-makers and practitioners were doing their best to think of new ways to deal with young offenders, and hoped that the work of the panel members was valued: 'The panel members seem very committed. These people are priceless.'

Fifth, from an organisational and administrative point of view, the lack of continuity of contact and lack of information provided by the YOT came in for some noteworthy criticism. In some cases, the lack of feedback had devalued the impact of the whole process:

> I had a real sense of closure at the panel but it was opened up again because nothing happened afterwards. It was half a procedure and it led to disappointment at the end.

This is in many ways very similar to the experiences victims report in relation to their contact with the police: relatively positive at first contact, but deteriorating over time particularly as information provision becomes more sporadic (see Shapland *et al.* 1985).

Sixth, as an early intervention, the referral order process was regarded as a positive initiative, but some thought that it might not be appropriate or effective for all victims or offenders, as the following corporate representative explained:

> This is not going to work for everyone. For some offenders it may not work or stop them offending, for some victims it may not be appropriate at all, especially in violent crimes. The idea of making offenders confront the people they have offended against is very good because it is about bringing people to account for their actions.

Nevertheless, two thirds of the victims agreed or strongly agreed that the referral order process in general was fair. This reinforces the high level of procedural satisfaction with regard to the victims' experiences of initial panel meetings noted earlier. However, the levels of agreement recorded here are somewhat lower than those specifically relating to initial panel meetings. This suggests that more victims found the experience of the initial panel meeting to be fair than they did in relation to the general referral order process as a whole.

A similar picture emerges with regard to the restorativeness of the panel process. Over half (53%) agreed or strongly agreed that the panel meeting had helped repair the harm caused by the offence. However, one fifth (19%) disagreed or strongly disagreed with this. One third agreed or strongly agreed that the panel process had helped restore a sense of security, although a quarter (24%) disagreed or strongly disagreed.

On a positive note, over half (56%) agreed or strongly agreed that if they were the victim of a young offender who was given a referral order in the future, they would choose to attend the panel meeting. For those who had not attended the panel meeting, a significant minority (40%) agreed or strongly agreed that they would attend if they were the victim of an offence committed by a young offender in the future.

Finally, in light of their experience of the referral order process as a whole, victims were asked whether their respect for the criminal justice process had changed. Responses were slightly mixed. Half felt that their respect for the criminal justice process had increased a little or a lot as a result of the way their case had been handled. Almost a quarter (24%) felt that their views had not changed and a similar number of those interviewed (26%) said that their respect for the criminal justice process had decreased a lot or a little (see Figure 11.2). Whilst for some the referral order had clearly increased their respect for criminal justice, the marginal place that victims have tended to occupy within traditional criminal justice means that changing attitudes broadly and the experience of victims specifically may require more fundamental reforms (see Shapland 2000).

Figure 11.2   Victims' respect for the criminal justice process

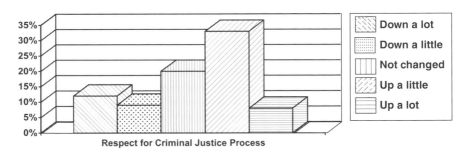

Respect for Criminal Justice Process

Conclusion

We sought to compare the responses and attitudes to certain key motivating factors of those victims who attended the panel and those who did not. Victims responded that they felt very strongly that these issues were important to them. Victims who did not attend the panel meeting were, on the whole, less curious to find out about the offender, and they were less inclined to find out from the offender why they had been victimised. Those who did not attend appeared to attach less significance to the opportunity to speak directly to the offender about how much they had been affected by the offence or to want the offender to make amends. However, fears that the offender might commit another offence against them were the same for both groups.

There is evidence from our findings that for victims participation may be as important as, if not more important than, the imposition of a particular sanction. Panels received high levels of satisfaction from victims on measures of procedural justice, including being treated fairly and with respect, as well as being given a voice in the process. In addition, there was indication of restorative movement on behalf of the victims as a consequence of panel attendance and input. However, compared to the high levels of satisfaction on measures of procedural justice, there was relatively less evidence of restorativeness. Victims benefited from attendance at panels. Those victims who were informed about the contents of contracts were generally of the view that these were fair, although there were some criticisms as to the appropriateness of particular forms of reparation and some concerns as to whether contracts were too lenient. Nevertheless, victims were largely very supportive of the idea and intentions of referral orders and particularly youth offender panels.

The low level of victim attendance across most of the pilot sites is a source of concern and should be the focus of significant work with YOTs during national implementation of referral orders. The fact that levels of victim involvement varied considerably among the pilots, together with evidence of restorative practices elsewhere, suggests that more can be done to facilitate victim attendance and input. Nevertheless, towards the end of the fieldwork (summer 2001) there were clear signs that victim contact work was being accorded a much higher priority. Across the pilot sites, a range of creative and innovative approaches to victim work were being developed and implemented.

However, the low level of victim participation in referral orders raises important questions about the cultural and organisational challenges presented by attempts to integrate victims into the heart of criminal justice processes. Most of the agencies involved in YOTs have been unaccustomed to working with victims. By contrast, many have an explicit offender-focus. For them, providing services for victims of crime is not their central purpose. New responsibilities for consulting and informing victims and witnesses can produce possible conflicts of interest with the existing duties and responsibilities of YOT staff. Where victim contact work is only a small aspect of a YOT member's wider responsibilities, it may well take second place to what are considered to be the primary aspects of the job. Often this secondary status of victim work will be a product of priorities as well as cultural assumptions and working practices. In some cases, however, there may even be outright resistance among YOT workers to victim consultation (Holdaway *et al.* 2001: 87). Whilst the criminal justice establishment may take on new ideas about victim involvement at the level of policy, implementation may serve to subvert these such that victim inclusion works towards meeting more traditional ends. The experience of the pilot suggests that the impact of victim involvement in the referral order process upon the wider work of the YOT is variable given the different models of service delivery. Clearly, some models of victim contact contain victim issues among a small number of specialist, trained staff, whilst other models prefer to disperse the work more generally throughout the YOT. Specialist victim liaison officers may be able to act as champions of the victims' perspective within YOTs but may do less to transform the culture and workings of the organisation as a whole. It is the broader implications of referral orders to which we now turn.

Notes

1 We have excluded from this calculation those cases where, for whatever reason, no panel meetings were held as it follows that no victims could attend in such instances.
2 This is made up of 84 cases in which a victim was contacted, did not attend but made some form of other input to a panel, 36 cases in which the victim was contacted, attended and made some other input, and 35 cases in which the victim was contacted, attended but made no other input.
3 In one area (Nottingham City) the deployment of Special Constables into the YOT specifically to work on victim contact was actively being considered. Although this would have short-term cost implications for training a sufficient number of officers, it was felt to offer a practical solution to tackling the excessive workload.
4 Within the sample of victims interviewed there were seven 'proxy' victims – six were parents of young victims who had either accompanied their child to the panel meeting, or had attended the meeting on their behalf. One corporate representative attended on behalf of her employee who was unable to attend as she was still recovering from the assault.
5 Research from New Zealand indicates that the most common reasons victims did not attend a family group conference were because they were not invited, were informed after the event or because the conference was held at a time that was not convenient for them. Very few victims did not wish to participate actively in the process (Morris *et al.* 1993).

6 Research from the 1998 British Crime Survey indicates that 41% of victims would accept the opportunity to meet the offender (Mattinson and Mirrlees-Black 2000).

7 This reinforces and reflects the findings of research from Australia with regard to conferences which have consistently shown that participants perceived the process to be fair and to treat victims with respect (Daly and Hayes 2001: 5).

8 The RISE project has shown that victims' sense of restorative justice (as measured for example by recovery from anger and embarrassment) is higher for those who went to conferences rather than to court (Strang *et al.* 1999; Strang 2001).

9 Research by Miers *et al.* (2001) found issues around reparation work particularly problematic.

10 For example, cleaning graffiti from public buildings could necessitate contact with potentially dangerous chemicals.

11 Research by Miers *et al.* (2001) found that victims wanted more information and feedback on cases. Research also indicates that victims benefit from continuity of contact and information (Shapland 2000).

Chapter 12

Implementing the new youth justice

In this chapter we explore a number of critical issues raised by the experience of the referral order pilots. We begin by considering some of the central dynamics within the referral order model and their potential implications, notably with regard to the distribution of responsibilities that the model entails and the involvement of lay members of the public within the panel process. We then go on to examine some of the broader policy tensions and ambiguities that find expression within the implementation of referral orders and youth offender panels and the manner in which they are likely to influence the future shape of developments. In so doing, we consider the integration of victim-sensitive restorative approaches to criminal justice. We conclude with some observations on the implications of our research findings for evaluation research and criminological analysis of youth justice reforms, as well as the significance of referral orders for restorative justice.

The Distribution of Responsibilities

'Responsibility' is one of the central themes of referral orders; one of the 3-Rs informing the operation of youth offender panels. Referral orders seek to responsibilise the principal parties to the offence, notably the young person and his or her parents/guardians but also the youth offending team and potentially the victim. At the same time as soliciting their involvement, the process confers responsibilities on them; contributing to the design of, ensuring the implementation of, and compliance with, the terms of the contract. The contract is a formal illustration of the fact that the parties have consented to meet certain obligations. The process assumes that people are more likely to abide by the terms of a contract in which they have actively participated. In this sense, the process is 'reflexive' as it seeks to achieve the compliance and co-operation of those subject to the regulation, through a form of self-regulation.

In this, referral orders intend to provoke *active*, rather than merely passive, responsibility. One of the limitations of traditional sanctioning processes is that participation as defendants, witnesses or victims usually involves passive responsibility, which is both after-the-event and backward-looking. Where an obligation exists, one is called to account afterwards for one's conduct or inaction (Braithwaite and Roche 2001). Active responsibility, by contrast, involves taking responsibility for addressing a problem. Prominence is given to action in the present and to the prevention of unwanted situations or events in the future. This translates into the question 'what *is* to be done?' (Bovens 1998: 27). Within the framework of the length of the referral order, this is the question that dominates youth offender panel meetings. Whilst passive responsibility is a necessary element in all forms of justice, the significant potential of deliberative forms of restorative justice is to be found in its stimulation of active responsibility.

However in doing so, restorative justice spreads responsibility across a broader range of actors, and this can also serve to confuse lines of accountability. A parent or carer may agree to active involvement in helping the young person to fulfil the agreed terms or monitoring the young person's compliance, but who is to be held accountable for their failure? Is the young person to be held accountable for the failings of others? If not, then how does a panel oblige parental compliance with the terms of the contract? Joint decisions and negotiated contracts tie the various parties into collective outcomes but often fail to identify lines of responsibility. The 'sharing' of responsibility can make it difficult to disentangle.

There are two other ways in which the referral order model blurs organisational responsibilities in terms of its delivery. Both these 'fault lines' are likely to be important dynamics in the manner in which referral orders develop in the future. First, as we have seen in the pilots, there is an ambiguous relationship between the role of the courts and that of youth offender panels. Managing this relationship so that there are good lines of information flowing between the two is a major challenge. On the one hand, there is the danger of magistrates resenting the loss of discretion and the delegation of powers to panels that the referral order entails. The experience of the pilots shows that this concern grew rather than diminished over time among magistrates surveyed. On the other hand, the fact that the court determines the length of the order without delegating a power to panels to terminate early (or extend) its duration may be perceived by panel members as unduly fettering their work. Furthermore, this may act as a disincentive for young people who strive to complete their contract in a timely manner.

One of the specific ways in which the operation of the court and the panel may be in tension is in the power of the court to accompany a referral order with certain ancillary orders, such as compensation orders, orders for costs and exclusion from football matches (s. 4(2) and (3)). This may constrain the role of the panel, which might (or might not) wish to attach such conditions to a contract. In practice, however, financial reparation has only ever played a relatively subsidiary role within restorative agreements in the British experience (unlike in North America). YOTs in some of the pilots made it clear from the outset that they were unwilling to get involved in financial reparation.

More fundamentally, the court's power offends the declared restorative intent of the panel process, as it imposes – through a coercive court order – something (namely compensation) which the young person might otherwise agree to voluntarily. Wonnacott notes: 'If the offender has already been the passive and resentful object of a criminal order for the offence, there is plainly little scope for the processes of restorative justice thereafter' (1999: 283). In practice, this probably overstates the situation, as the independent status and different working practices of the panel allow it to start a new dialogue with the young person, his or her parents and relevant others. This is not to suggest that the panel process is not influenced by the court experience. It clearly is. Rather it is to suggest that the panel can go some way towards opening up a deliberative and inclusive examination of how to deal with the aftermath of the offence and its implications for the future, *despite* its coercive setting. However, there remain clear possibilities of conflicting provisions in the court order and the panel contract.

One of the ways in which the power of the court to award an order of compensation and/or costs may influence panel deliberations is the manner in which it subsequently constructs the parent as secondary victim. As the parent is responsible for paying the compensation or costs awarded against the young person, the parent may arrive at the panel as a new injured party of the young person's offence. In such a situation, finding a way for the offender to repay costs to the parent may become a focus of the panel's discussions and subsequently a condition (either voluntary or not) of the contract. This not only potentially alters the ways in which the panel members interact with the young offender and his or her parent(s), but may also place an unnatural limit on the involvement of the victim. The existence of court-ordered compensation may have the consequence of limiting the extent to which the panel – and possibly the victim – feel that further material reparation can be made, or even be discussed.

A second way in which the referral order model blurs responsibility is in the relationship between the YOT member of the panel and the lay panel members. As we have noted, this is a crucial relationship in the operation of panels. According to the *Guidance*, the role of the YOT panel member is to advise on the potential components of the contract, the availability of suitable interventions and to ensure proportionality. And yet, the YOT panel member is also enlisted into the decision-making process. This is different from the role of the Reporter in Scottish Children Hearings, for example. There, all the members of the hearing are lay people, assisted by a Reporter who has no decision-making role. The youth offender panel, by contrast, introduces a dynamic, if potentially tense, relationship in which different organisational and cultural understandings, aims, ways of working and power differences can clash. Is the YOT member accountable for decisions arrived at by community panel members or is he or she just there to provide information? This was a question that YOT members themselves posed during the pilots, particularly concerned that they may be held responsible for agreements arrived at by a panel which subsequently go wrong, resulting in harm to one of the parties. None the less, as we have argued, this blend of lay people and professionals within the panel framework, if responsively managed, also affords an exciting dynamic within the work of panels.

Untapping the Potential of Lay Involvement

Youth offender panels offer an interesting way of trying to involve the public more intimately in criminal justice processes. This is an important endeavour given: first, the emotions that crime (particularly youth crime) and justice excite; second, the low (and declining) levels of public confidence in the criminal justice system as revealed by social surveys (Mirrlees-Black 2000: 1–2); third, the systemic misperceptions and misunderstanding that much of the public has about crime problems and the operation of criminal justice (Hough and Roberts 1998: vii); fourth, the crucial role that the public plays in responses to crime and its prevention, in the provision of information as witnesses or victims and through networks of informal social control; and finally, the historic decline of public participation.

There are strong arguments for greater public involvement in criminal justice – notably youth justice – as a cultural and political restraint against more punitive policies and the growing resort to penal exclusion. It may challenge the presupposition in policy discourse that public opinion, at every turn, demands more punishment. Whilst broad opinion surveys do often reveal a more punitive public, we need to distinguish between 'public opinion' and 'public judgement'. The former is impromptu, not informed by serious discussion or weighing the facts and the arguments of others. Neither is it followed by taking responsibility for the argued-for position. Public judgement incorporates all these characteristics. Research suggests that when provided with more information about offenders and the circumstances under which they offend, the public is more tolerant and less punitive than politicians would have us believe (Hough 1996). People tend to respond in more moderated and thoughtful ways to events and issues about which they are well informed or personally involved than those to which they are more abstractly connected. Certainly, the experience of the youth offender panels, in the pilots, is a testimony to the seriousness and thoughtfulness that lay people can bring to such forums and to the task of facilitating discussion. They may go a small way towards restoring the deliberative control of justice to citizens.

Failure to involve the public may exacerbate legitimacy deficits and facilitate crises of confidence. By contrast, informed public debate and dialogue as a central aspect of criminal justice potentially allow for regulated ways in which people can deliberate upon, and search for ways of resolving, conflict. As Girling *et al.* note:

> if the punitive passions (and actions) of citizens are the impotent cries of spectators watching dramas in which they play little part, and for whose outcomes they exercise no responsibility, then keeping such sentiments 'in the shadows' also has its costs. It leaves the impassioned demands of citizens undiscussed and unchallenged and does nothing to make good the legitimation deficits suffered by institutions from whose actions attentive, concerned citizens have been excluded. (2000: 177)

The participation of ordinary citizens in the deliberative processes of criminal justice can also help to ensure that proceedings which may otherwise be dominated by technical, bureaucratic or managerial demands also accord to the emotional and expressive needs of responses to crime. It can facilitate the 'opening up' of otherwise introspective professional cultures, which militate against greater public participation. Significant community participation can act to open up processes which may otherwise see professionals guided by detached and disinterested performance standards often of a kind which are more concerned with internal organisational legitimacy than responsiveness to public interests. It can help break down inward-looking cultures and paternalistic attitudes held by professionals and in their place encourage responsiveness to the concerns articulated by citizens, as the guidance of professionals. Lay involvement can counter scepticism on the part of participants – notably offenders – that decision-makers are removed from their concerns and understandings, precisely because of their professional attachments. Community panel members at meetings often emphasised their sincerity in their concern for the welfare of the offender, victim and wider community on a human or relational rather than a professional level. This they reinforced through reference to their own status as volunteer, implying something unique and important about the voluntary participation of local citizens. As such, community involvement may act as a safeguard against some of the excesses of the managerialisation of criminal justice.

Furthermore, community participation may also help to cement relations and encourage greater synergy between formal and informal systems of control. It affords processes of restorative justice to operate through informal relations of interdependencies and mutual understanding. In so doing, it promotes the importance of local capacity. Lay participation may bring with it local knowledge and an attachment to 'the affective and effective world of local affairs' (Shapiro, cited in Doran and Glen 2000: 10). This local knowledge can be a rich source for norm-clarifying and norm-reinforcing purposes. However, it implies that lay participants are genuinely embedded in local interactions, interests and normative orderings. The extent to which this is evident from the youth offender panels remains uncertain as the pilots highlight the practical difficulties of ensuring the representativeness of lay participants.

Competing Dynamics within Youth Justice

As suggested in Chapter 1, contemporary youth justice is a confluence of differing penological philosophies, rationalities and principles. The traditional dichotomies of welfare/punishment and care/control are now overlain with other disparate strains. These are particularly to be found infusing the implementation of referral orders and youth offender panels.

Here we wish to draw attention to seven of the most visible competing dynamics within contemporary youth justice.

Lay involvement versus the professionalisation of justice

Ironically, the significant investment in lay involvement within youth justice heralded by the recruitment, training and support for community panel members is occurring at precisely the same time as countervailing pressures towards the professionalisation of justice. For example, the central practices of participatory democracy at the heart of traditional criminal justice – namely the jury system and the lay magistracy, both of which share the notion of 'judgement by one's peers' – are currently under threat like never before (Raine 2001). The use of juries is being curtailed in criminal cases, whilst there are pressures to increase the number of stipendiary magistrates. The recent managerialist and modernising agendas of government have implied a reduction in lay participation in court processes and an increased reliance on paid and legally qualified professionals. In the broader picture, this leaves community panel members as something of an anomaly.

Local justice versus centralised control

Similarly, there is a tension between, on the one hand, the devolution of authority to local institutions of criminal justice, such as local magistrates courts, YOTs and community safety partnerships and, on the other hand, the greater centralisation of control exerted through standard-setting and performance monitoring, backed by regimes of audits and inspections. The managerialist concern with performance measurement and efficiency gains has often led to a move away from 'local justice' and encouraged greater centralisation, in which government departments and related agencies closely govern local practices. This tension is particularly apparent in the implementation of referral orders where the philosophy of youth offender panels evokes the importance of local knowledge, local people contributing to the handling of cases in their own local area, and hence the importance of local normative orders, and local service provision. In many ways, youth offender panels (in the broad restorative justice tradition) appeal to a form of 'legal pluralism' (Merry 1988), which is sensitive to local conditions and needs, but is at odds with the close central steering of initiatives by government departments. On the one hand, there is the centralist desire to control, to issue guidance, to ensure minimum standards, and to authorise, license and inspect the doings of others. On the other hand, there is the fluid and creative potential of party empowerment that informs the principles of restorative justice and which demand flexibility, deliberation and adaptation to circumstances. This appears to illustrate some of the limits of the shift towards 'governing at a distance'. It is as if government is apprehensive about the creation of 'self-steering networks' over which it has little control or else has little faith in the ability of such networks to deliver services appropriately. As such, governments resort to traditional interventionist strategies. This is symptomatic of a broader ambiguity within government of governing 'at arm's length but hands on' (Crawford 2001b: 63). As Rhodes notes, for government '"hands off" is the hardest lesson of all to learn' (2000: 361).

Rights versus responsibilities

Some commentators have argued that the human rights agenda, stimulated by the incorporation of the ECHR into domestic law, poses a number of direct challenges to the incorporation of restorative justice ideas into the juvenile justice system. These challenges may take the form both of substance and of principle. The impact of these challenges may lead to the long-term dilution of restorative ideals. Clearly, at one level the informality of the youth offender panel would appear to conflict with the emphasis upon formal legal rights and due process to be found in the Human Rights Act. Pressures to formalise youth offender panels, which may have their origins in administrative and managerial imperatives as suggested by the experience of the pilots, may be further stimulated by challenges under the human rights legislation. Whilst, to date, there have been no challenges to youth offender panels under the legislation, in a recent Scottish case, S v Miller (2001 SLT 531), the court found that the restrictions on access to legal aid in Children's Hearings were incompatible with art. 6 of the ECHR. This prompted one commentator to describe this as potentially 'the end of the Children's Hearing system as we know it' (Edwards 2001).[1] Despite the already noted differences between Children's Hearings and youth offender panels, this demonstrates the capacity for conflict. The non-involvement of lawyers in youth offender panels in the pilot sites was generally not an issue. However, the availability of legal aid, were this to be established, might encourage their greater involvement, potentially rendering youth offender panels more adversarial and formal. The fear here would be that interest-based and party-centred negotiations might be undermined by rights-based and lawyer-centred proceedings. This would, clearly, run counter to the initial intentions of referral orders.

Nevertheless, it would be wrong to suggest that the 'rights versus responsibilities' debate is a zero sum game, whereby more responsibilities equals fewer rights and vice versa. Formal legal rights and due process can act as bounding mechanisms that empower and constitutionalise informal processes. They can foster responsibilities within a context of checks upon the arbitrary exercise of power.

Speeding up justice versus time for party-centred input and deliberation

Pressures to speed up justice in the name of efficiency, effectiveness and economy may be in tension with the restorative urge to incorporate diverse stakeholders, to provide them with time for party-centred input and deliberation, and to attend to the relational and human aspects of dispute resolution through negotiation. One of the central appeals of youth offender panels over courts is that they should accommodate sufficient time for the parties to engage with and voice the 'things that matter to them'. Not rushing justice is an implicit facet of restoration. As Daly notes, restorative interventions necessitate 'time for anger and forgiveness', among other things, to be expressed (2000). This appears to conflict with the current emphasis on speed through the system and the reduction of delay, through fast-tracking and the introduction of statutory time limits. As the referral order pilots highlight, there is a potential tension between speeding up justice (through the imposition of national standards) and victim consultation and input, both of which often take time if victims are not to be pressurised unduly and their needs are to be addressed sensitively. Fast-tracking may hinder the institutionalisation of a victim-centred approach if it becomes a dominant end in its own right.

Rationalisation of justice and the affective expression of emotions

This raises a broader tension within criminal justice between the urge to rationalise justice and the need to respond to the emotions and expressive demands that crime evokes, especially for victims. To some extent, restorative justice by involving the immediate parties to a conflict in party-centred deliberation seeks to accommodate both dynamics, at least, more so than the traditional court. We have seen how, in the implementation of youth offender panels, administrative demands of rational management often conflict with desires to allow space for appropriate local involvement, inclusive attendance and extensive deliberation. That panels were not held in sufficiently informal or community-based locations and did not incorporate appropriately proximate community panel members was often due to the administrative challenges associated with managing such complex events. The low level of victim input was often explained in terms of the administrative (rather than ideological) challenges that it presented to YOT staff. Rotas of community panel members, for example, were not ideal ways of constituting youth offender panels, but presented a rational way of managing them. So too did the strategy of scheduling numerous panels, one after the other. Nevertheless, they all served potentially to limit the restorative potential of panels. In practice, balancing the demands of rational management and accommodating the expressive, morally-toned and human dimensions of justice constitute a fundamental but precarious dynamic in implementing youth offender panels. The manner in which this is played out will often depend upon local circumstances and the values of the people entrusted with implementing them, for as Rutherford notes, 'the expression of humane values within criminal justice ultimately resides within practitioners' (1993: xii).

Greater interventionism and the quest for cost reductions

There are concerns that the greater interventionism in young people's (and their parents') lives potentially heralded by referral orders – but certainly fostered by some of the other recent changes to youth justice[2] – has significant funding implications. These implications both in the short and longer term may not have been sufficiently thought through by government. This 'poverty of resource thinking' (Downes 1998: 196) is likely to be exposed if the reforms do not produce quick and significant reductions in reoffending rates. There is a dangerous assumption that restorative justice is cheap. Whilst in some instances this may be so (see Miers *et al.* 2001), it is not inevitably the case. Restorative justice interventions are also labour and time intensive, requiring significant preparation with potentially a greater number of parties. The idea that they may rely on unpaid volunteers (such as community panel members) or that they tap underexploited community resources does not, necessarily, mean cost savings. As the referral order pilots highlight, there are significant costs associated with training, advice and information provision for volunteers as well as with other supporting infrastructures which are required simply because volunteers are involved. Moreover, the referral order experience also suggests that tapping community resources is itself time-consuming and difficult.

Reconciling the past and the future

As we have seen, 'doing justice' is bound up with both looking to reorder the past by correcting a symbolic moral equilibrium that has been disturbed by the event of crime and reducing threats to security in the future. In a contemporary context, this Janus-faced logic of justice is evoked particularly forcefully in the future-focused concerns over 'risk', 'dangerousness' and 'public protection', all of which clash potentially with the past-oriented and expressive preoccupations of 'just deserts' and retributive notions of proportionality. Once again, as was argued in Chapter 3, restorative justice attempts to reconcile these tensions by combining both the risk-based and instrumental approach to 'governing the future' with a moral and symbolic space for confronting the past. The findings from the research documented in this book suggest that the practice of restorative justice, through referral orders, rather than reconciling these tensions in any simple or coherent way, actually articulates this strain in both visible and tangible ways. In some senses, this dichotomy is to be found in the two preoccupations at the heart of youth offender contracts. The requirement to repair the harm done through victim or community reparation looks to the past and the hurt suffered, even if the response is only to be a symbolic apology. By contrast, the requirement for a programme of activities designed primarily to prevent further offending looks to the future. Hence, in practice, as Daly (2000) notes, restorative interventions express 'several justice principles – not just one'. This may be precisely what is so interesting about practical manifestations of restorative justice: their attempt to reconcile, albeit rarely wholly successfully (and why should it?), fundamental tensions within the practice of 'doing justice'.

The interplay between these tensions and competing dynamics is likely to structure the manner in which the future shape and direction of referral orders and youth offender panels unfold.

Victims and Restorative Justice

In the last two decades the victim has re-emerged as a central figure within criminal justice policy. Where previously the individual victim's interests were subsumed within, and often sidelined by, the general 'public interest', now the current political orthodoxy has moved victims to the position of a central fulcrum in criminal justice policy debate. For example, latest government proposals (in the Queen's speech, 13 November 2002), according to the Prime Minister, are designed to create a 'victim justice system'. To this end, politicians increasingly invoke the hurt, stories, feelings and interests of victims as the basis of legitimacy upon which new criminal justice initiatives are founded. This has seen an array of governmental activity and initiatives that have sought to integrate or take account of victims in various different ways: by giving victims greater access to information; by providing victims with the opportunity for greater involvement in their case; by giving testimony to how the crime has affected victims' lives through personal statements; and by conveying victims' views or concerns to decision-makers both before and after sentencing. The referral order represents a particularly important step in this process.

And yet, the implications of incorporating victims and introducing a victim perspective within the delicate balance between state and offender are often ill understood. The place of the victim within criminal justice raises far wider questions about the role and purpose of criminal justice. As such, victims' interests often become caught up in much larger political and philosophical debates about the meaning of criminal justice. Organisations that had developed an early stake in the provision of services to victims, such as Victim Support, have become wary as more and different organisations and initiatives have jostled each other on an increasingly crowded pitch. Consequently, in many of the pilot sites, the involvement of Victim Support in the implementation of referral orders was limited and on occasions the relationship between them and the YOT was precarious.

There is often an apparent lack of co-ordination between initiatives for victims as well as between the statutory agencies charged with providing services to victims. The police, Crown Prosecution Service, youth offending teams and probation service all have separate responsibilities for contacting victims under different auspices. There is considerable scope for confusion and overlap, as victim services often lack coherence, communication and synergy. Perversely, recent managerialist pressures have served to increase the isolation and introspection of many criminal justice agencies. They have done so because, first, they accord little attention to negotiating shared purposes and collaboration, particularly where there is no hierarchy of control. Second, they focus attention upon narrowly construed service delivery to 'customers' of a particular segment of criminal justice at a given time and place within the process, rather than upon cross-cutting, horizontal accountabilities and responsibilities. Hence, victims tend only to be considered relevant in so far as they relate to narrow core responsibilities, with little regard to the relation between the victim and criminal justice as a 'systemic' whole. The new Victim Ombudsman, with powers to investigate and comment on the way a case or an individual has been handled,[3] might also act as a champion of victims' interests in general, for example, by recommending improvements to agencies' procedures to ensure they are victim sensitive. As such, the Victim Ombudsman may go some way to assist in countering co-ordination deficits, but is unlikely to address organisational and cultural impediments to coherent victim integration within criminal justice.

Providing victims with an enhanced role in the disposition of their cases may impose new obligations upon them. As the JUSTICE Report on the role of victims in criminal justice stated: 'The criminal justice system must not place further duties on citizens without meeting its own responsibilities for the consequences of introducing those duties' (1998: 110). Furthermore, victim involvement may unrealistically or falsely raise expectations of what justice can deliver (Crawford and Enterkin 2001). Victims in some of the pilots, who had been invited to a panel only to be asked to leave once the panel had dealt with issues of reparation and were keen to focus on discussions about the programme of activities for the young person – which it was not deemed appropriate for victims to participate in – were reminded of their secondary status within the process. In this context, victims may see themselves as a 'prop' in an offender-focused drama. Moreover, victims may actually be 'used' in the service of rehabilitation or enlisted in the demands of the justice system itself, for example in processing offenders or as information providers.

In addition to recognising these dangers, there is a need to acknowledge that there may be limitations to victim involvement. Daly (2003) sheds important light on the limitations of conferences in Australia, notably with regard to limits on both victims' capacities to see offenders in a positive light and offenders' interests to repair the harm. Notable among the reasons for victims' negative judgements of offenders were the offender not showing remorse and not taking responsibility for what he or she had done. These findings would appear to be supported by our own study.

Nevertheless, it is also clear from this study and others (Strang 2002) that, where sensitively treated, victims have much to benefit from restorative approaches to justice, particularly at an emotional level. However, the low level of victim participation in referral orders raises important questions about the cultural and organisational challenges presented by attempts to integrate victims into the heart of criminal justice processes.

Implementing and Evaluating Referral Orders

Although considerable energy is expended by criminologists in the UK in studying and analysing the latest criminal justice and penal policy developments, the focus of such activity rarely strays from the formal instruments of policy: legislation, advice and guidance from central government and so on. And yet, all policy instruments have to be implemented 'on the ground'. It is less usual for criminologists to focus on the nature of the process of implementation, with the exception of formal outcome-oriented evaluations that describe 'implementation failures' in great detail. We return to this issue later in the chapter. First, however, we wish to offer a few observations on the circumstances under which the referral order pilots were implemented and on the nature of the evaluation itself.

There are a number of practical aspects of the implementation of referral orders that are worth commenting on briefly here. The first relates to issues of timescale. As we outlined earlier, the YOTs selected as the sites for the pilots were informed early in 2000 that they had been chosen. Delay within the Home Office in receiving full confirmation of funding for the pilots meant that some YOTs did not receive full, formal confirmation until March that year. The timetable set for implementation required that the first orders be operational in July 2000. In practice, that meant that the pilot YOTs had to recruit or appoint a referral order co-ordinator, advertise for, recruit and train sufficient community panel members to cope with the first influx of orders and liaise with the courts in the space of little more than three months. Anyone familiar with local authority appointments procedures will appreciate that this was, to put it mildly, an ambitious timetable.

Not only was the timetable ambitious but it was also effectively inflexible. The primary reason for that was a commitment had already been made by ministers that referral orders would be rolled out nationally in early 2002. In practice, therefore, almost from the outset national roll-out set the agenda for the pilots, the reverse of what might often be expected to be the relationship. The pressing timescale for national roll-out had one further major impact. This was to reinforce and increase the degree of central oversight and control exerted over the pilots. Careful and close observation of local developments by the Home Office and the Youth Justice Board would be expected in relation to an initiative such as referral orders. However, the fact that national implementation had been promised, and was to be budgeted for early in the life of the pilots (late summer 2000), meant that officials took a particular interest in progress. Visits by officials to the pilots were frequent. Telephone contact between officials and referral order co-ordinators took place weekly at some stages. Data on referral orders were sent directly from pilot areas to the multi-agency steering group chaired by the YJB that oversaw the pilots. In short, the management of the pilots by the centre was very much 'hands on'.

In some respects the same was true of the relationship between the evaluation and officials. Though the relationship was very positive for the most part, both the Home Office and YJB took a very keen interest in the evaluation and the data collected. The evaluation team was represented on the Steering Group, which met monthly throughout the pilot period, in addition to the regular research meetings, ad hoc meetings and interim reports that form part of most evaluations. This close oversight was also related to the need to ensure that the integrity of the implementation was maintained and that the timetable for national roll-out did not slip. As such, the evaluation was intimately bound up with the process of implementation, and in ways that some evaluators may find unusual. This in itself we do not take to be problematic. That is not to say that it was without problems. There were difficulties and these in large part stemmed from what we perceived to be insufficient clarity – at least at certain points – about the purpose(s) of the evaluation.

There is a broad range of reasons for undertaking evaluations. Eleanor Chelimsky (1997) groups these into three broad conceptual frameworks of evaluation:

- *evaluation for accountability* (e.g. measuring results or efficiency);

- *evaluation for development* (e.g. providing evaluative help to strengthen institutions); and

- *evaluation for knowledge* (e.g. obtaining a deeper understanding in some specific area or policy field).

Evaluation for accountability generally involves providing information about effectiveness and efficiency. By contrast the development perspective, which usually involves process evaluations, is generally conducted to understand and improve the performance of particular institutions or processes. Finally, the knowledge perspective is concerned with increasing understanding of 'the factors underlying public problems, about the "fit" between these factors and the policy or program solution proposed, and about the theory and logic (or their lack) that lie behind an implemented intervention' (*ibid.*: 103).

Each of these approaches to evaluation has overlaps in terms of the methods they may use and the questions they may ask. However, the ways in which the methods are employed will – or at least should – differ depending on the purpose of the evaluation (Newburn 2001). Moreover, and importantly for our purposes here, evaluations such as the one discussed in the body of this book, may serve more than one end simultaneously. Indeed, the evaluation of the introduction of referral orders into the youth justice system displayed, to some degree, aspects of all three of Chelimsky's ideal types. Thus, in relation to the accountability perspective the evaluation contained a number of elements designed specifically to see how each of the pilot sites were implementing the new systems and, more particularly, how cost-effectively they were doing this.

Each of the major activities was costed, including recruitment and training of community panel members, the running of youth offender panels, and the activities undertaken in support of contracts. This information was fed back to the commissioning bodies and was used by them to calculate the public expenditure bid required to support national roll-out of referral orders.

The original timetable for the introduction of referral orders included not only the establishment of the pilots but also for national implementation. The legislation had been passed and there was effectively no question that referral orders would go national. The pilots, consequently, were not primarily about assessing whether local experiments showed sufficient promise to be replicated more widely. Rather, they were about understanding how local experience could be utilised, and wherever possible, improved to aid national implementation. As a result, the evaluation was at least in part concerned with supporting the Home Office Juvenile Offenders Unit and the YJB in their goal of managing the smooth, and cost-efficient, roll-out of referral orders to all YOTs, i.e. it had a significant *development* role.

Finally, the evaluation did of course also have an important knowledge component. Both the Home Office and the YJB were concerned to understand how this restorative justice-influenced initiative worked within the youth justice system and, more particularly, to assess the extent to which it had an impact on the participants involved in the process. That this was the case is illustrated in the wealth of data reported in this book, and also by the fact that a reconviction study is to be undertaken following on from the initial evaluation. However, as this brief description should have made clear, this knowledge component – often assumed to be at the heart of academic evaluations – was only one part of the overall task, and arguably may not have been the most important. We return to this below.

Many of those that read evaluation reports, and indeed many that commission evaluations, take as read the *purpose* of evaluation. That is to say, it is often the case that those responsible for initiating and/or funding evaluation research are either not aware that evaluation may have numerous functions or, if they are so aware, choose for whatever reason not to make the particular purpose explicit. When the purpose of evaluation is unclear a number of problems may result. Two of the most frequent concern the confusion that is potentially caused by the existence of multiple purposes and the problem of differing interpretations. In the former, difficulties occur when the need to satisfy accountability demands (the need to deliver management information in the relatively short term for example) or development demands (should changes be made to the operation of a particular institution or initiative) clashes with the need to satisfy more traditional evaluation for knowledge demands (the need to deliver outcome information over the medium and long term). In the second, a related problem occurs when different actors in the process (the customer and the contractor for example) hold different views of the purpose of the evaluation. Unless the purpose of evaluation is clearly specified and understood at the outset it is relatively easy for parties to find themselves with dissonant views of what the evaluation is intended to achieve.

Awareness that the referral orders study contained diverse elements – including, as we suggest, of all three of Chelimsky's evaluation perspectives – was not uniformly or equally spread across all those that had an interest in it. From time to time the different perspectives were in a certain amount of tension with each other. Put crudely (and this is of necessity something of a caricature), the Juvenile Offenders Unit (JOU) in the Home Office was concerned primarily with the development and accountability aspects of the evaluation. It had responsibility for national roll-out and, for example, relatively early in the life of the evaluation sought information about the set-up costs so as to calculate the size of the bid that the Home Office needed to make to the Treasury to finance the process. Whilst assessing set-up costs was part of the contract of research, in practice the timetable was considerably foreshortened because of the demands of the public expenditure round. The YJB, which chaired the Steering Group set up to oversee the pilots, was especially concerned with development issues. The Steering Group contained representatives from the police service, the Magistrates' Association, the Lord Chancellor's Department, Victim Support, NACRO and the Restorative Justice Consortium. Each had particular concerns – compliance with the legislation, protection of victims' interests, impact on sentencing and magistrates' courts and so on – and saw the evaluation as a source of information about each of these. Finally, the Research, Development and Statistics Directorate of the Home Office, who were the primary customer, had concerns that spread across all three perspectives but which were focused more directly on the knowledge aspects than was the case with any of the other major stakeholders.

We raise these issues here for a number of reasons. First, they are intrinsically important. Too often the term evaluation is used as if its meaning is self-evident. As we have attempted to suggest this is very often not the case. Moreover, it is not only the case that evaluation in general may play a number of different functions, but a particular evaluation may also do so. This evaluation did so. Second, the fact that the referral orders evaluation had an important developmental aspect is itself worthy of comment. The successful implementation – success in the ways we have described it in earlier chapters – was in part aided by the evaluation. The nature and delivery of training, the recruitment of volunteers, the levels of funding available to YOTs, and the management of panels were all affected by the feeding in of data from the evaluation as it progressed. Third, where there is a development aspect to evaluation, successful implementation and successful evaluation both depend in part on clarity of purpose. As Browne and Wildavsky (1984: 204) have noted:

> The evaluator collects and analyses data to provide information about program results. The implementer consumes this information, using it to check on past decisions and to guide future actions. Implementation is … about learning from evaluation. It is in their production and consumption of information (that is, learning) that implementers and evaluators engage in complementary relationships.

These relationships, we would argue, are both complementary and in some ways overlapping. It is not simply that implementers may use the 'results' of evaluation to guide future action, but that evaluators may be relatively closely involved in the process of making judgements and recommendations on the basis of evaluation data and encouraging changes to practice whilst the evaluation is ongoing.

Implications for the Study of Youth Justice

In a provocative essay a decade and a half ago, Jock Young (1986) focused on what he felt was the 'failure' of contemporary criminology and outlined the consequent need for a 'radical realism'. In particular, Young suggested that the demise of positivism and social democratic reformism opened up a space in which the new 'administrative criminology', with its empiricist concern with rational choice and deterrence, emerged. Though Young's argument may have contained something of a caricature of this supposed 'administrative criminology', nonetheless in drawing attention to the declining interest in causes, in social justice and in rehabilitation, and to the increasing interest in surveillance, policing and control, he was some way ahead of the 'new penologists' who identified similar trends some years later.

Young argued that the paradigm change affecting criminology at that point was a consequence of an 'aetiological crisis' – the continued, rapid rise in crime in and since the 1960s despite the diminution of social disadvantage through better social welfare, housing, education, health services and lower unemployment, all traditionally seen as major social 'causes' of crime. Though a 'nothing works' pessimism was dominant for a significant period, as we outlined in Chapter 1, recent years have seen something of a rebirth of interest in the social causes of crime and the possibility of rehabilitation – albeit in significantly reworked form. The rise of the 'what works' movement and the emergence of New Labour with its avowed attachment to evidence-led policy and practice, has led to a very significant expansion in research activity in many areas of criminal justice, including youth justice.

The study of youth justice and young offenders in the UK is currently dominated by three, somewhat unconnected, bodies of work. There is, first, writing of a largely theoretical and abstract kind that focuses on the analysis of policy together with what are generally polemical critiques of the politics of youth justice. Second, and by contrast, there are the highly empirical, relatively technically sophisticated longitudinal studies, and other studies of risk and protective factors, that have underpinned much of the 'what works' movement. Finally, and the most recent development, there is the burgeoning market in, what are often small-scale, empirical studies of local practice. This latter body of work constitutes a new form, or variant of 'administrative criminology'. Its concerns tend to be highly localised. The approach taken in such work is often predictable – being replicated again and again in different parts of the country, often under-pinned by very small research budgets and technically unsophisticated approaches to methodology.

One of the consequences of this 'topography' of youth justice/youth crime research is that, for varying reasons, frequently it fails to engage with the relationship between politics, policy and practice in a meaningful manner. Earlier in the chapter we noted the tendency within con-temporary criminology for policy be taken 'as read'. That is, too often those writing about the state of criminal justice generally, and youth justice in particular, tend in their work to elide policy prescription and professional practice. Accounts of contemporary developments either tend to rely on a reading of formal instruments or formal statements (legislation, green and white papers, consultation documents, press releases, speeches by government ministers, etc.) or they focus on the minutiae of practice. Relatively seldom, it seems, is attention paid to both. Rarer still, is the attempt to examine the dissonance between the two. Why should this be?

There seem to us to be several possible reasons. First, and most fundamentally, whilst much of the criminological community is interested in the 'politics of criminal justice' there tends to be little engagement with the literatures of policy-making and policy implementation. This is a two-way street. Just as criminologists pay scant attention to the literature of social policy and administration, so social policy scholars treat crime and criminal justice very much as a side-issue (where they acknowledge it at all).[4] Second, there continues to exist a rather unhelpful division in criminology between those engaged in largely theoretical scholarship and those that are more empirically-minded. It remains all too rare that the two meet. This has led to the emergence of what Bottoms (2000) has called a 'pragmatic division of labour' in which the theoretically-minded do theory and the empirically-minded analyse data. Though possibly pragmatic, as he goes on to argue, this is a dangerous division of labour. First, criminologists cannot, and should not, avoid theory. Second, 'there is indeed a real world, and … criminologists cannot avoid engagement with that world, whether they like it or not' (and some do not like it much) (*ibid.*: 16).

The emergence of something akin to such a 'pragmatic division of labour' links with the third factor underpinning the lack of a full engagement with the politics, policy and practice nexus in youth justice. This is what we take to be the relationship of contemporary British criminology to the politics of crime control. In crude terms, we would suggest that British criminology largely fails to grapple with real-world criminal justice and penal politics. In practice, there is little substantive conversation between British criminology and government (certainly when compared with other areas of social science and government policy). In large part, this is because too often work in the area is either too abstractly theoretical, too minutely empirical or too focused on formal policy rather than emergent practice to have, or be perceived to have, much relevance.

The arrival of referral orders is illustrative of some of these tensions. Their proposed introduction gave rise to a somewhat hostile response from some commentators. Muncie (2002), for example, argued that some of the dangers and difficulties in contemporary youth justice are the result of the unthinking transposition of policies from other jurisdictions to the UK. In particular, he suggested that the positive potential of restorative justice was being undermined by the dominant influence of North American punitiveness – and, in particular, the impact of the 'what works' ideology. Ball, occupying similar territory, argued that 'the coercive nature of the approach so evident in the 1998 [Crime and Disorder] Act permeates the referral order provisions in a way that is likely to result in their failing to achieve the declared objectives of restorative justice' (2000: 215). Wonnacott (1999) went further, describing the contract to be drawn up by youth offender panels as 'counterfeit'. She elaborated upon this as follows: 'Notwithstanding that the imagery is overwhelmingly consensual, in substance the contractual basis of the referral order is a sham, because all the negotiating power is in the hands of the youth offender panel' (*ibid.*: 281). Though Wonnacott and others are right to examine and where appropriate, to criticize, policy recommendations and legislation, there is a tendency in much of this literature to assume that the way in which policy will be implemented in practice is predictable and can be read directly from the formal policy instrument. This, it strikes us, is naïve.

Whatever view one takes of the policy-making process – analysing it as a set of stages (Rose 1973) or in terms of streams (Kingdon 1984) – there is a part, best thought of as *implementation*, which is just as much part of the process as agenda-setting or decisions between alternatives. As Anderson notes, 'policy is made as it is being administered and administered as it is being made' (1975: 79). In this, the activities of what Lipsky (1980) called 'street-level bureaucrats' is central. As Lipsky notes:

> Too often social analysts offer generalizations about organisational and governmental actions without concretely explaining how individual citizens and workers are affected by the actions, how the behaviour of the individuals, when aggregated, gives rise to the actions, or how and why the actions in question are consistently reproduced by the behaviour of individuals. (*ibid.*: xi)

As we have sought to illustrate in this book, youth justice practitioners – the primary street-level bureaucrats in this story – had a significant impact on the ways in which the Youth Justice and Criminal Evidence Act was implemented. In numerous ways they acted to transform, subvert or redirect the intentions of policy in different ways: sometimes inadvertently, sometimes due to administrative necessity and sometimes for ideological reasons. These 'reworkings' covered, among others, such areas as the nature of the training provided to community panel members, the ways in which panels were managed and run, the content of contracts, and responses to failure to comply with the terms of the contract. In some respects, it was such activities that helped realise some of the more restorative and inclusive aspects of the referral orders process. In this way, some of the expectations of Whitehall were modified and given positive and concrete form in Swindon and Nottingham, Cardiff, London and elsewhere.[5]

Against the expectation of many commentators (Wonnacott 1999; Ball 2000), referral orders seem to us to come remarkably close to fulfilling at least some of the criteria outlined by John Pitts (2000) as likely to provide the basis for a constructive and thoughtful youth justice. They do seem to 'offer children who get caught up in the criminal justice system a stake in, and a hand in, shaping their futures' (*ibid.*: 12). The fact that the principles of 'inclusivity, reciprocity, appreciation and tolerance' are potentially found in the referral orders process does not of course necessarily mean they will be effectively operationalised. However, our research suggests that considerable efforts are being made to ensure that this is the case. That commentators have previously ignored this, we think, is a product of the tendency to rely solely on formal policy instruments as their guide to what is happening, and failure to take account of how these instruments are put into practice by street-level bureaucrats and, in the case of community panel members, volunteer citizens.

At a time when there is no over-riding philosophy within youth justice it is especially difficult to form an overall judgement as to its possible future. Nonetheless, it remains valuable to attempt some assessment of current trends and likely trajectories. New Labour's youth justice policy has met with far from unanimous acclaim within criminological and other circles. The continued expansion of the numbers of young people in prison, the introduction of new penalties such as child curfews and ASBOs, together with the emphasis on anti-social behaviour by those below the age of criminal responsibility, have led to particular concern about the punitive and interventionist direction of youth justice policy. We share many of these concerns. Yet, as we have sought to illustrate, this is not the whole story. By contrast with the largely punitive thrust to many developments there has also been a very real attempt by New Labour to utilise some restorative justice-inspired approaches within the youth justice arena. As we have outlined, doing so in such a context has its tensions and indeed contradictions. Nonetheless, the referral order and youth offender panel, for all the difficulties associated with their implementation, hold real promise for greater involvement of young people's families, the victims of crime and the wider community and for more constructive, deliberative, inclusive and participative ways of responding to youthful offending.

Referral Orders and Restorative Justice

The introduction of referral orders and youth offender panels in the pilot areas presented a number of fundamental challenges for those charged with their implementation. The context was, and remains, one of constant change with new programmes and funding initiatives being launched whilst practitioners attempt to get to grips with, and understand the lessons of, previous waves of reform. Referral orders were introduced in the pilot areas just as they were trying to come to terms with the radical institutional changes delivered by the creation of youth offending teams, the Youth Justice Board and the swathe of new sentences and programmes heralded by the Crime and Disorder Act 1998 as well as the Narey reforms. During the pilot period, further new initiatives came into effect, such as the Intensive Supervision and Surveillance Programmes, drawing human and material resources away from referral orders.

In this context, it might not have been surprising had there been little stomach or enthusiasm for the introduction of yet another change to the youth justice system, in the form of the referral order. Nevertheless, referral orders and youth offender panels were well received and embraced by most charged with their implementation, including magistrates, court clerks, YOT staff and community panel members, as well as those who became the subject of them, notably young offenders, their parents and victims (where they attended). In large part, this positive reception was due to the restorative justice ideals and values that were intended to inform the referral order. It offered an informal, inclusive and party-centred way of responding to crime that allowed for constructive ways to address the offending behaviour of young people. By and large, youth justice practitioners (including magistrates) saw, in the referral order, a chance to 'do something different' with victims, offenders and their parents.

Nevertheless, the implementation of referral orders and youth offender panels presented a number of fundamental challenges to the culture and organisational practice of youth justice. First, working with victims presents deep-rooted difficulties for YOTs, whose staff are not accustomed to working with victims. Integrating victims as people and a victim perspective as a way of working into the core of their services is no easy task, and may appear to sit awkwardly alongside concerns for the young people with whom they work. Presenting victims with real choices over attendance, input and participation in the future requires some reworking of cultural assumptions and working practices. This was a particular challenge for police service members of YOTs who were very often those charged with the responsibility for liaising with victims.

Second, working with lay people as equal partners in an open and inclusive process presents real challenges to the way in which professional YOT staff work. Youth offender panels in the pilot sites, though making significant progress, only uncovered a small part of the potential contribution of community panel members. There is clearly still much more that can be done in relation to their involvement in the deliberative process and as a broader resource in delivering a form of community justice that links panels to wider communities in which they are located and the latent forms of social control that reside therein. Third, organising youth offender panels presents a considerable number of administrative hurdles that challenge traditional ways of working. Holding panels in the evening and at weekends requires different working patterns; facilitating the attendance of the diverse stakeholders presents difficulties of organisation and timing; and finding appropriate venues challenges the extent to which panels are rooted in local community infrastructures. Moreover, administering panels creatively and flexibly often sits awkwardly within a risk-averse professional culture.

These challenges, this research suggests, will take some considerable time, effort and institutional learning to address and, as we have sought to show, there are countervailing dynamics – most notably a managerialist ethos with its emphasis upon standardisation, efficiency and economy – that can serve to undermine or limit the capacity of those seeking to confront them. That said, as we have also attempted to show, within a relatively short period of time youth justice practitioners have begun to come to terms with many of these challenges and have been actively looking for ways to address them. In terms of involving victims, working with community members and offering young people the opportunity to participate in a more deliberative forum, the desire among YOT staff in the pilots to work with restorative ideals and values was strong.

As the review of restorative justice initiatives presented in Chapter 2 highlights, the referral order represents both a particular and a rather peculiar hybrid attempt to integrate restorative justice ideas and values into youth justice practice. It does so in a clearly coercive, penal context that offends cherished restorative ideals of voluntariness. Yet, by establishing an almost mandatory sentence of the court (for young offenders appearing in court for the first time), the referral order delivers a steady supply of cases to youth offender panels. In so doing, the referral order circumvents the fundamental stumbling block for most restorative justice initiatives, namely the problem of insufficient referrals. Unlike most initiatives that deal with very small caseloads and remain peripheral to the coercive system, the referral order moved centre stage almost overnight. Coercion provided the capacity to move certain restorative values to the very heart of the youth justice system, and the loss of voluntariness was the price paid. The coercive nature of the referral order undoubtedly constrains the work of youth offender panels. However, the evidence from the pilot sites suggests to us that they were nevertheless able to engage young people and their parents in a very different, and more positive, process of communication and reasoning from that found generally in the criminal courts.

Thus one of the positive lessons for restorative justice is that despite the coercive context, and possibly partly as a consequence of it, change in the direction of delivering a more deliberative process can be realised. However, we should note at this point that the experience with regard to the inclusiveness of the parties to the deliberations was mixed.

One question that the sceptic might reasonably ask is to what extent did the terms of youth offender contracts differ from the types of sentences that young offenders might have received through the courts? In some respects there were clear differences, notably with regard to the emphasis upon reparation. Panels have a wider creative script upon which to work. However, in reality much of the reparation was indirect rather than direct. It was frequently reparation by way of work in the community, such as through Community Payback schemes. The creative potential of contract terms was often limited by concerns about supervision, health and safety or insurance. As a consequence, the programmes of activities designed to address the young person's offending behaviour sometimes resembled the kind of work that a young person might receive through an action plan order or other community penalty.

Panels are not only forums for deliberation about the harm and its consequences, but also act as a means of monitoring contract compliance and championing reintegration. In this regard, referral orders accord a more central role to the panel beyond the initial meeting at which the contract is agreed, than do many other restorative interventions. The story here is also mixed. On the one hand, YOTs did not run the level of review meetings suggested by strict adherence to the Home Office *Guidance*. The data show that in only half the cases was a review meeting held and in nearly a third of cases there was no final meeting. Furthermore, in practice it became difficult to arrange for the same panel members to be present at the review meeting as had attended the initial meeting. Many sites accepted that in practice they could only work to the norm of at least one member appearing in all panels in a case to ensure some kind of consistency, overview and rapport with the parties involved. On the other hand, this points to one of the enduring lessons of the pilot experience, the capacity of practitioners working with the community panel members to ensure that programmes were not over-intensive or overly interventionist. In the process of implementation – in other words in giving practical effect to government policy – YOTs in the pilot areas did much to limit the nature of the referral order as a sentence, particularly in less serious cases where the administrative demands, personnel commitment and intervention in the lives of those affected often appeared out of proportion to the nature of the offending. This expressed itself in a number of ways. First, work done by some YOTs with Youth Court magistrates encouraged the use of longer referral orders only in exceptional cases. Moreover, some YOTs particularly encouraged magistrates to refrain from 12-month referral orders so that if a young person reoffended, either before the panels had met or soon thereafter, the order could be lengthened by the court rather than abandoned. Second, YOT staff worked hard with community panel members to keep the contractual terms to a minimum (as evidenced by the findings in Chapter 8) so that they could realistically be achieved. In training and in practice the YOT staff sought to keep in check any benevolent, yet overly intrusive, desires on behalf of community panel members to intervene in the lives of the young people and their parents. Third, as noted above, where young people adhered to their contractual commitments, YOT staff preferred not to organise too many review meetings, particularly as they were often well aware of the progress that the young person had made. In practice, where contracts had been successfully completed YOT staff did not continue to hold further meetings.

The low level of victim attendance suggests that on most occasions youth offender panels are only ever 'mostly restorative' according to McCold's typologies (see Chapter 3, Figure 3.1) as they involve only two of the three key stakeholders: victim, offender and community. However, one further broad lesson for restorative justice from the experience of youth offender panels may be that in practice there can be a tension between community involvement and victim participation. The involvement of community representatives can serve to dilute the central importance of the victim. The community, it may be felt, is capable of bringing a victim perspective through its own role as an indirect or secondary victim of the crime. This expanded notion of victim feeds into restorative justice models of harm, but may limit the involvement of actual victims. This is not to suggest that community involvement will always function in this way, but rather that in an 'unwilling system', community participation can be used as an excuse for victim non-attendance. What this research and others (JUSTICE 1998; Crawford and Goodey 2000; Strang 2002) show is that there is much more to learn about the best ways to provide victims with both greater agency and voice within public responses to crime. We need to know more about what kinds of victims, under what circumstances, are more likely to benefit from active participation in restorative programmes and how best to facilitate this. Despite some of the findings emerging from RISE about the differential impact of different types of victims on offenders (Sherman 2002), there is a need to be wary of programmes that seek to justify victim involvement solely on the basis of the impact upon recidivism rates. At the same time, we need to acknowledge that there may be limits to both victims' capacities to see offenders in a positive light and young offenders' capacity to repair the harm and/or acknowledge the legitimacy of the victim.

A careful reading of the early experience of the introduction of referral orders requires, as we have argued, an acknowledgement of mixed success – certainly if one is judging by the standards of what we might think of as 'restorative justice ideals'. Though acknowledging some of the difficulties – not least of which is the so far limited involvement of victims – we have nonetheless sought to show that there is much that is positive in these developments. From the recruitment, training and involvement of community volunteers to the establishment of relatively informal, deliberative panel meetings, the introduction of referral orders intimates that it may just be possible to do youth justice differently.

Notes

1 Article 6 states that everyone charged with a criminal offence has the right to legal assistance and to be given it free of charge if he or she does not have sufficient means to pay for it. In Scotland, legal aid was not available for the Children's Hearing itself, as a result very few children were accompanied by a legal representative. However, it has been available at proof hearings and appeals.
2 Such as changes to the cautioning system, ASBOs, child curfews, parenting orders, etc.
3 But who is unable to comment on or intervene in judicial or other legally based decisions.
4 By way of illustration, nowhere in two of the major social policy textbooks, Hill's (2000) *Understanding Social Policy* or Glennerster's (2000) *British Social Policy since 1945*, is there any reference to criminal justice or penal policy.
5 In their classic, though more pessimistic, work on implementation, Pressman and Wildavsky (1984) subtitled their book *How Great Expectations in Washington are Dashed in Oakland*.

References

Abel, R. (1981) 'Conservative Conflict and the Reproduction of Capitalism: The Role of Informal Justice', *International Journal of the Sociology of Law*, 9, 245–67.

Alder, C. and Wundersitz, J. (1994) (eds) *Family Conferencing and Juvenile Justice*, Canberra: Australian Institute of Criminology.

Anderson, J.E. (1975) *Public Policy-Making*, New York, NY: Praeger.

Ashworth, A. (2000) 'Victim's Rights, Defendant's Rights and Criminal Procedure', in A. Crawford and J. Goodey (eds) *Integrating a Victim Perspective within Criminal Justice*, Aldershot: Ashgate, 185–204.

Ashworth, A. (2002) 'Responsibilities, Rights and Restorative Justice', *British Journal of Criminology*, 42(3), 578–95.

Audit Commission (1996) *Misspent Youth*, London: Audit Commission.

Auld, Lord Justice (2001) *Review of the Criminal Courts of England and Wales*, London: HMSO.

Bailey, V. (1987) *Delinquency and Citizenship: Reclaiming the Young Offender 1914– 1948*, Oxford: Clarendon Press.

Ball, C. (2000) 'The Youth Justice and Criminal Evidence Act 1999, Part I', *Criminal Law Review*, 211–22.

Bazemore, G. and Schiff, M. (2001) (eds) *Restorative Community Justice: Repairing Harm and Transforming Communities*, Cincinnati, OH: Anderson Publications.

Bazemore, G. and Walgrave, L. (1999) (eds) *Restorative Juvenile Justice*, Monsey, NY: Criminal Justice Press.

Beck, U. (1992) *Risk Society: Towards a New Modernity*, London: Sage.

Bottoms, A.E. (1974) 'On the Decriminalisation of English Juvenile Courts', in R. Hood (ed.) *Crime, Criminology and Public Policy*, London: Heinemann, 319–46.

Bottoms, A.E. (1995) 'The Philosophy and Politics of Punishment and Sentencing', in C. Clarkson and R. Morgan (eds) *The Politics of Sentencing Reform*, Oxford: Oxford University Press, 17–49.

Bottoms, A.E. (2000) 'The Relationship between Theory and Research in Criminology, in R. King and E. Wincup (eds) *Doing Research on Crime and Justice*, Oxford: Oxford University Press, 15–60.

Bovens, M. (1998) *The Quest for Responsibility*, Cambridge: Cambridge University Press.

Braithwaite, J. (1989) *Crime, Shame and Reintegration*, Cambridge: Cambridge University Press.

Braithwaite, J. (1995) 'Inequality and Republican Criminology', in J. Hagan and R. Peterson (eds) *Crime and Inequality*, Palo Alto, CA: Stanford University Press, 277–305.

Braithwaite, J. (1998) 'Restorative Justice', in M. Tonry (ed.) *Handbook of Crime and Punishment*, New York, NY: Oxford University Press, 323–44.

Braithwaite, J. (1999) 'Restorative Justice: Assessing Optimistic and Pessimistic Accounts', *Crime and Justice: A Review of Research*, 25, 1–127.

Braithwaite, J. (2002a) *Restorative Justice and Responsive Regulation*, Oxford: Oxford University Press.

Braithwaite, J. (2002b) 'Setting Standards for Restorative Justice', *British Journal of Criminology*, 42(3), 563–77.

Braithwaite, J. and Mugford, S. (1994) 'Conditions of Successful Reintegration Ceremonies: Dealing with Juvenile Offenders', *British Journal of Criminology*, 34(2), 139–71.

Braithwaite, J. and Pettit, P. (1990) *Not Just Deserts: A Republican Theory of Criminal Justice*, Oxford: Oxford University Press.

Braithwaite, J. and Pettit, P. (2000) 'Republicanism and Restorative Justice', in H. Strang and J. Braithwaite (eds) *Restorative Justice: Philosophy to Practice*, Aldershot: Ashgate.

Braithwaite, J. and Roche, D. (2001) 'Responsibility and Restorative Justice', in G. Bazemore and M. Shiff (eds) *Community and Restorative Justice: Cultivating Common Ground*, Cincinnati, OH: Anderson Publications, 63–84.

Browne, A. and Wildavsky, A. (1984) 'What Should Evaluation Mean to Implementation?, in J.L. Pressman and A. Wildavsky (eds) *Implementation: How Great Expectations in Washington are Dashed in Oakland, or, Why it's Amazing that Federal Programs Work at all, this be a Saga of the Economic Development Administration*, Berkeley, CA: University of California Press, 181–205.

Cain, M. (1985) 'Beyond Informal Justice', *Contemporary Crises*, 9, 335–73.

Carlen, P. (1976) *Magistrates' Justice*, London: Martin Robertson.

Cavadino, M. and Dignan, J. (1992) *The Penal System: An Introduction*, London: Sage.

Chelimsky, E. (1997) 'Thoughts for a New Evaluation Society', *Evaluation*, 3(1), 97–118.

Christie, N. (1977) 'Conflicts as Property', *British Journal of Criminology*, 17(1), 1–15.

Clear, T.R. and Karp, D.R. (1999) *The Community Justice Ideal: Preventing Crime and Achieving Justice*, Boulder, CO: Westview Press.

Coates, R.B., Umbreit, M. and Vos, B. (2000) *Restorative Justice Circles in South Saint Paul, Minnesota*, Saint Paul, MN: Center for Restorative Justice, University of Minnesota.

Cohen, S. (2001) *States of Denial*, Oxford: Polity Press.

Consedine, J. (1995) *Restorative Justice: Healing the Effects of Crime*, Lyttleton, New Zealand: Ploughshares Publications.

Crawford, A. (1996) 'Alternatives to Prosecution: Access to, or Exits from, Criminal Justice?', in R. Young and D. Wall (eds) *Access to Criminal Justice: Lawyers, Legal Aid and the Defence of Liberty*, London: Blackstone Press, 313–44.

Crawford, A. (1997) *The Local Governance of Crime*, Oxford: Clarendon Press.

Crawford, A. (1998) 'Community Safety and the Quest for Security: Holding back the Dynamics of Social Exclusion', *Policy Studies*, 19(3/4), 237–53.

Crawford, A. (1999) 'Questioning Appeals to Community in Crime Prevention and Control', *European Journal on Criminal Policy and Research*, 7(4), 509–30.

Crawford, A. (2000) 'Justice de Proximité – The Growth of "Houses of Justice" and Victim/Offender Mediation in France: A Very UnFrench Legal Response?', *Social and Legal Studies*, 9(1), 29–53.

Crawford, A. (2001a) *Public Matters: Reviving Public Participation in Criminal Justice*, London: IPPR.

Crawford, A. (2001b) 'Joined-up but Fragmented: Contradiction, Ambiguity and Ambivalence at the Heart of Labour's "Third Way" ', in R. Matthews and J. Pitts (eds) *Crime Prevention, Disorder and Community Safety: A New Agenda?*, London: Routledge, 54–80.

Crawford, A. (2002) 'The State, Community and Restorative Justice: Heresy, Nostalgia and Butterfly Collecting', in L. Walgrave (ed.) *Restorative Justice and the Law*, Cullompton: Willan Publishing, 101–29.

Crawford, A. (2003) 'The Prospects for Restorative Youth Justice in England and Wales', in K. McEvoy and T. Newburn (eds) *Criminology, Conflict Resolution and Restorative Justice*, Houndmills: Palgrave, 256–315.

Crawford, A. and Clear, T.R. (2001) 'Community Justice: Transforming Communities through Restorative Justice?', in G. Bazemore and M. Shiff (eds) *Restorative Community Justice: Repairing Harm and Transforming Communities*, Cincinnati, OH: Anderson Publications, 127–49.

Crawford, A. and Enterkin, J. (2001) 'Victim Contact Work in the Probation Service: Paradigm Shift or Pandora's Box?', *British Journal of Criminology*, 41(4), 707–25.

Crawford, A. and Goodey, J.S. (2000) (eds) *Integrating a Victim Perspective within Criminal Justice*, Aldershot: Ashgate.

Daly, K. (2000) 'Revisiting the Relationship between Retributive and Restorative Justice', in H. Strang and J. Braithwaite (eds) *Restorative Justice: From Philosophy to Practice*, Aldershot: Dartmouth, 33–54.

Daly, K. (2001) 'Conferencing in Australia and New Zealand: Variations, Research Findings and Prospects', in A. Morris and G. Maxwell (eds) *Restorative Justice for Juveniles*, Oxford: Hart Publishing, 59–83.

Daly, K. (2002) 'Restorative Justice: The Real Story', *Punishment & Society*, 4(1), 55–79.

Daly, K. (2003) 'Mind the Gap: Restorative Justice in Theory and Practice', in A. von Hirsch, J. Roberts, A.E. Bottoms, K. Roach and M. Schiff (eds) *Restorative Justice and Criminal Justice: Competing or Reconcilable Paradigms*, Oxford: Hart Publishing, 219–36.

Daly, K. and Hayes, H. (2001) 'Restorative Justice and Conferencing in Australia', *Australian Institute of Criminology, Trends and Issues in Crime and Criminal Justice*, no. 186, February.

Daly, K. and Immarigeon, R. (1998) 'The Past, Present, and Future of Restorative Justice', *Contemporary Justice Review*, 1, 21–45.

Davis, G. (1992a) *Making Amends: Mediation and Reparation in Criminal Justice*, London: Routledge.

Davis, G. (1992b) 'Reparation in the UK: Dominant Themes and Neglected Themes', in H. Messmer and H.-U. Otto (eds) *Restorative Justice on Trial*, Dordrecht: Kluwer, 445–60.

Davis, G., Boucherat, J. and Watson, D. (1988) 'Reparation in the Service of Diversion: The Subordination of a Good Idea', *Howard Journal*, 27(2), 127–34.

Dignan, J. (1992) 'Repairing the Damage: Can Reparation be Made to Work in the Service of Diversion?', *British Journal of Criminology*, 32, 453–72.

Dignan, J. (1999a) 'The Crime and Disorder Act and the Prospects for Restorative Justice', *Criminal Law Review*, 48–60.

Dignan, J. (1999b) 'Restorative Crime Prevention in Theory and Practice', *Prison Service Journal*, 123, 2–5.

Dignan, J. (2000) *Youth Justice Pilots Evaluation: Interim Report on Reparative Work and Youth Offending Teams*, London: Home Office.

Dignan, J. (2002) 'Restorative Justice and the Law: The Case for an Integrated, Systemic Approach', in L. Walgrave (ed.) *Restorative Justice and the Law*, Cullompton: Willan Publishing, 168–90.

Dignan, J. and Lowey, K. (2000) *Restorative Justice Options for Northern Ireland: A Comparative Review*, Belfast: HMSO.

Dignan, J. and Marsh, P. (2001) 'Restorative Justice and Family Group Conferences in England', in A. Morris and G. Maxwell (eds) *Restorative Justice for Juveniles*, Oxford: Hart Publishing, 85–101.

Doran, S. and Glenn, R. (2000) *Lay Involvement in Adjudication*, Belfast: HMSO.

Downes, D. (1998) 'Toughing it Out: From Labour Opposition to Labour Government', *Policy Studies*, 19(3/4), 191–8.

Duff, R.A. (1992) 'Alternatives to Punishments or Alternative Punishments', in W. Cragg (ed.) *Retributivism and its Critics*, Stuttgart: Franz Steiner, 44–68.

Duff, R.A. (2002) 'Restorative Punishment and Punitive Restoration', in L. Walgrave (ed.) *Restorative Justice and the Law*, Cullompton: Willan Publishing, 82–100.

Edwards, L. (2001) 'S v Miller: The End of the Children's Hearing System as We Know It', *Scots Law Times*, 41, 23 May.
Etzioni, A. (1993) *The Spirit of Community*, New York, NY: Simon & Schuster.
Evans, R. and Puech, K. (2001) 'Reprimands and Warnings: Populist Punitiveness or Restorative Justice?', *Criminal Law Review*, 794–805.

Fairclough, N. (2000) *New Labour, New Language?*. London: Routledge.
Family Policy Studies Centre (1998) *The Crime and Disorder Bill and the Family*, London: Family Policy Studies Centre.
Farrington, D.P. (1997) 'Human Development and Criminal Careers', in M. Maguire, R. Morgan and R. Reiner (eds) *The Oxford Handbook of Criminology*, Oxford: Clarendon Press, 361–408.
Feeley, M. and Simon, J. (1994) 'Actuarial Justice: The Emerging New Criminal Law', in D. Nelken (ed.) *The Futures of Criminology*, London: Sage, 173–201.

Gardner, J., von Hirsch, A., Smith, A.T.H., Morgan, R., Ashworth, A. and Wasik, M. (1998) 'Clause 1 – The Hybrid Law from Hell?' *Criminal Justice Matters*, 31 (Spring), 25–7.
Garland, D. (2001) *The Culture of Control*, Oxford: Oxford University Press.
Girling, E., Loader, I. and Sparks, R. (2000) *Crime and Social Change in Middle England: Questions of Order in an English Town*, London: Routledge.
Glennerster, H. (2000) *British Social Policy since 1945*, Oxford: Blackwell.
Goldblatt, P. and Lewis, C. (1998) *Reducing Offending: An Assessment of Research Evidence on Ways of Dealing with Offending Behaviour*. Home Office Research Study 187, London: Home Office.
Goldson, B. (2000) (ed.) *The New Youth Justice*, Lyme Regis: Russell House.
Graham, J. (1998) 'What Works in Preventing Criminality', in P. Goldblatt and C. Lewis (eds) *Reducing Offending: An Assessment of Research Evidence on Ways of Dealing with Offending Behaviour*. Home Office Research Study 187, London: Home Office.

Haines, J. (2000) 'Referral Orders and Youth Offender Panels: Restorative Approaches and the New Youth Justice', in B. Goldson (ed.) *The New Youth Justice*, Lyme Regis: Russell House, 58–81.
Hall, S. (1980) *Drifting into a Law and Order Society*, London: Cobden Trust.
Hallett, C. and Murray, C., with Jamieson, J. and Veitch, B. (1998) *The Evaluation of Children's Hearings in Scotland. Volume 1*, Edinburgh: The Scottish Office Central Research Unit.
Hassall, I. (1996) 'Origin and Development of Family Group Conferences', in J. Hudson, A. Morris, G. Maxwell and B. Galaway (eds) *Family Group Conferences: Perspectives on Police and Practice*, Annandale, NSW: Federation Press, 17–36.

Hayes, H., Prenzler, T. and Wortley, R. (1998) *Making Amends: Final Evaluation of the Queensland Community Conferencing Pilot*, Brisbane: Griffith University.

Hill, M. (2000) *Understanding Social Policy*, Oxford: Blackwell.

Hines, J., Holdaway, S., Wiles, P., Davidson, N., Dignan, J., Hammersley, R. and Marsh, P. (1999) *Interim Report on Youth Offending Teams*, London: Home Office.

Holdaway, S., Davidson, N., Dignan, J., Hammersley, R., Hine, J. and Marsh, P. (2001) *New Strategies to Address Youth Offending: The National Evaluation of the Pilot Youth Offending Teams*, London: Home Office.

Home Office (1997a) *Community Safety Order: A Consultation Paper*, London: Home Office.

Home Office (1997b) *Getting to Grips with Crime*, London: Home Office.

Home Office (1997c) *New National and Local Focus on Youth Crime: A Consultation Paper*, London: Home Office.

Home Office (1997d) *No More Excuses – A New Approach to Tackling Youth Crime in England and Wales*, Cm 3809, London: Home Office.

Home Office (1997e) *Tackling Delays in the Youth Justice System: A Consultation Paper*, London: Home Office.

Home Office (1997f) *Tackling Youth Crime: A Consultation Paper*, London: Home Office.

Home Office (1998) *Summary of the Response to the Comprehensive Spending Review of Secure Accommodation for Remanded and Sentenced Juveniles*, London: Home Office.

Home Office (2000) *Implementation of Referral Orders – Draft Guidance for Youth Offending Teams*, London: Home Office.

Home Office (2001) *Implementation of Referral Orders – Guidance for Youth Offending Teams*, London: Home Office.

Hough, M. (1996) 'People Talking about Punishment', *Howard Journal*, 35(3), 191–214.

Hough, M. and Roberts, J. (1998) *Attitudes to Punishment: Findings from the British Crime Survey*. Research Study 179, London: Home Office.

Hoyle, C., Young, R. and Hill, R. (2002) *Proceed with Caution: An Evaluation of the Thames Valley Police Initiative in Restorative Cautioning*, York: JRF.

Hudson, J., Morris, A., Maxwell, G. and Galaway, B. (1996) (eds) *Family Group Conferences: Perspectives on Police and Practice*, Annandale, NSW: Federation Press.

Jackson, S. (1998) 'Family Group Conferencing in Youth Justice', *Howard Journal*, 37(1), 34–51.

Johnstone, G. (2002) *Restorative Justice: Ideas, Values, Debates*, Cullompton: Willan Publishing.

Jones, R. (1984) 'Questioning the New Orthodoxy', *Community Care*, 11 October, 26–9.

JUSTICE (1998) *Victims in Criminal Justice*. Report of the Committee on the Role of the Victim in Criminal Justice, London: JUSTICE.

Karp, D.R. (2000) 'Harm and Repair: Observing Restorative Justice in Vermont', unpublished manuscript, New York, NY: Department of Sociology, Skidmore College.

Karp, D.R. and Walther, K. (2001) 'Community Reparative Boards in Vermont', in G. Bazemore and M. Schiff (eds) *Restorative Community Justice*, Cincinnati, OH: Anderson Publishing, 199–217.

Kilchling, M. and Loschnig-Gspandl, M. (2000) 'Legal and Practical Perspectives on Victim/Offender Mediation in Austria and Germany', *International Review of Victimology*, 7, 305–32.

Kingdon, J. (1984) *Agendas, Alternatives and Public Policies*, Boston, MA: Little Brown & Co.

Kurki, L. (2000) 'Restorative and Community Justice in the United States', *Crime and Justice*, 27, 235–303.

Labour Party (1996) *Tackling Youth Crime, Reforming Youth Justice*, London: Labour Party.

LaPrairie, C. (1995a) 'Altering Course: New Directions in Criminal Justice', *Australian and New Zealand Journal of Criminology*, 78–99.

LaPrairie, C. (1995b) 'Community Justice or Just Communities? Aboriginal Communities in Search of Justice', *Canadian Journal of Criminology*, 37, 521–45.

LaPrairie, C. (1999) 'Some Reflections on New Criminal Justice Policies in Canada: Restorative Justice, Alternative Measures and Conditional Sentences', *Australian and New Zealand Journal of Criminology*, 32, 139–52.

Law Commission of Canada (1999) *From Restorative Justice to Transformative Justice, A Discussion Paper*, Ottawa: Law Commission.

Leng, R., Taylor, R. and Wasik, M. (1998) *Blackstone's Guide to the Crime and Disorder Act 1998*, London: Blackstone Press.

Levrant, S., Cullen, F., Fulton, B. and Wozniak, J. (1999) 'Reconsidering Restorative Justice: The Corruption of Benevolence Revisited?', *Crime & Delinquency*, 45(1), 3–27.

Lilles, H. (2001) 'Circle Sentencing: Part of the Restorative Justice Continuum', in A. Morris and G. Maxwell (eds) *Restorative Justice for Juveniles*, Oxford: Hart Publishing, 161–79.

Lipsky, M. (1980) *Street-level Bureaucracy: The Dilemmas of the Individual in Public Services*, New York, NY: Russell Sage Foundation.

Marshall, T.F. (1996) 'The Evolution of Restorative Justice in Britain', *European Journal on Criminal Policy and Research*, 4(4), 21–43.

Marshall, T.F. (1999) *Restorative Justice: An Overview*, London: Home Office.

Marshall, T.F. and Merry, S. (1990) *Crime and Accountability*, London: HMSO.

Masters, G. (2002) 'Family Group Conferencing: A Victim Perspective', in B. Williams (ed.) *Reparation and Victim-focused Social Work*, London: Jessica Kingsley.

Matthews, R. (1988) 'Assessing Informal Justice', in R. Matthews (ed.) *Informal Justice?*, London: Sage, 1–24.

Mattinson, J. and Mirrlees-Black, C. (2000) *Attitudes to Crime and Criminal Justice: Findings from the 1998 British Crime Survey.* Research Study 200, London: Home Office.

Maxwell, G. and Morris, A. (1993) *Families, Victims and Culture: Youth Justice in New Zealand,* Wellington: Institute of Criminology, Victoria University of Wellington.

Maxwell, G. and Morris, A. (1996) 'Research on Family Group Conferences with Young Offenders in New Zealand', in J. Hudson, A. Morris, G. Maxwell and B. Galaway (eds) *Family Group Conferences: Perspectives on Police and Practice,* Annandale, NSW: Federation Press, 88–110.

Maxwell, G. and Morris, A. (2001) 'Family Group Conferences and Reoffending', in A. Morris and G. Maxwell (eds) *Restorative Justice for Juveniles,* Oxford: Hart Publishing, 243–63.

McCold, P. (1996) 'Restorative Justice and the Role of Community', in B. Galaway and J. Hudson (eds) *Restorative Justice: International Perspectives,* Monsey, NY: Criminal Justice Press, 85–101.

McCold, P. (2000) 'Towards a Mid-range Theory of Restorative Criminal Justice: A Reply to the Maximalist Model', *Contemporary Justice Review,* 3(4), 357–414.

McCold, P. (2001) 'Primary Restorative Justice Practices', in A. Morris and G. Maxwell (eds) *Restorative Justice for Juveniles,* Oxford: Hart Publishing, 41–58.

McCold, P. and Wachtel, B. (1998) *Restorative Policing Experiment: The Bethlehem Pennsylvania Police Family Group Conferencing Project,* Popersville, PA: Community Service Foundation.

McConville, M., Hodgson, J., Bridges, L. and Pavlovic, A. (1994) *Standing Accused,* Oxford: Clarendon Press.

McElrea, F. (1996) 'The New Zealand Youth Court: A Model for Use with Adults', in B. Galaway and J. Hudson (eds) *Restorative Justice: International Perspectives,* Monesy, NY: Criminal Justice Press, 69–84.

Merry, S.E. (1988) 'Legal Pluralism', *Law and Society Review,* 22(5), 869–96.

Michael, A. (1998) Speech to the Crime Concern Parliamentary Discussion Group, London, 7 July.

Miers, D. (2001) *An International Review of Restorative Justice.* Crime Reduction Research Series Paper 10, London: Home Office.

Miers, D., Maguire, M., Goldie, S., Sharpe, K., Hale, C., Netten, A., Uglow, S., Doolin, K., Hallam, A., Enterkin, J. and Newburn, T. (2001) *An Exploratory Evaluation of Restorative Justice Schemes. Crime Reduction Research Series Paper 9,* London: Home Office.

Mirrlees-Black, C. (2000) *Confidence in the Criminal Justice System: Findings from the 2000 British Crime Survey. Research Findings* 137, London: Home Office.

Moore, D. and O'Connell, T. (1994) 'Family Conferencing in Wagga Wagga: A Communitarian Model of Justice', in C. Alder and J. Wundersitz (eds) *Family Conferencing and Juvenile Justice,* Canberra: Australian Institute of Criminology, 45–86.

Morris, A. (2002) 'Critiquing the Critics', *British Journal of Criminology,* 42(3), 596–615.

Morris, A. and Gelsthorpe, L. (2000) 'Something Old, Something Borrowed, Something Blue, but Something New? A Comment on the Prospects for

Restorative Justice under the Crime and Disorder Act 1998', *Criminal Law Review*, 18–30.

Morris, A. and Giller, H. (1987) *Understanding Juvenile Justice*, Beckenham: Croom Helm.

Morris, A. and Maxwell, G. (2000) 'The Practice of Family Group Conferences in New Zealand: Assessing the Place, Potential and Pitfalls of Restorative Justice', in A. Crawford and J. Goodey (eds) *Integrating a Victim Perspective within Criminal Justice*, Aldershot: Ashgate, 207–25.

Morris, A. and Maxwell, G. (2001a) (eds) *Restorative Justice for Juveniles*, Oxford: Hart Publishing.

Morris, A. and Maxwell, G. (2001b) 'Implementing Restorative Justice: What Works?', in A. Morris and G. Maxwell (eds) *Restorative Justice for Juveniles*, Oxford: Hart Publishing, 267–81.

Morris, A., Maxwell, G. and Robertson, J. (1993) 'Giving Victims a Voice: A New Zealand Experiment', *Howard Journal*, 32(4), 304–21.

Morris, N. and Tonry, M. (1990) *Between Prison and Probation: Intermediate Punishments in a Rational Sentencing System*, New York, NY: Oxford University Press.

Muncie, J. (2000) *Youth and Crime: A Critical Introduction*, London: Sage.

Muncie, J. (2001) 'A New Deal for Youth? Early Intervention and Correctionalism', in G. Hughes, J. Muncie and E. McLaughlin (eds) *Crime Prevention and Community Safety*, London: Sage, 142–62.

Muncie, J. (2002) 'Policy Transfers and "What Works": Some reflections on Comparative Youth Justice', *Youth Justice*, 1(3), 27–35.

Nellis, M. (2002) *Creating Community Justice*, Cullompton: Willan Publishing.

Newburn, T. (1998) 'Tackling Youth Crime and Reforming Youth Justice: The Origins and Nature of "New Labour" Policy', *Policy Studies*, 19(3/4), 199–211.

Newburn, T. (2001) 'What Do We Mean by Evaluation?', *Children and Society*, 15, 5–13.

Newburn, T., Crawford, A., Earle, R., Goldie, S., Hale, C., Masters, G., Netten, A., Saunders, R., Sharpe, K. and Uglow, S. (2001a) *The Introduction of Referral Orders into the Youth Justice System*. RDS Occasional Paper 70, London: Home Office.

Newburn, T., Crawford, A., Earle, R., Goldie, S., Hale, C., Masters, G., Netten, A., Saunders, R., Sharpe, K., Uglow, S. and Campbell, A. (2001b) *The Introduction of Referral Orders into the Youth Justice System: Second Interim Report*. RDS Occasional Paper 73, London: Home Office.

Newburn, T., Crawford, A., Earle, R., Goldie, S., Hale, C., Masters, G., Netten, A., Saunders, R., Sharpe, K. and Uglow, S. (2002) *The Introduction of Referral Orders into the Youth Justice System*. Home Office Research Study 242, London: Home Office.

O'Malley, P. (2003) *Risk, Uncertainty and Government*, London: Cavendish.

Patton, M.Q. (1986) *Utilization-focused Evaluation*, Newbury Park, CA: Sage.

Pearson, G. (1983) *Hooligans: A History of Respectable Fears*, Basingstoke: Macmillan.

Penal Affairs Consortium (1995) *The Doctrine of Doli Incapax*, London: Penal Affairs Consortium.

Pitts, J. (2000) 'The New Youth Justice and the Politics of Electoral Anxiety', in B. Goldson (ed.) *The New Youth Justice*, Lyme Regis: Russell House, 1–13.

Pitts, J. (2001) 'The New Correctionalism: Young People, Youth Justice and New Labour', in R. Matthews and J. Pitts (eds) *Crime, Disorder and Community Safety*, London: Routledge, 167–92.

Pollard, C. (2000) 'Victims and Criminal Justice System: A New Vision', *Criminal Law Review*, 5–17.

Pollard, C. (2001) 'If your only Tool is a Hammer, all your Problems will Look like Nails', in H. Strang and J. Braithwaite (eds) *Restorative Justice and Civil Society*, Cambridge: Cambridge University Press, 165–79.

Pranis, K. (1998) 'Engaging the Community in Restorative Justice', Balanced and Restorative Justice Project, OJJDP, Department of Justice, at http://ssw.che.umn.edu/rjp/Resources/Documents/cpra98a.pdf.

Pratt, J. (1989) 'Corporatism: The Third Model of Juvenile Justice', *British Journal of Criminology*, 29(3), 236–54.

Pressman, J.L. and Wildavsky, A. (1984) *Implementation: How Great Expectations in Washington are Dashed in Oakland; or, Why it's Amazing that Federal Programs Work at all, this Being a Saga of the Economic Development Administration as Told by Two Sympathetic Observers who Seek to Build Morals on a Foundation of Ruined Hopes*, Berkeley, CA: University of California Press.

Putnam, R. (2000) *Bowling Alone*, New York, NY: Touchstone.

Quill, D. and Wynne, J. (1993) (eds) *Victim and Offender Mediation Handbook*, Leeds: Save the Children/West Yorkshire Probation Service.

Raine, J.W. (2001) 'Modernizing Courts or Courting Modernization?', *Criminal Justice*, 1(1), 105–28.

Reeves, H. (1984) *The Victim and Reparation*, London: Victim Support.

Reeves, H. and Mulley, K. (2000) 'The New Status of Victims in the UK: Opportunities and Threats', in A. Crawford and J. Goodey (eds) *Integrating a Victim Perspective within Criminal Justice*, Aldershot: Ashgate, 125–45.

Reichman, N. (1986) 'Managing Crime Risks: Towards an Insurance Based Model of Social Control', *Research in Law, Deviance and Social Control*, 8, 151–72.

Renshaw, J. and Powell, H. (2001) *The Story So Far: Emerging Evidence of the Impact of the Reformed Youth Justice System*, London: Youth Justice Board.

Restorative Justice Consortium (1998) *Standards for Restorative Justice*, London: National Council for Social Concern.

Rhodes, R.A.W. (2000) 'The Governance Narrative: Key Findings and Lessons from the ESRC's Whitehall Programme', *Public Administration*, 78(2), 345–63.

Roach, K. (2000) 'Changing Punishment at the Turn of the Century: Restorative Justice on the Rise', *Canadian Journal of Criminology*, 42(3), 249–80.

Roche, D. (2002) 'Restorative Justice and the Regulatory State in South African Townships', *British Journal of Criminology*, 42, 514–33.

Rose, R. (1973) 'Comparing Public Policy: An Overview', *European Journal of Political Research*, 1(1), 67–94.

Rosenbaum, D.P. (1988) 'Community Crime Prevention: A Review and Synthesis of the Literature', *Justice Quarterly*, 5(3), 323–93.

Rutherford, A. (1993) *Criminal Justice and the Pursuit of Decency*, Oxford: Oxford University Press.

Rutherford, A. (1986a) *Growing out of Crime: Society and Young People in Trouble*, Harmondsworth: Penguin Books.

Rutherford, A. (1986b) *Prisons and the Process of Justice*, Oxford: Oxford University Press.

Rutter, M. and Giller, H. (1983) *Juvenile Delinquency: Trends and Perspectives*, Harmondsworth: Penguin Books.

Rutter, M., Giller, H. and Hagell, A. (1998) *Antisocial Behaviour by Young People*, Cambridge: Cambridge University Press.

Sampson, R.J., Raudenbush, S.W. and Earls, F. (1997) 'Neighborhoods and Violent Crime: A Multi-level Study of Collective Efficacy', *Science*, 277, 918–23.

Sarat, A. (1988) 'The New Formalism in Disputing and Dispute Processing', *Law and Society Review*, 21, 695–715.

Sarat, A. (1997) 'Vengeance, Victims and the Identities of Law', *Social and Legal Studies*, 6(2), 163–89.

Savage, S. and Nash, M. (2001) 'Law and Order under Blair', in S.P. Savage and R. Atkinson (eds) *Public Policy Under Blair*, Basingstoke: Palgrave, 102–22.

Sebba, L. (2000) 'The Individualisation of the Victim', in A. Crawford and J. Goodey (eds) *Integrating a Victim Perspective within Criminal Justice*, Aldershot: Ashgate, 55–76.

Shapland, J. (1988) 'Fiefs and Peasants: Accomplishing Change for Victims in the Criminal Justice System', in M. Maguire and J. Pointing (eds) *Victims of Crime: A New Deal?*, Milton Keynes: Open University Press, 187–94.

Shapland, J. (2000) 'Victims and Criminal Justice: Creating Responsible Criminal Justice Agencies', in A. Crawford and J. Goodey (eds) *Integrating a Victim Perspective within Criminal Justice*, Aldershot: Ashgate, 147–64.

Shapland, J., Willmore, J. and Duff, P. (1985) *Victims in the Criminal Justice System*, Aldershot: Gower.

Shearing, C. (2001a) 'Transforming Security: A South African Experiment', in H. Strang and J. Braithwaite (eds) *Restorative Justice and Civil Society*, Cambridge: Cambridge University Press, 14–34.

Shearing, C. (2001b) 'Punishment and the Changing Face of Governance', *Punishment & Society*, 3(2), 203–20.

Sherman, L. (2002) Paper presented to the international workshop 'Doing Restorative Justice', University of Keele, 16 July.

Sherman, L. and Strang, H. with Woods, D. (2000a) *Recidivism Patterns in the Canberra Reintegrative Shaming Experiment (RISE)*, Canberra: Centre for Restorative Justice, ANU.

Sherman, L. and Strang, H. with Woods, D. (2000b) 'Captains of Restorative Justice: Experience, Legitimacy and Recidivism', paper presented to the International Conference on Restorative Justice, Tubingen ,1–4 October.

Silbey, S. and Merry, S. (1986) 'Mediator Settlement Strategies', *Law and Policy*, 8, 7–32.

Skelton, A. and Frank, C. (2001) 'Conferencing in South Africa: Returning to Our Future', in A. Morris and G. Maxwell (eds) *Restorative Justice for Juveniles*, Oxford: Hart Publishing, 103–19.

Smith, D. (2000) 'Corporatism and the New Youth Justice', in B. Goldson (ed.) *The New Youth Justice*, Lyme Regis: Russell House, 129–43.

Sparks, C. and Spencer, S. (2002) *Them and Us? The Public, Offenders, and the Criminal Justice System*, London: IPPR.

Stevenson, S. (1989) 'Some Social and Political Tides Affecting the Development of Juvenile Justice 1938–64', in A. Gorst, L. Johnman and W.S. Lucas (eds) *Post-war Britain: Themes and Perspectives*, London: Pinter Press and the Institute of Contemporary British History, 68–94.

Strang, H. (1995) 'Replacing Courts with Conferences', *Policing*, 11(3), 212–20.

Strang, H. (2001) 'Justice for Victims of Young Offenders: The Centrality of Emotional Harm and Restoration', in A. Morris and G. Maxwell (eds) *Restorative Justice for Juveniles*, Oxford: Hart Publishing, 183–93.

Strang, H. (2002) *Repair or Revenge: Victims and Restorative Justice*, Oxford: Clarendon Press.

Strang, H., Barnes, G., Braithwaite, J. and Sherman, L. (1999) *Experiments in Restorative Policing*, Canberra: ANU.

Strang, H. and Braithwaite, J. (2001) (eds) *Restorative Justice and Civil Society*, Cambridge: Cambridge University Press.

Straw, J. and Boateng, P. (1997) 'Bringing Rights Home', *European Human Rights Law Review*, 2(1), 71–80.

Stuart, B. (1994) 'Sentencing Circles: Purpose and Impact', *National Canadian Bar Association*, 13.

Stuart, B. (1996) 'Circle Sentencing: Turning Swords into Ploughshares', in B. Galaway and J. Hudson (eds) *Restorative Justice: International Perspectives*, Monesy, NY: Criminal Justice Press, 193–206.

Stuart, B. (2001) 'Guiding Principles for Designing Peacemaking Circles', in G. Bazemore and M. Schiff (eds) *Restorative Community Justice*, Cincinnati, OH: Anderson Publishing, 219–41.

Stubbs, J. (1995) ' "Communitarian" Conferencing and Violence against Women: A Cautionary Note', in M. Valverde, L. MacLeod and K. Johnson (eds) *Wife Assault and the Canadian Criminal Justice System: Issues and Policies*, Toronto: Centre of Criminology, University of Toronto, 260–89.

Tilley, N. (2001) 'Evaluation and Evidence-led Crime Reduction Policy and Practice', in R. Matthews and J. Pitts (eds) *Crime, Disorder and Community Safety*, London: Routledge, 81–97.

Trimboli, L. (2000) *An Evaluation of the NSW Youth Justice Conferencing Scheme*, Sydney: Bureau of Crime Statistics and Research.

Tyler, T. (1990) *Why People Obey the Law*, New Haven, CT: Yale University Press.

Umbreit, M., Coates, R.B. and Vos, B. (2001) 'Victim Impact of Meeting with Young Offenders: Two Decades of Victim Offender Mediation Practice and Research', in A. Morris and G. Maxwell (eds) *Restorative Justice for Juveniles*, Oxford: Hart Publishing, 121–43.

Umbreit, M. and Roberts, A. (1996) *Mediation of Criminal Conflict in England: An Assessment of Services in Coventry and Leeds*, St Pauls, MN: University of Minnesota.

United Nations (2000) *Basic Principles on the Use of Restorative Justice Programmes in Criminal Justice Matters*, Vienna: United Nations.

Van Ness, D. and Strong, K.H. (1997) *Restoring Justice*, Cincinnati, OH: Anderson Publishing.

Victim Support (1995) *The Rights of Victims of Crime*, London: Victim Support.

von Hirsch, A. (1993) *Censure and Sanction*, Oxford: Clarendon Press.

Walgrave, L. (2000) 'Extending the Victim Perspective towards a Systemic Restorative Justice Alternative', in A. Crawford and J. Goodey (eds) *Integrating a Victim Perspective within Criminal Justice*, Aldershot: Ashgate, 253–84.

Walgrave, L. (2001) 'On Restoration and Punishment', in A. Morris and G. Maxwell (eds) *Restorative Justice for Juveniles*, Oxford: Hart Publishing, 17–37.

Walgrave, L. (2003) 'Imposing Restoration Instead of Inflicting Pain: Reflections on the Judicial Reaction to Crime', in A. von Hirsch, J. Roberts, A.E. Bottoms, K. Roach and M. Schiff (eds) *Restorative Justice and Criminal Justice: Competing or Reconcilable Paradigms*, Oxford: Hart Publishing, 61–78.

Walklate, S. (1989) *Victimology*, London: Unwin Hyman.

Wachtel, T. and McCold, P. (2001) 'Restorative Justice in Everyday Life', in H. Strang and J. Braithwaite (eds) *Restorative Justice and Civil Society*, Cambridge: Cambridge University Press, 114–29.

Weiss, C.H. (1998) *Evaluation*, Upper Saddle River, NJ: Prentice Hall.

Weitekamp, E. (1999) 'The History of Restorative Justice', in G. Bazemore and L. Walgrave (eds) *Restorative Juvenile Justice*, Monsey, NY: Criminal Justice Press, 75–102.

Weitekamp, E. (2001) 'Mediation in Europe: Paradoxes, Problems and Promises', in A. Morris and G. Maxwell (eds) *Restorative Justice for Juveniles*, Oxford: Hart Publishing, 145–60.

Whyte, B. (2000) 'Between Two Stools: Youth Justice in Scotland', *Probation Journal*, 47(2), 119–25.

Wilkinson, T. (1995) '*Doli Incapax* Resurrected', *Solicitors Journal*, 14 April, 338–9.

Wilson, J.Q. and Kelling, G. (1982) 'Broken Windows: The Police and Neighbourhood Safety', *The Atlantic Monthly*, March, 29–37.

Windlesham, Lord (2001) *Dispensing Justice: Responses to Crime, Volume 4*. Oxford: Oxford University Press.

Wonnacott, C. (1999) 'The Counterfeit Contract – Reform, Pretence and Muddled Principles in the New Referral Order', *Child and Family Law Quarterly*, 11(3), 271–87.

Wright, M. (1991) *Justice for Victims and Offenders*, Milton Keynes: Open University Press.

Wynne, J. (1996) 'Leeds Mediation and Reparation Service: Ten Years Experience of Victim–Offender Mediation', in B. Galaway and J. Hudson (eds) *Restorative Justice: International Perspectives*, Monsey, NY: Criminal Justice Press, 445–61.

Wyvekens, A. (1997) 'Mediation and Proximity', *European Journal on Criminal Policy and Research*, 5(4), 27–42.

Young, J. (1986) 'The Failure of Criminology: The Need for a Radical Realism', in R. Matthews and J. Young (eds) *Confronting Crime*, London: Sage, 4–30.

Young, R. (2000) 'Integrating a Multi-victim Perspective through Restorative Justice Conferences', in A. Crawford and J. Goodey (eds) *Integrating a Victim Perspective within Criminal Justice*, Aldershot: Ashgate, 227–51.

Young, R. (2001) 'Just Cops Doing "Shameful" Business?: Police-led Restorative Justice and the Lessons of Research', in A. Morris and G. Maxwell (eds) *Restorative Justice for Juveniles*, Oxford: Hart Publishing, 195–226.

Young, R. and Goold, B. (1999) 'Restorative Police Cautioning in Aylesbury – From Degrading to Reintegrative Shaming Ceremonies?', *Criminal Law Review*, 126–38.

Youth Justice Board (2001) *Good Practice Guidelines for Restorative Justice Work with Victims and Young Offenders*, London: Youth Justice Board.

Zedner, L. (1994) 'Reparation and Retribution: Are they Reconcilable?', *Modern Law Review*, 57, 228–50.

Zehr, H. (1990) *Changing Lenses*, Scottdale, PA: Herald Press.

Index

outcome versus process in restorative
justice, 44–5

Panel Matters, 67, 68n, 74, 137
panel meetings
  attendance at multiple, 177–8
  legal representation, 103
  length, 119, 120t
  location, 60–1, 116–19
  number held per young person,
    113t
  participation of victims, 172–4
  research team observations, 122–30
  time held, 114–5
  victim attendance, 184–6
  see also breach panels; final panels;
    initial panels; review panels
panels, 59, 107–8
  administration, 143–4
    by YOTs, 80–4
  assessment data, 113–4
  composition, 60, 61–2, 120–1
  experience of young people and
    parents, 178–81
    criticisms, 181–2
  as forums of justice, 166–71
  implementation, 237–9
  information given to young people
    and families, 160
  process issues, 147–9
  relationship between YOTs, Youth
    Courts and, 95–8
  role in contract compliance and
    reintegration, 240–1
  victim involvement, 185
  working relationships, 144–7
  see also community panel members
parents
  attendance at subsequent panel
    meetings, 177–8
  attitudes to participation of victims,
    173–4
  experience of initial panel meetings,
    164–5
    comparisons with Youth Courts,
      165–6, 168t

as forums of justice, 169, 171
experience of referral orders,
  178–81
  criticisms, 181–2
experience of Youth Courts, 159–60
information supplied about referral
  orders and panels, 160–3
and the referral order process, 157
  interview sample, 157–9
as secondary victims, 218–9
views on contracts, 171, 175–6, 177t
participation
  in the referral order process, 156–7
  in restorative justice, 22–3, 41
passive responsibility, 217
peace committees, 35
pilots for referral orders *see* referral
  order pilots
'populist punitiveness', 10
procedural justice in panels, 169
process versus outcome in restorative
  justice, 44–5
professionalisation of justice, 222
public involvement *see* community
  involvement
punishment
  proportionality, 48–9
  and restorative justice, 45–7

rationalisation of justice, 224–5
referral order pilots, 63
  evaluation, 229–31
  research design and methods,
    62–6
  research process, 66–8
  timescale, 229
referral orders, 5, 108–9, 236–7
  impact, 98–105
  information given to youth people
    and parents, 160
  origin and intention, 59–63
  and restorative justice, 237–9
  theme of responsibility, 216–9
  view of victims, 210–12, 212f
  views of magistrates, clerks and
    YOT staff members, 92–5